Kenny Riley and
Black Union Labor Power
in the Port of Charleston

ALSO BY TED REED

Carl Furillo, Brooklyn Dodgers All-Star (McFarland, 2011)

BY TED REED AND DAN REED

American Airlines, US Airways and the Creation of the World's Largest Airline (McFarland, 2014)

Kenny Riley and Black Union Labor Power in the Port of Charleston

TED REED *and*
JOHN J. YURECHKO

McFarland & Company, Inc., Publishers
Jefferson, North Carolina

ISBN (print) 978-1-4766-7772-9
ISBN (ebook) 978-1-4766-3928-4

LIBRARY OF CONGRESS AND BRITISH LIBRARY
CATALOGUING DATA ARE AVAILABLE

Library of Congress Control Number 2020008516

© 2020 Ted Reed and John J. Yurechko. All rights reserved

No part of this book may be reproduced or transmitted in any form or by any means, electronic or mechanical, including photocopying or recording, or by any information storage and retrieval system, without permission in writing from the publisher.

On the cover: Kenny Riley presides over the Port of Charleston, the fourth busiest container port on the East Coast and ninth busiest in the U.S. (Jeff Siner)

Printed in the United States of America

*McFarland & Company, Inc., Publishers
Box 611, Jefferson, North Carolina 28640
www.mcfarlandpub.com*

To our families
Ale, Teresa, Gabriela, Chad (TR)
Jane, Christine, Alice, and Janie (JY)

Table of Contents

Preface by Ted Reed   1

Introduction   3

1. We Lived in Our Own Little World   9
2. Getting an Education, Separate Not Equal   21
3. Charleston the Slave Port   31
4. A City Is Born: It Grows on the Backs of Slaves   38
5. The War for Freedom Leaves Many Enslaved   48
6. South Carolina Declares War on the United States   54
7. Ex-Slaves Form a Labor Union and It Folds   65
8. Charleston Rots and Then Rebounds   74
9. George Washington German Brings the Union Back   82
10. On the Waterfront   93
11. Containers Take Over the World   103
12. A Sixties Kid Takes Over Local 1422   113
13. A World Beyond Charleston   120
14. The Charleston Five   130
15. Lessons Learned from the Charleston Five   139
16. A Charleston Guy Finds Allies in New York and San Francisco   150
17. The Family Politics of Local 1422   159

Table of Contents

18. For Labor, South Carolina Is Tough, but "The Union Is Anomalous" — 168
19. Riley Looks to Retirement — 179

Chapter Notes — 187
Bibliography — 197
Index — 201

Preface
by Ted Reed

In the late 1990s and early 2000s, I was a *Charlotte Observer* reporter and my beats included organized labor. For Labor Day, I would sometimes write a story about labor in the Carolinas: Because Charlotte is on the North Carolina/South Carolina border, we covered both states. The Charleston Five event in January 2000 made Kenny Riley and International Longshoremen's Association Local 1422 an obvious story topic.

Kenny's charisma, dedication and ease with reporters quickly became clear to me and I realized that he would be a good subject for a book, which I started to work on 18 years later.

I asked John Yurechko, a classmate at Wesleyan University, to write about the history of Charleston. John has a Ph.D. from the University of California at Berkeley, where he specialized in military history. He wrote most of chapters 3 through 8.

Jeff Siner, a photographer for the *Charlotte Observer* since 1989, took most of the photographs for the book during a trip to Charleston in November 2018. He was North Carolina Press Photographer of the Year in 2002.

For his thesis at Harvard, Charleston attorney Eli Poliakoff wrote about Kenny and Local 1422. Chapters 8 and 9 are based largely on Eli's work.

The primary editors were Audrey Williams June, a former *Charlotte Observer* reporter now at the *Chronicle of Higher Education,* and my wife, Ale Jenkins. Other editors and proofreaders included Andrew Goldman, Douglas Praul, Gabriela Reed, Alice Yurechko, Christine Yurechko and Janie Yurechko.

I have been grateful for the continuing coverage of the Port of Charleston by the *Charleston Post and Courier.* Charleston is fortunate to

Preface by Ted Reed

be served by a high-quality, family-owned newspaper that has not been as excessively vulnerable to financial pressures as many publicly traded newspapers. I have quoted extensively from the newspaper's coverage. In addition, I have been encouraged and assisted by David Wren, who now covers the port, and by Tony Bartelme, his predecessor.

When I started to work on this book, David told me that Kenny can be hard to reach. I was reminded of this advice many times. Kenny is a self-confessed workaholic who is constantly busy with the myriad responsibilities of a local and national union leader, a port power, a father and a dedicated provider of care at an orphanage in Gbarnga, Liberia. He told me once that when Barack Obama was president, many acquaintances had described him as "harder than Obama to reach." This remains true.

At one point in 2018, Kenny had added an extra job: He was serving temporarily as trustee for the International Longshoremen's Association (ILA) local in Miami after local leadership had been removed due to potential legal problems. We were together in Charleston when Kenny got a phone call saying that Miami members could not cash their paychecks because money had not been transferred to the proper bank account. Kenny was already having a busy day. Suddenly he had a one-more-thing-I-have-to-fix-because-everything-is-my-responsibility moment. It seemed briefly that even Kenny could be overwhelmed. He fixed it.

As I worked with Kenny, I gradually became aware that he has a great sense of humor. I did not notice this initially. I think it is something he keeps hidden until he knows you. Two people who mentioned it to me as I worked on the book were his daughter, Marnique Riley Strickland, and his attorney, Peter Wilborn.

Writing Kenny's story gave me the chance to better understand black life in the segregated South of the 1950s and 1960s; the history of Charleston, one of the South's most fascinating cities; and the labor movement's ability to provide members and others with better lives.

I like to think the book makes the point that one man can make a big difference.

Introduction

They came to Charleston as cargo. Now, Charleston's cargo cannot move without them.

The transformation represents the heart of the story of International Longshoremen's Association (ILA) Local 1422, a powerful black union at what was once the United States' largest slave port, the point of arrival for 40 percent of all the slaves who came to America. Today, the union local is among South Carolina's most powerful black institutions. The approximately 800 members, who can earn upper middle-class incomes, are generally politically united. They are led by a charismatic elder labor statesman named Kenny Riley who is dedicated not only to their continued financial and career success, but also to participation in civil rights and labor struggles and to charitable work on behalf of black children in Africa. Among Kenny Riley's Christmas gifts in 2018 was a study of his genealogy. It revealed that his ancestors were from Guinea-Bissau, a West African coastal country located a few hundred miles from Liberia, where he journeys several times each year to work at an orphanage. This is the work he hopes to pursue when he retires as union president at a still undetermined date, after taking office in 1997.

"We always talk about this narrative: We were the cargo on the earlier ships that came here, and ironically now we control the cargo that comes off these ships," said Leonard Riley, Kenny's brother. "In fact, we are in control of the world economy: If we stop work, it will have a ripple effect throughout the world. We are the descendants of slaves, but now we are able to be a springboard for other descendants in achieving the American dream, and if we don't utilize this opportunity afforded us by being in this position, then it is all for naught."[1]

Leonard is slightly older than Kenny, born about a year earlier. The brothers have been at one another's side throughout lives that began in the rural, segregated South. In their formative, teenaged years, they matured

Introduction

as the civil rights movement seized imaginations and ignited hopes. They were among the first wave of young black students to attend colleges, in their case the College of Charleston, that had been entirely white. That could easily have led to white-collar jobs: Kenny studied business management and Leonard prepared to be a doctor. But their father had been a longshoreman, and they were drawn to the docks, where they stood out as college-educated civil rights advocates in a work group that had not been characterized by either. Both rose to leadership, but in different realms. Leonard focused on Charleston, where the solidarity and financial strength of a strong union could reinforce the black community in multiple battles against a white power structure. Kenny engaged in the ILA, embracing a commitment to change in a union that lacked black leadership even though its membership was majority black.

A labor confrontation at the Port of Charleston in January 2000 thrust Kenny Riley onto the world stage. There he emerged as an articulate leader of an international movement to provide a legal defense for five union members—four black, one white—who had been arrested after protesting a shipping line's effort to use non-union workers to fill jobs that historically were staffed by the union. The cause of the Charleston Five and the slogan "Free the Charleston Five" became internationally known, and Riley rallied unionists around the world. The confrontation escalated to the level that unionized longshoremen threatened a global one-day work stoppage if the five dockworkers were found guilty of the felony charges initially filed against them by South Carolina's attorney general, who sought to burnish his record as an ideological, anti-union, anti-liberal representative of white South Carolina. The attorney general provided a perfect foil as backers of labor and civil rights mobilized. Had his charges stuck, the five dockworkers might have gone to jail and lost their jobs. "In the Charleston Five incident, Kenny Riley was able to go on TV and say that the day this comes to trial is the day that all commerce stops all over the world," said Bill Wise, a South Carolina resident and a general chairman of the International Association of Machinists. "He could say that because he took months to fly all over the world to get it set up. That's true power there."[2] Eventually, the felony charges against the Charleston Five were reduced to misdemeanors involving fines of a few hundred dollars, and the five workers walked free after enduring months of house arrest.

Local 1422's rise to power was not an easy one. After the Civil War ended, black people in the South continued to be oppressed. In many cases, they remained oppressed even after improvements enabled by the

Introduction

civil rights movement. But two unique institutions bolster 1422. One is the ILA, one of the country's most distinctive and powerful labor unions. The other is Charleston, one of the South's most distinctive cities.

It may seem to be an overstatement when Leonard Riley says that longshoremen have control of the world economy. Or perhaps it is an overstatement only until tested, as occasionally happens, by labor action. Roughly 90 percent of the world's goods are transported by sea, with more than 70 percent carried as containerized cargo. In Europe and the United States, longshoremen are unionized and have the ability to largely halt the movement of cargo, a reality that is recognized by shippers, who only occasionally seek to challenge the authority of the various longshoremen's unions, even though—as in many industries—automation constantly threatens union jobs. Historically, the biggest threat to union dockworker jobs was the move to cargo containerization in the 1960s. That transition led to the loss of tens of thousands of jobs, yet it also empowered the union workers who remained.

Containerization represented the vision of one man, a North Carolina trucking-firm executive named Malcolm McLean, who realized that it was more efficient to transport cargo in large containers than to individually carry large rolls of paper, sets of tires and crates of machinery, each manually unloaded from trucks and onto ships by dockworkers. One key to the importance of the Port of Charleston is that in the early 1960s, very quickly after a visit by McLean, it became one of the first ports to install cranes in order to adapt to container shipping.

The ILA could not stop containerization. But, led by resolute New Yorker Teddy Gleason, it devised a method to guarantee income for longshoremen whose jobs were lost and, perhaps more importantly, to provide container royalties to compensate the remaining workers for cargo movements through their ports. "I still marvel at the fact that this guy had so much insight and was able to get this done," said ILA President Harold Daggett. "No other dockworkers union anywhere in the world negotiated a container royalty."[3] Another benefit for Charleston's dockworkers is that the ILA regularly negotiates a national contract with shippers, setting national pay scales. As a result, South Carolina's rabid anti-unionism has little impact on dockworker compensation. For its part, the management of Charleston's port generally chooses to accept and participate in the dictates of global shipping. This approach has enabled Charleston to remain one of the principal U.S. ports, just as it was 400 years ago, although the nature of the cargo has changed.

Introduction

What particularly distinguishes the Riley brothers is that the combination of the labor movement with the civil rights movement provided a moral foundation for their engaged lives. "As the descendants of slaves, we have the obligation to keep this flavor in the labor movement," Leonard Riley said. "When I think about unions, I think about how the labor movement provides a balancing act for the many, as opposed to the many opportunities that are provided for the few. I think of the labor movement as the best anti-poverty machine."[4]

Through its long history, Charleston has both nurtured and tormented black people and their labor union. Charleston first flourished as a colonial city before the Revolutionary War. Tens of thousands of slaves arrived at its port. The Civil War began in Charleston Harbor as an effort to preserve slavery. Today it is possible to stand at Charleston's battery, a defensive seawall surrounded by homes that are centuries old, and to look out over Fort Sumner much as residents did when they watched the war's first shots being fired in April 1861. Yet despite enabling the horribly destructive conflict, Charleston has long had a degree of openness. Blacks participated in its commerce for centuries, starting before the American Revolution. The city has been home to men like J. Waties Waring, a U.S.

Kenny Riley was first elected to be president of International Longshoreman's Local 1422 in Charleston in 1997 (Jeff Siner).

Introduction

District Court judge, and Joe Riley, its mayor for 40 years. Waring realized in the 1940s that a segregated South was failing to provide black people with rights guaranteed under the Constitution. Joe Riley sought to make the city hospitable to all of its residents and in recent years has dedicated himself to raising money to build a museum that will tell the story of the slaves brought to Charleston. Joe Riley, who is white, is not related to Kenny Riley.

"Charleston is an open city, a port city," Joe Riley said. "Port cities usually are oriented more outward than inward. Centuries ago, Charleston was engaged in reaching out and connecting with other countries and in bringing commerce to and from other countries. There was immigration to Charleston by many people, including the forced migration of Africans who came against their will. They helped shape the city, with their character, language, food and music. The descendants of those slaves have a sense of ownership here; they had that even during times of segregation."

"The reason I sought the job of mayor in 1975 was to build bridges in the community," Joe Riley said. "I didn't want Charleston to be a Southern city divided by race. I ran for mayor to make Charleston a city for everyone. We worked hard on that. Kenny Riley has been part of that. I have known him since early in my tenure. He's a very skilled leader. He's inspiring, he's charismatic, and he works hard for the people he represents. I think the great progress the waterfront has experienced over the last few decades, because of its tremendous efficiency—that's his leadership. Members of the ILA believe in him."[5]

An open city it may be, but Charleston also remains a southern city, in which some have opposed racism while others have long embraced it. A well-known recent episode is the 2015 shooting of nine black people at Emanuel African Methodist Episcopal Church by a 21-year-old white nationalist. The reaction to this massacre underscores the ingrained conservatism of South Carolina politics. Widespread abhorrence led to the state legislature's decision to remove the Confederate flag from the grounds of South Carolina's capitol building, a move backed by Governor Nikki Haley, whose political profile was enhanced as a result. Yet Haley remains a virulent adversary of the union labor movement.

Charleston is also the city where Kenny and Leonard grew up in a segregated world, rarely interacting with white people; where as teenagers they saw a black man beaten up because he would not give up his seat on a bus and where, after advancing all the way to high school in an all-black school, they attended a newly integrated high school where a majority

Introduction

of white students and faculty seemed to oppose their every effort to belong, not to mention to try to perform well in their classes. The following year, their situation improved when they moved to a newly opened school where the effort at integration was embraced by black and white students as well as faculty. Middleton High School set a better model for the lives they would lead.

Although a sometimes-tolerant city and a sometimes-supportive labor union benefited the two brothers, it is clear to anyone who knows them that the biggest advantage they were given in life was their parents. Their father Leonard was a longshoreman who ran small companies in a half dozen other industries: trucking, manpower contracting, laundry pickup and delivery, farming and moonshine production. Among the experiences he provided his sons was an opportunity as teenagers to pick crops, including cucumbers and pickles on land he farmed in Long Island, New York. His dedication to work was passed on: "All of the Riley men are workaholics,"[6] says Kenny Riley's daughter Marnique.

Additionally, Leonard Riley, Sr., benefited from following one of life's most basic precepts: He married up. In 2019, at age 87, his widow Corine Riley radiated wisdom, drove a new car and was rarely at home during the day. She had infused her children with awareness and commitment regarding the civil rights struggle, with a desire to become educated and with religious commitment, a quality she shared with her husband. When I met Corine in 2018, she told me that she had attended an all-black school in Charleston as she prepared for high school. But there was a charge for black children to attend the white high school, and she did not want to impose that burden on the woman who cared for her as she grew up. So Corine, who had always gotten excellent grades in school, attempted to get low grades so that she would not incur unaffordable costs. In this attempt she failed, because the one thing Corine Riley could not do was act unintelligently.

It is an attribute she passed on to her children.

1

We Lived in Our Own Little World

Kenny Riley, a veteran of the civil rights struggle who became an internationally known labor leader, still lives in the West Ashley area of Charleston, about two miles from the house where he was born, which is a few hundred yards from where his mother still lives. The house he inhabits today was his great-grandmother's house. It has of course been updated, but it remains a flat, one-story, synthetic wood house of about 1,000 square feet, now mustard colored and well-tended. It sits on an acre of land that is covered with neatly cut grass and shaded on two sides by towering oak trees. What is unique about the house is that it is part of a semi-rural oasis that is nearly surrounded by urban Charleston, with a low-slung warehouse-like structure next door, an auto-body shop across the street and Sam Rittenberg Boulevard—a busy urban street filled with traffic and strip malls and fast food restaurants—a few hundred yards away. When Riley took me to see the house in the fall of 2018, he seemed somehow not to see the urban sprawl, but rather to see the past—the old neighborhood, entirely African American; the trees; the creeks; the ponds; the snakes; the alligators; and the many hours he spent walking with his brother Leonard.

For anyone who has seen a modern city grow up on top of the neighborhood they once inhabited, the feelings are probably similar, but Riley has fought harder than most to preserve them. He remarked that on the weekends, when the body-shop compressor shuts down and the traffic on the nearby boulevard is less dense, he can go outside, hear remarkable silence, walk around the borders of his property, watch the birds and the squirrels and feel like nothing has changed from the day when he was young. Back then, St. Andrew's Parish was rural, and no one—at least no one except for his mother—ever imagined that he would be renowned in

Kenny Riley and Black Union Labor Power

South Carolina and in the International Longshoreman's Association, one of the world's best-known and most successful labor unions.

When Riley is at home, it seems, the singularity of his story occurs to him, at least in the sense that he realizes that, perhaps a week earlier, he occupied a room in a nice hotel in London or New York or Miami, conducting union business, and now he is home in a far more humble environment, and it is "absolutely quiet, and I can walk to a nice dinner" at one of the Sam Rittenberg Boulevard restaurants, and "I'm in the country, but I'm also in the city."[1] His daughter Marnique Riley Strickland said, "Dad really enjoys the solitude there; I think it rejuvenates him. He likes walking through the woods, spotting different birds and different trees, even though the area is developed now."[2] A visitor cannot help but think that the city life is all around, while the rural aspect of the area exists primarily in Riley's memory, an indication that his youth in black Charleston remains his emotional anchor. While he now travels broadly, he has spent the vast majority of his life in an enclave, and it comforts him. Most of his extended family—including his mother, his siblings, two of his four children, and his ex-wife—lives in Charleston, generally close to his home. While the city has grown enormously, Riley's sense of Charleston has changed very little.

Charleston is among a select group of New South cities where enormous growth has resulted from a series of beneficial trends, including lower costs, pleasant climate, a commitment to corporate recruiting and a continuing southern civility that at times thinly masks the racism that still characterizes segments of the region. Charleston has not grown much in importance, as Charlotte and Nashville and Raleigh-Durham have done, only because Charleston has always been important. *Gone with the Wind*, the classic novel of the antebellum South, focuses primarily on Atlanta, but secondarily on Charleston. Yet some outside the South are still coming to understand Charleston's importance.

It is in part Charleston's self-image that enables the familiar characterization of North Carolina as "a valley of humility between two mountains of conceit," referring to the pride of South Carolina and Virginia. However, the state's long-standing tendency to self-aggrandize has not always extended to African American Charleston, a community that has long included a high proportion of slaves and later of their descendants, and which has provided a nurturing environment for Kenny Riley throughout his life.

The story of how Riley came to own his house is revealing. In the

1. We Lived in Our Own Little World

early 1980s, while he was working as a longshoreman and serving as recording secretary for Local 1422, Riley would come by the house—which was then occupied by his grandfather's sister—and cut the grass with a push lawnmower. In 1984, when his grandfather's sister moved to a retirement home, she gave him the house. The incident underscores Riley's sense of obligation to others. The house he lives in was given to him as a reward for good deeds. It fits into a worldview that includes intense lifelong involvements in the church, in the civil rights movement and in the labor movement.

Riley was born September 8, 1953, in the home of Celia Gethers, the sister of his deceased grandmother. Throughout Riley's life, Gethers acted as his grandmother, a particularly important role in African American families. The home was in St. Andrew's Parish, which stretches west about 20 miles from the Ashley River and from downtown Charleston. The Rileys inhabited a section known more specifically as the Savage Road area and also known as "the hill." The section where Kenny Riley now lives is Jenkins Woods, named after one of the early African American families in the region. In the 1950s, the area was undeniably rural. The Riley family

Kenny Riley departs his mother's house on Savage Road. The house is a few hundred yards from the house where he was born (Jeff Siner).

still holds about 20 acres in the area, the largest single tract of undeveloped land inside the 526 beltway that now encircles Charleston.

"Savage Road was a dirt road, muddy when it rained, and it was out in the country," Riley said. "You could go miles and miles and never hit a paved road. There were cows, sheep, chicken, ducks, even alligators. We would hunt rabbits and squirrels and birds in the backyard. It was about five or six miles from downtown Charleston. When you came into town and you said you were from that area, they said you were country. We were as country as it gets." Over time, he said, "the city came to us."[3]

Kenny's brother Leonard, Jr., recalls that his experience in squirrel hunting was limited to a single encounter when he was about 12. "I wanted to shoot a squirrel because that's what the older guys were doing—you would sometimes see guys coming out of the woods with their hunting conquests on their belts—and my dad sometimes talked about it, although I never saw him come in the house with a bunch of dead squirrels," Leonard said. "I snuck the rifle out of the house, and shot a squirrel and then I tried to take the skin off. You were supposed to burn it off. I didn't get far—that was a disaster. I never even got to the point of cooking it and I never shot another squirrel."[4]

Even after the first white development was built on Savage Road, the area remained segregated. "At Halloween, when we would go trick or treating, our parents would tell us 'Do not go to the white section,'" Kenny Riley recalled. "Orleans Road was perpendicular to Savage Road, and there was a little wooden bridge there, and if you crossed over it you would get into the white section. We knew not to go across, but on Halloween, we would start slipping into that white section. There were five or six houses on either side of the street. We were hoping that no one would bother us, because they could afford more candy."[5]

The Riley family lacked financial wealth, but it possessed the type of richness defined by two hard-working, motivated parents, with a paternal legacy augmented by a commitment to longshore work, a profession that could be passed on, while the maternal lineage included high intelligence—also passed on. All five children went to college. Kenny, the second oldest son, "was always a deep thinker," Corine Riley recalled in 2018. "Sometimes he'd be sitting in a corner and you didn't want to disturb him."[6] Her five children grew up neither hungry nor disadvantaged enough to feel they were poor. "We knew what we could afford," Kenny Riley said. "You had one set of clothes you would get to start school each year, and one set a year for Easter Sunday." Rice was a staple, because it

1. We Lived in Our Own Little World

could be bought cheaply in bags weighing 25 or 50 pounds. "For black folks, rice was a must," Riley said. "Whites ate a lot of rice too, because a lot of black cooks cooked for the white families."[7]

Four predecessors were most important in Riley's life: father, mother, brother and grandmother. Leonard Riley, Sr., was born in 1929 and died of a stroke in 2005. "He was a warrior," Kenny Riley said.

> I didn't appreciate what he was able to do, with his work ethic and entrepreneurial spirit, until I did the math before he died. Dad was always working. He provided for us and took care of his family. He started working when he was 10 or 12 years old. He was a career longshoreman, but he built the houses we lived in. He was a long-distance trucker and he was a contractor for the farms on the island: he provided all the labor to work the fields in Charleston and the islands [Edisto Island, James Island, Johns Island and Wadmalaw Island]. He also had a modified bread delivery truck, which my mom, Leonard and I used to pick up and deliver clothes to the rural areas for Lyles Cleaners, a laundry company that cleaned the workers' clothes. Dad would work late in the packing sheds, so in the middle of the night we had to take the truck home. Mom would drive and Leonard and I would ride with her. All of those areas were pretty much secluded. Sometimes alligators would be walking across the road.
>
> After the season ended here, Dad would leave with trucks and buses and crews and go to Salisbury, Maryland, and work the fields there and when that season ended, we would go up to Bridgehampton, Long Island [New York] and we would pick those fields, cucumbers and pickles, and then we would have to come back here and go to school. But dad kept a crew in Long Island, migrant workers living in labor camps, until late January for the white potato harvest. They would ship those potatoes all over the country.[8]

The boys' work was not 100 percent legitimate: Leonard Riley had a sideline business as a moonshiner. "He had stills in old abandoned houses in the woods," Kenny Riley said. "He and his uncles had about three stills in the woods, and he also built a mini-still that he set up in our home in the bathroom. That drove my mother crazy. My brother Leonard and I would change the mason jars all night long as they got filled with moonshine."[9]

Strickland said the dedication to work was passed from her grandfather to her father, her Uncle Leonard and her brother Kenny, Jr. "All of the Riley men are workaholics," she said. As for her father, Kenny, Strickland said, "Even when he's not working, he's working. He's always fixing things or going to help somebody at church. He's not going to walk by a branch that doesn't need to be moved."[10]

Leonard Riley, Jr., recalls that on some nights his father would come home from work exhausted. "Dad was a muscular guy, but he would be whipped because he did awesome backbreaking work," Leonard said. "When he got home from work, he'd get a foot tub. He would take off his shoes and we would soak and wash his feet. I thought it was an honor for me to wash his feet because he got so tired. Another thing he did, he would kneel by the side of the bed and pray out loud and he would ask God to take care of each of his five kids, and he would name us one by one. We all saw that he was working so he could take care of his family. He worked on the farm, he drove trucks, he did a little moonshine—he did everything he could to take care of his five kids. He wanted them to be in a better situation than he was."[11]

Kenny Riley's mother, Corine Gethers, was born June 1, 1932, across the street from her current home on Savage Road. She was raised by an aunt, Celia Gethers, because her mother had died young. She was the great-granddaughter of a slave, Phoebe Jones, who arrived in Charleston on a slave ship and worked in a plant nursery on a plantation. "I remember Phoebe sitting in a rocking chair on the porch and making quilts," Corine said. Another relative, whom she recalls meeting just once, was her great-grandfather Amos Magwood. The relationship between Phoebe Jones and Amos Magwood is unclear, but Corine recalls that "after Lin-

This Riley family portrait shows Leonard, Sr., and Corine (seated). Standing are their children: Michael, Laurie Ann, Leonard, Jr., Sonya and Kenny (courtesy Kenny Riley).

1. We Lived in Our Own Little World

coln freed the slaves, Phoebe had a choice to make—she could go different places—so she lived here," perhaps because Charleston provided opportunities for blacks during Reconstruction.[12]

Corine Gethers attended elementary school at St. Andrew's School. "It was an old wooden school with two rooms," she said. "We walked to school. We had to help the teacher pick up branches to put in the stove to heat the room. Each room had three or four classes in it." At the time, black students had to pay to go to high school. Corine knew that Celia Gethers, who was raising her, didn't have enough money to pay the tuition, so she tried to avoid graduating from elementary school. "I was making A's, but then I tried to flunk eighth grade so I could stay another year," she said. "But they had me at the head of the school and I couldn't do it."[13] Eventually, Corine attended Burke High School, a black high school. She didn't graduate, but in the 1950s she obtained a high school diploma by mail.

By 2019, when she was 87, Corine Riley was still active, rarely home, possessed of vivid recall, and a careful driver of a Lincoln MKC Crossover that her children had bought for her. "She's wise: she has so much wisdom and awareness," said granddaughter Marnique Strickland. "Sometimes she just calls out of the blue and has some words to say that fit the situation, whatever it is. She's also very religious."[14]

Corine married Leonard Riley in 1952. "When my mom married my father, I don't think she knew what she was getting into," Kenny Riley said. "When we did the migrant work for my dad, Mom would be in the fields working. On one of the farms on Edisto Island, Dad had crews working in the fields and the packing shed while Mom ran the shack that fixed lunch. She made fried chicken and other kinds of sandwiches, and I was the kid at the window taking the money. They couldn't cheat me because I knew how to count very well. Dad would make Mom keep the place open late at night."[15]

Besides working with her husband, Corine Riley had a career as a cook at the Wallace School, created in 1953 when a couple of smaller schools consolidated to create a single school, serving first grade through high school, for the black students of St. Andrew's Parish. It stands today as Ashley River Creative Arts Elementary School at 971 Wallace School Road. At age three, Kenny Riley was able to start a year early at Mrs. Kattie Robinson's private kindergarten because, when his mother took Leonard to school, Kenny wouldn't stop crying. "My brother was leaving me for the first time," he said. "I would cry so long and so hard that when my mother was dropping him off, the teacher said to let me come, even though you were supposed to be four."[16]

Corine Riley had five children. The oldest, Leonard Riley, Jr., was born August 27, 1952. Kenny was second. A third son, Michael, lives in the Los Angeles area and has been a musician and stage worker in the music industry. A daughter Laurie died in 2006 of a brain hemorrhage; the youngest child, daughter Sonya, is a physical therapist in Charleston. Corine Riley has said that even though Leonard, Jr., is a year older than Kenny, it sometimes seems that Kenny is the older one, because Leonard often follows Kenny's lead. But Leonard, Jr., said, "It's more that we had a partnership as well as a brotherhood. We have thought patterns that are very similar, and most of the time we arrive at the same conclusion on the issues."[17] Kenny says he has always looked up to his brother, as they have gone through life together, attending the same schools and remaining aligned as they rose through the ranks as longshoremen. Both are workaholics, following in the footsteps of their father, but Leonard, Jr., seems to be at a uniquely high level in terms of his dedication to the job.

"I work every day, usually seven days a week, and I have been doing that for 40 years," Leonard, Jr., said in a 2019 interview. "When I got to the point when I could work regularly, that's what I did." When he was young, he said, he was trying to get to 700 hours a year, the minimum for seniority and benefits. Leonard recalls that his dad would say, "When the ships come in, that is when you work. You can only work them when they are here." By early 2019, Leonard had a seniority number among the top dozen of Charleston's 900 longshoremen, generally allowing him to choose when and where to work. He prefers the job of lashing, putting rods on containers to hold them down on the ship's deck. Leonard generally tries to work every day, sometimes twice a day when ships come in late. In some years, he has worked 4,000 hours. One year his brother told him, not surprisingly, that he had accumulated the most hours of any longshoreman in Charleston. "We've always been sort of driven," Leonard acknowledged.[18]

Leonard Riley, Sr., is at the center of his oldest son's thinking. "People imitate their heroes," the son said. "I could not be who I am today without the things my father did." Sometimes Leonard, Jr., drives by the cemetery on Highway 61 where his father is buried. "I am so thankful when I ride by," he said. "I make a fist and a thumbs up, and I say, 'Thank you, Daddy.' Thank you for the work ethic and self-confidence. They are the foundation of my success."[19]

1. We Lived in Our Own Little World

Corine Riley sits with her son Kenny. The granddaughter of a slave, she shared deep faith and sharp intelligence with her children (Jeff Siner).

Celia Gethers raised Corine and assumed the role of grandmother to Corine's children. Gethers provided for the family by foraging in the county dump on Savage Road. When the Riley boys were young, they would accompany her. Kenny Riley's recollection, from when he was about four years old, is that "all those old ladies who were squatters at the dump had huts there where they kept hoe forks." Riley recalled,

> They would go to the dump every day and bring their grandkids and they had everybody digging into the piles of trash and separate what we found into sacks. Food, clothes, pieces of metal—they would all go into different sacks. Old scrap food that had gotten all moldy, that would go into a sack and it would be used to feed the chickens and the few hogs we had around the house. But there were times when we found packs of old stale frankfurters, and we would take them to a nearby pond and wash them, build a fire, put them on a stick, cook them and eat them. You would also find old clothes, and take them home and wash them in big pots, and then we would wear them if they were good enough—some kids would tease you then for wearing clothes from the dump—or else we would sell them to the rag man, who would sell them for reprocessing. But he wouldn't take filthy material so you had to wash it. And any type of metal we found, like iron rods or copper, we would put in another sack to sell it to the junkman.

Kenny Riley and Black Union Labor Power

This was all in the days before trash compactors: all the garbage was thrown over the sides of the trucks. When trash compactors came in, that revolutionized the dump, because there was three times the amount of garbage to dig through. We could tell by the sound of the motor on the trucks coming down the dirt road what kind of truck it was, and when we heard those motors, we would yell, "The packer is coming," and everybody would get excited because we would know we had a lot of trash to dig through.

At the end of the day, the grandmothers would put the sacks on their heads and we would all walk home, and they would be carrying the sacks on their heads. I go to Africa now and I see the same thing. Recently I was in Gambia, and we were driving from one town to another, and I was watching women with these piles on their heads. I felt like I was looking at myself. It was surreal to me to see, in the face of those people, the exact same thing that we had over here. The scent was familiar to me too. People apologized to me for the scent, but I said it was not offensive to me, not at all. Now sometimes I sit in Paris, at some fabulous hotel, and you look at the place and you think about how far you have come, because at four years old you were scavenging at the dump.[20]

Churchgoing was a major component of life in Charleston's black community. Besides his father and his brother, the male who most influenced Riley was a priest. In Riley's earliest days, his church was St. Andrew's Episcopal Mission. It was a black church founded in 1845 by the congregation of St. Andrew's Parish Church in order to accommodate slaves, who had previously joined whites in worship, even though the church was nominally segregated. Slaves worshipped in the balcony.

"I grew up in that church," Riley said. "My mom was the organist. We went to church on Sunday, to prayer service on Tuesday and to Bible study on Thursday. The best part was that because our church could not afford a full-time priest, the bishop would allow the priest from Calvary Episcopal in downtown Charleston to service our mission twice a month, on the first and third Sundays, and I got to hear the beautiful hymns, pre-written and calm and quiet. It was a formal Episcopal service, and it was the opposite of our own church, which was a shouting, raucous, good times–type church. We would fellowship with the other black churches: sometimes we would sing and worship at their church and sometimes they would sing and worship at ours. For me, it meant I got the best of both worlds. I got both experiences—the Episcopalian form of worship and the black Baptist. They were so different. I appreciated both equally. Even now, I say I am Baptist—Baptist by circumstance—but truly in my heart, I am Episcopalian."[21]

St. Andrew's Episcopal Mission was headed by the Rev. Stephen Mackey when Riley was a teenager. "He was the perfect gentleman; he was

1. We Lived in Our Own Little World

so polished; he could sing in so many different voices," Riley said. "He was highly educated, but he was a people person [who] could identify with a little old lady who had no education at all." Riley and his brother Leonard became acolytes. Once a week, the two brothers would take the bus into Charleston to visit Calvary Episcopal, ostensibly to study to be acolytes but practically to absorb broader life lessons.

"Reverend Mackey would tell us stories about when he was growing up; we learned so much from him," Riley said. Mackey also arranged for the boys to attend a church summer camp on Pawleys Island, S.C. When Mackey was away, a substitute, the Rev. Price Graham, would step in: he too influenced the Riley brothers. Graham "was a God-fearing man who was influenced by his dreams. If he had a dream that involved you, he would call and say 'Listen, I need to see you. I need to meet you at church. You know you are doing some things wrong.' One time he told me, 'I saw you in a dream last night, I saw you going through a dark tunnel.' He was trying to help me. The three men with the most influence on me were my father, Father Mackey and Father Graham."

After Mackey retired, the Bishop of the Diocese appointed in succession two new priests who failed to connect with the congregation. The first appointee sought to eliminate the Baptist influence; the second seemed committed primarily to building a new structure to secure his own legacy. "His primary focus was to build a new church, even though the parishioners were extremely satisfied with their old historic structure, upfitted with heating and air conditioning," Riley said.[22]

Then a mysterious fire ended the controversy. "One night around 2:30 to 3:00 a.m. a call went out throughout the community that our crown jewel, St. Andrews Episcopal Mission, Magwood Chapel, as it was known, was on fire," Riley said. "Because it was a wood structure, the entire church burned down all the way to the floor. Many of us held on to the hope that we would rebuild and that the church family would once again be able to worship in peace and in love as we had done for so many years. But very soon the reality began to set in. St. Andrews Episcopal Mission would never be the same and families begun to seek refuge at other churches, none of which were Episcopalian."[23] One day, a group of five women gathered in Corine's kitchen to try to figure out what to do next. "We were five little ladies and we got on our knees and started talking to Father and he did the rest," Corine recalled.[24] Out of that moment grew a new church, Bible Way Baptist Church.

Riley's early years were spent almost entirely in a segregated black world. He had little contact with white people and, therefore, little contact with the harsh racism of the Jim Crow South. But there was one ugly incident that stands out. In 1966 or 1967 (Riley does not recall the precise date) he and his brother were taking their weekly ride from Wallace School, which they attended, to downtown Charleston for piano lessons—one more indication that Corine Riley had aspirations for her children. It was a 45-minute ride. Although the Montgomery bus boycott had successfully concluded in 1955 with desegregation of the privately owned city buses, Charleston had managed to avoid similar reform on its buses, operated by South Carolina Electric and Gas.

"Blacks still had to ride at the back of the bus," Riley said.

> If you were seated in front of the side door and a white person entered, you would have to move to the back, behind the side door. On this particular day, Leonard and I were sitting in the back. A guy we knew, who we called "Dungeon"—he was a carpenter—was sitting in front of the back door. The bus went one stop and then came to a second stop and a white lady entered the bus. Dungeon was sitting by a window and the seat beside him was open. The white lady went to that seat and stood without saying a word. The driver of the bus said, "Sir, you have to move to the back of the bus." And Dungeon said, "I'm going to sit right here; she can sit in the seat beside me." They went back and forth at least twice. And that was unacceptable to the bus driver. Then the bus driver moved the bus to the side of the road and put on the brakes and came back to Dungeon and said, "Sir, are you going to move to the back of the bus?" And Dungeon said, "I'm seated here; she can sit beside me."
>
> The driver had a blackjack, a leather club that you used to beat people. He came out with that thing and hit Dungeon a couple of times, and Dungeon reached into his back pocket, where he had a folding ruler. He took it out and a fight broke out between him and the bus driver and everybody started getting off the bus. A white person went to a phone booth and called the police. They had to treat the bus driver, who was beaten, and they took Dungeon to jail. We knew we were not going to make it to piano that day, so we walked back home.
>
> This was not my first exposure to Jim Crow. As a little kid, I loved going to the movies on King Street, and I could not understand why we could not go into the theater through the front door, where the ticket booth and the marquee and all the lights were. We had to enter through a side door. And I knew of some of the issues going on in the Deep South, issues going outside of Charleston. We were still seeing cross burnings 20 miles outside of town. I knew that you don't get any deeper south than South Carolina. But I wasn't really too impacted by it. We lived in our own little world. We knew where we were supposed to go and where we were not supposed to go. That incident on the bus was the first time I saw violence.[25]

2

Getting an Education, Separate Not Equal

In the fall of 1969, Charleston public schools were desegregated.

The move came 15 years after the United States Supreme Court's unanimous *Brown v. Board of Education of Topeka* ruling, on May 17, 1954, that separate but equal schools for black and white students were unconstitutional, and 14 years after a second, year-later *Brown* decision in which states should desegregate "with all deliberate speed." Like many southern states, South Carolina chose a course that did not lead to rapid desegregation. In many parts of the state, white private academies opened so that white students could continue to evade integration.

Nevertheless, St. Andrew's Parish could not prevaricate forever. In the spring of 1969, Kenny Riley completed 10th grade at Wallace School. That summer, Riley began 11th grade at newly integrated St. Andrew's High School. Riley's year in 11th grade was among the worst in his life because, for the first time, he had daily confrontations with racism. For his senior year, he would attend Middleton High School, an integrated school that was created in 1970. Middleton, for Riley, was a joyous place that attempted to fulfill the promise of integration. It provided a stark contrast to St. Andrew's High School.

For varying reasons, integrated schools weren't necessarily what either black students or white students wanted. Wallace had provided a nurturing environment for its several hundred black students. "Leaving Wallace was traumatic," Riley said.

> We felt like, man, we have to go to that white school, and the white students were saying "those kids are coming here" to their school. Besides that, I felt deep pain leaving the school I had known for 10 years. One of the things we enjoyed at Wallace was that, even starting out in the first grade, I knew people in 12th grade. One

Kenny Riley and Black Union Labor Power

wing was first through sixth; another was seventh through 12th. We all came to school together. I would watch guys I knew playing football, and I knew who their girlfriends were. These couples were the stars of the school. I couldn't wait to play football and basketball and to have one of those girlfriends.

While at Wallace I never failed a test; I never failed a grade. The girls were always smart, and on parent-teacher day, they gave out awards for all the kids who made the honor roll. Most of those honored were girls, but two of us, Allen Parker and I, decided we were going to make honor roll and to make our parents proud. One of the greatest memories of my life was when I made honor roll in the seventh grade and my mom came out of the kitchen, where she was working, to see me get an award.

St. Andrew's was different. That year (11th grade) was very contentious. There was a lot of racism, a lot of tension, a lot of fighting. Personally, for me, I learned quickly that the books the black kids were learning from were books that were outdated as far as the white schools were concerned; we were separate but we were definitely not equal. My education was held back because of this. At Wallace, I was getting great grades, and when I left there, I had 10 credits. You needed 18 credits to graduate. At St. Andrew's I decided to take six credits, because that way, my senior year would be a breeze—I would need only two credits. But when I took those six courses, I failed four. I had never been so devastated in all my life. I had never failed at anything before. How could I have done so well at Wallace, where I made the honor roll, and then the minute I get to an integrated school, I fail four out of six classes? I had never even needed help before. But then, when I changed schools, I was far behind. Fortunately, I was still on track to be a senior. You needed 12 credits to become a senior, and that is what I had after getting just two credits for the entire year at St. Andrew's.

The whole experience was very traumatic. It was the first time I had to experience Jim Crow on a daily basis. I grew up in that period, but at St. Andrew's I was staring it in the face every day, from the teachers on down to the students. I had very little contact with white people before that. When I think back, the only previous experience I had with white people was when we worked on the farms, sharecropping or doing migrant work with my dad, not only in the South but also when we went North: the big farmers were white. What happened at St. Andrew's was not a good first experience. It changed my outlook on life.

One of the problems at St. Andrew's was massive, continuing fighting. A big reason was that a black guy, Earl Grant, was dating a white girl: she was the daughter of the head of the school cafeteria. Folks were getting jumped and beaten. Usually, all the blacks would go to the big oak trees behind the school. This is a plan that was put together by my brother and others: all the blacks should go to the trees. We took the area over: all you would see there was black folk. This was our safe haven. But one day, Earl didn't follow the plan and the football players caught him and beat him real bad. After that, my brother and a guy called "Tank," a slender guy who was very athletic, a fighting machine, ran into Earl and he said that the white guys had beaten him, and Tank said, "Let's go." Those white guys had gone into the cafeteria, and we went in there and a fight started and soon it was a riot, everybody fighting. You could hear the sirens coming from everywhere. A lot of people were beaten, black and white, but no one went to jail. I remember that very distinctly.[1]

2. Getting an Education, Separate Not Equal

Leonard Riley recalled that one of the white football players involved in beating Grant had an after-school job driving the bus that transported black kids. "He was a white guy who drove a bus route through the black community," Leonard said. "But after they hustled him off the campus, they couldn't get the kids home; they needed someone to drive the bus. I was also a bus driver, so they called me." Leonard, however, wouldn't accept a one-day assignment. Rather, "I used the leverage I had and I got the bus route for the rest of the year." The first day on the route, however, was challenging. As Leonard prepared to drive the bus out of the school parking lot, a half dozen white students got together and prepared to block the bus by standing in the road in front of it. "I pulled up to them, and then I had to stop," Leonard said. "One had a knife. I was about to come out of the bus, when Kenny came running over and hit the guy before I could step out. Then Kenny grabbed the knife and I drove away."[2]

Following the incident, the black students of St. Andrew's developed an emergency plan. "We decided that if anybody gets in any trouble, we would pull the fire alarm," Kenny Riley said.

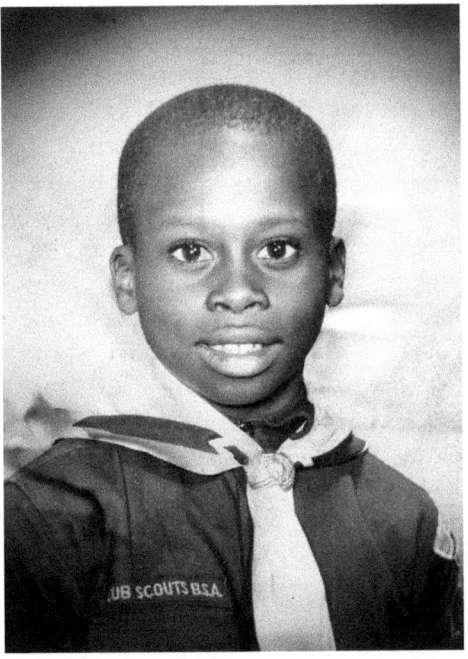

During the time he was a third grader at Wallace School, Kenny Riley was a Cub Scout. He attended all-black Wallace for 10 years (courtesy Kenny Riley).

A few weeks later I was in a chemistry class, there was a fight right outside the classroom, the fire alarm was pulled, the chemistry teacher said, "Don't go out," and I said, "Please, sir, let me out," and I went out. We were in survival mode. We didn't have a formal African American group, but it was informal and it was successful; it gave us security among each other. On break time you would go to those trees.

Going to classes, you would go up and down the stairs—it was our first time in a school with two stories—and you would get hit with spitballs and all kinds of things. We would say "Who did that?" and white folks would start laughing. Some blacks, when they got hit, they would turn on the first white person they saw. But I didn't think that was right. A lot of whites were sympathetic. Unless I could tell who did it, I wouldn't do anything. At that school, about 20 percent of the whites were helpful, another 20 percent kept quiet, and 60 percent were against us. I always thought, I never want to hit an innocent person. I could take a lot.

It was tough. I went to geometry class, and I was doing badly, and so were some other students. So the teacher said that those who needed help should stay after school: "I will meet with you and try to help you." So my friend Mary Green and I got in line, she was three or four ahead of me, and when she got to the front she turned around and started crying. I didn't ask why. But when I got to the front I told the teacher I needed help and I asked could I schedule time to meet with him, and he said, "I can't. Don't you have someone at home who can help you, like your mother, father, sister or brother?" and I realized why Mary was crying. I had a lump in my throat then.[3]

Leonard had a similar experience with a math teacher at St. Andrew's. One morning, he went to an algebra and trigonometry class, and saw white students gathered around the teacher's desk. "The teacher's first remark to me was 'I think you're in the wrong class,'" he recalled. "I told her that I was taking the class because it was required for people going to college and I had been accepted to College of Charleston. But she said, 'You're not going to pass this class.' Then I went to the guidance counselor, who was a little more accepting, and I got out of that class. It was hard because Wallace, the school I had come from, had our best interests at heart. But St. Andrew's was the segregated South."[4] Fortunately, the Rileys' tenure at St. Andrew's lasted only one year.

Middleton High School generally gave everyone the opportunity to start with a clean slate, although catching up academically—especially after a lost year at St. Andrew's—could still be a problem for black students. It was a new school—it took over the campus of a former white middle school—so black students didn't have to try to integrate an existing white school. "When we went to St. Andrew's, the white kids and teachers would say we were coming to their school," Kenny Riley said. "At Middleton, nobody could say it was their school. Over the summer, the students decided on the colors and the mascot." In this way, the Middleton Razorbacks were born. About a third of Middleton students were black. "The difference from St. Andrew's was day and night," Riley said. "There was peace and folks got along. I could have stayed there forever."

In the classrooms, they "had new, more open-minded teachers, teachers who were trying to teach to succeed," he said. "It was a whole different experience. We had a very strong athletic program. We were tough in basketball and tough in football. Everything there was wonderful. Of the white students, some were sympathetic to us: they understood what

2. Getting an Education, Separate Not Equal

we were going through. I'd say there were about 20 percent who were out front and helpful, and others were sympathetic but passively. But I always knew I could never attack someone in retaliation because they happened to be white: I knew too many classmates who were trying to make us feel comfortable."

At Middleton, Riley had his first girlfriend. Her name was Elizabeth Heyward; she too lived on Savage Road. "We had known each other forever; our families knew each other," Riley said. Their romance developed at Middleton, in particular under an oak tree in an area that was designated as the school's "senior lawn." If the oak trees of St. Andrew's defined an area where black students had to go for their own safety, the oak tree of Middleton was something entirely different: the centerpiece of an area for seniors, black and white. The kids under the trees provided a dramatic illustration of the differences in the schools' environments.

"The senior lawn was a place where only seniors could go: the only way an underclassman could go there was to be escorted by a senior," Riley said. "Lizzie wanted to come into that area and I was her pass. We would hang out there, and we would walk home together, and we found out we liked each other. We dated for three or four years. But then something happened: we found out that we were distant cousins. In those days, you would call everybody 'cousin,' the greeting everybody would use was 'Hey, cuz.' But we found out that we really were cousins. It was very difficult, but we ended it right there."

Despite all of the positives at Middleton, the school's first graduating class in 1971 included only about a half dozen black students, out of perhaps 100 graduates. "A lot of folks had suffered before we got to Middleton, and that held them back," Riley said. "Folks had suffered so much that junior year at St. Andrew's, being held back by racism and academics and the textbooks that were outdated, textbooks we got only when the white schools got newer ones." In his own case, Riley was able to pass all six courses he took, which brought him to the required total of 18, but not every black student was so successful. "I felt so unprepared at Middleton," he said. "I had some white friends, but I never went to a class reunion. The five or six blacks who graduated, if we ever wanted to get together, we could just go out to dinner."[5]

After high school, Riley's intent was to go to work. He elected to study computer programming at a for-profit college, Massey Business College in Jacksonville, Fla., one of a chain of about a dozen business colleges in the South. "I wanted to get out and do something and go to work," Riley said.

Kenny Riley and Black Union Labor Power

"I wanted to go to a two-year school and get some experience and go to work. Massey was recruiting in South Carolina and Georgia: a guy from there came to Charleston and made the place look a whole lot better than it was."

Riley arrived in Jacksonville in the summer of 1971, a time of racial unrest and riots in the North Florida city.

> I took the train from Charleston. When I arrived in Jacksonville, the city was literally on fire, with fires, riots and curfews. Massey College had no campus: the student housing was with people in the community. My housing was literally in the hood in a boarding house with some other kids. The very first night there, these kids wanted to show me a short cut to the school. So we walked over there, and before we got to the spot, police cars came from two directions. They boxed us in and wanted to know why we were violating the curfew.
>
> I had a habit of hanging my hands off the corner of my pockets, with my thumb in the pockets and my hands hanging out, when I was talking. So my hands went to do that, and the cop took the palm of his hand, slammed me into the car, pulled out his .38 revolver, pushed it in my nose, and said, "Don't ever put your hands in your pockets when you are talking to an officer." Then he spun me around, slammed me against the car, and kicked my legs apart, and started patting me down. Then he decided to let us go. He said, "Get off the street" and they drove away. Had it not been for the big going-away party that I had the night before, I would have gotten on the train and gone right back to Charleston.[6]

Much of what Riley learned in Jacksonville resulted not from the time he spent in classes but rather from the time he spent outside of them. "Being in Jacksonville was an experience I value to this day," he said. "I was on my own. I was living in the ghetto, in the Jefferson Street projects. I was learning to survive. I played basketball in the projects and also in a gym at the community school where I got a job cleaning up. Everybody came in there, all kinds of people, and I had to figure out who should I try to get along with, among these kids—no matter how good they were, or how bad they were. I felt like I was well received there. They gave me the nickname 'Short Rib' because of my height; all of these guys were a little taller than I was."

Before integration, Jacksonville's Ashley Street had been known as the Harlem of the South, a center of black life because of its nightclubs, visited by musicians like Louis Armstrong and Duke Ellington; movie theaters; retail stores; and hotels. "There were bus excursions from Charleston; people went there to have a good time and to party on the weekends," Riley said. "It was like Bourbon Street in New Orleans." By the 1970s the area had started to deteriorate. "When I was there it was full of pimps, prostitutes, drug addicts and folks who were starting to come out as trans-

2. Getting an Education, Separate Not Equal

sexual," Riley said. "I saw it all. I would sit on the porch of the boarding house where I lived and watch. Anytime there was news of a robbery, the suspects would run towards the Jefferson Street projects and the police would run into the projects looking for suspects. Besides that, there were the riots and there were a lot of civil rights demonstrations. That's why they had the curfew the night I arrived there. Things were going on at night. Sometimes they would still be burning buildings. It was all very eye-opening, very sobering. But I knew that whatever it was, I was going to survive. I was not going to give up. I was going to make it right there."[7]

One day late in 1972, as the Vietnam War was slowly winding down, Riley's mother called to tell him that he had been drafted. At the time, a lottery used birth dates to determine the order in which young men were drafted. Riley remembers his number—97—and he felt sure he was about to be sent to war. But like many, he was saved from going to Vietnam by the gradual diminution of the draft and war, which ended in 1975. Riley went on to graduate from Massey with an associate's degree in computer programming and then returned to Charleston. After a year and a half in Jacksonville, he was convinced that Charleston was the best place for him.

> After I graduated, I had several job offers from companies in Jacksonville—big insurance companies and also the CSX railroad tried to recruit me. But I didn't want to stay there. I realized once I got to Jacksonville that I didn't know I could miss Charleston so much. Every three months I would come home, and it was like so much had passed me by. I made up my mind that I would never again in my life leave Charleston. The problem was that, unlike Jacksonville, Charleston didn't have big companies that needed computer skills. So I decided I would go back to college at College of Charleston and get a bachelor's degree. Back in that time, people you would encounter would say, 'Let me be honest with you, if you want to get a good job when you graduate, don't go to a historically black school, go to a white college like College of Charleston or the Citadel.' So I did that. As it turned out, none of the credits I earned in Jacksonville could be transferred, so it was like starting all over. But that was fine with me. I went back to Charleston and I started at College of Charleston in January 1973.[8]

Unfortunately, College of Charleston more closely resembled St. Andrew's than it did Middleton. Founded in 1770, it remained primarily a college for the young men of Charleston until the early 1900s, when it began to admit women and to seek students from other parts of the state. The first black student enrolled in 1967. In 1970, the college became part of the state's educational system. Nevertheless, according to Leonard, who had started at the school in 1971 while Kenny was in Jacksonville, "This was a school that didn't really want us. It had started to accept blacks, but in almost every class I attended, I was the only black person there." At the time, Leonard aspired to be a dentist or doctor and he pursued pre-med classes, including trigonometry and physics, for which his pre-college education had not prepared him. "It was extremely tough the first couple of years," he said. "I felt so disadvantaged. I had to work overtime to get C's and D's. I would study crazy hours: I was determined and I couldn't imagine a situation where somebody in our family wouldn't be successful. But this was a situation where confidence met reality."[9]

At the same time, Leonard was working part-time on the docks. It may not have been a white-collar job, but it paid well and he enjoyed the work, and his interest in becoming a doctor began to wane—particularly when his application to the Medical University of South Carolina was rejected. "I really began to immerse myself in the waterfront when I didn't get in," he said. "I fell in love with it. I realized, if you had a bachelor of science degree and you applied for a job, you might make $16,000 or $17,000 a year, and I could make that in a couple of months. Mom would have loved to see me become a doctor or something professional, but Dad wanted to see me take care of myself."

Eventually, Leonard left College of Charleston and enrolled in Baptist College (now Charleston Southern University). He graduated in 1976. In retrospect, Leonard said, "I loved college," but the racial and cultural divisions of the day had made college difficult for him. "I had a beard and an Afro and I spoke the way I speak; I'm black and I sound black, and when we wrote essays in science, I didn't always use the right tense—I expected my instructor to say he's got the concept. But it seemed like all of those things put me at a disadvantage with the white instructors." Despite the difficulties,

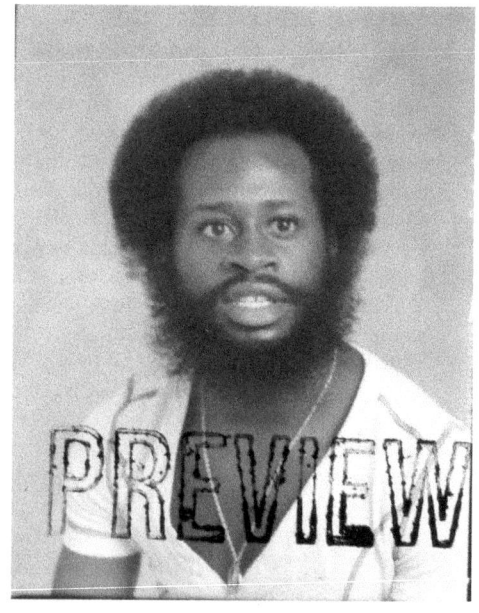

Kenny Riley attended the College of Charleston in the mid–1970s, graduating in 1977. The college was about 10 percent black and he was among the first black graduates (courtesy Kenny Riley).

2. Getting an Education, Separate Not Equal

Leonard urged his younger brother to join him in Charleston—largely, he concedes, so he would not be so alone. "I wanted that partnership, that tag team," he said. "It always worked for both of us."[10]

Kenny's experience at College of Charleston was similar to Leonard's. "My years at College of Charleston were the darkest days of my life," he said.

> I was under so much pressure. It was the only time in my life that I had an ulcer. I didn't know how to navigate those years. Early on, I loaded up with heavy courses, not knowing that you were supposed to have some heavy and some light. I took so much math, so much science, and I also took courses in history and English and a foreign language because those were the core courses I needed for a BA. No one gave me guidance; I took the courses that other students told me I needed to take. When I took subjective courses like English or history, I didn't do well. I would answer questions and I would think my answers were on target, but I didn't get good grades. I believe it was about race. I felt that some of the education deficiencies that came as a result of attending all black schools caught up with us. We thought we were getting a real good education, but it turned out to be not as good as we thought. We were not well prepared. The struggle to make it through was difficult.
>
> Also, the College of Charleston was still being integrated. They were recruiting blacks to fill a quota and I was among the first. The school was less than 10 percent black and there were just a few black kids. Every semester you would get excited that a lot of blacks were coming. But they would last only one semester, then they would be punched out, expelled from school because of grades. It was really a revolving door. There was nothing for blacks other than classes. There was no social life. Leonard and I formed an Afro-American society. We also formed a chapter of Kappa Alpha Psi, about a dozen of us. The school gave us a fraternity house. If we had a party and there were ten girls who attended, we were doing well: there were not that many to go around.
>
> A few things helped me get through. I was determined that I would finish, that they were not going to be able to run me off. I was not going to transfer to an easier school. In the fraternity, we had a sense of comfort. We would be on each other: "Listen, man, you got to hit the books."

As for white people, "there were enough white people who understood that we had to improve our social lives if we were going to stay there," which explained why the college provided a black fraternity house. But Riley did not have any white friends.[11]

Riley's parents paid his tuition, but he had to earn money for housing and other expenses. He held a variety of jobs: in the cafeteria kitchen, in the marine biological laboratory, as a bus driver for the county health department, as a driver for nurses to rural areas, and, of course, occasionally as a dockworker. He had started working on the docks as a casual worker in 1971, while attending high school; he joined ILA Local 1422 in 1975,

Kenny Riley and Black Union Labor Power

while attending college. He graduated from College of Charleston in December 1977 with a degree in business administration and accounting. Early the next year, he began to work full-time on the docks.

A 1998 profile in the *Post and Courier* described Riley's gradual realization of the course his life seemed destined to take: "Kenneth Riley envisioned himself as a hotshot in the white-collar world when he picked up his degree in business management from the College of Charleston," the newspaper said. "He would wear a tie, land a corner office, make it big. Out-of-town companies recruited him but didn't offer enough for him to leave his hometown. Until he could find an office job in Charleston, he decided to work at the docks with his father and older brother, loading and unloading cargo ships. Riley never left the waterfront. Sure, he questioned his decision when he watched his business school buddies, nice and pressed, drive by to their banks and companies, or when he squeezed into a packed bathroom on cold days, toes frozen, just to stay warm on break. Twenty years later, though, he knows he did the right thing."[12]

3

Charleston the Slave Port

Sullivan's Island in the 21st century is a magnet for tourists seeking an oceanside vacation paradise. It boasts thousands of properties for rent or purchase. Multibedroom condominiums, beachfront houses, even sprawling villas can be rented for anywhere from $200 to $500 per day. Some offer their own swimming pools and tennis courts. During the summer, the surrounding area overflows with visitors whose social calendars include July 4 fireworks ceremonies, boardwalk activities, and fun-in-the-sun lounging.[1]

Sullivan's Island, however, has a very dark past. It was the point of entry for approximately 160,000 African slaves brought to the colonies and United States during the 17th, 18th, and 19th centuries. It operated as a quarantine facility, where slaves were processed and sorted. Some were then sent into Charleston and the surrounding areas; others were transported to the other colonies and states, even as far as New York and New Jersey, before slavery was outlawed there.

Charleston's location was ideal for the slave trade business. The harbor was excellent, and Sullivan's Island provided an efficient entryway for the incoming human cargoes. Charleston was close to the Caribbean, which was also an integral part of the "triangular trade" business. This business moved European manufactured goods to Africa to be exchanged for slaves, who were then sent to the Caribbean and Charleston as tender for raw materials, which were in turn sent back to Europe to fuel the economies there. The Charleston-Caribbean-and-in-between route came to be known as the "Middle Passage." The finances supporting this business were enormous, as were the profits. Business flourished.[2]

The mechanics of this commerce evolved into a self-sustaining dynamic. The demand for raw materials placed on the local economy in South Carolina by European merchants fostered a demand for more labor, which was supplied by the African slave traders. The raw materials fed the

Kenny Riley and Black Union Labor Power

The calm waters of Charleston Harbor provide a perfect, protected location for shipping (Jeff Siner).

production of end-product manufactured goods, which provided for the acquisition and transport of African slaves.

Charleston Harbor and its port evolved as well to facilitate the slave trade business. Besides the quarantine and sorting processes on Sullivan's, various small businesses in the port emerged to support the visiting ships and the movement and dispersion of their human freight. Eventually some of the slaves themselves became an integral part of this microeconomic landscape. Slaves became trained harbor pilots, who guided the slave ships through the various shoals and passageways so the ships could unload safely. Other slaves provided small transport and shuttle services to move slaves and ship crew from Sullivan's to the city proper. Along Charleston's portside, slaves worked the wharves and docks in unloading and uploading supplies for the fleets of boats. Other slaves, men and women alike, worked along the docks in numerous jobs that helped to directly sustain and provide for the slavers' business. They became carpenters, blacksmiths, seamstresses and food servants.[3]

The tentacles of slavery did not just stop at the port. The port and the surrounding city and the surrounding countryside were intertwined. Once ashore and released from quarantine, the slaves went to market and were sold. They then had to be transported to their plantations. Again, slaves were used to move slaves. As the slaves worked the land, the fruit of their labor would be collected and brought to port, often by slaves sailing the local waterways and overland routes. By the early 19th century, the complex, brutal economic operation had become highly efficient.[4]

3. Charleston the Slave Port

The city merchants negotiated deals between the plantation owners and the slave trading companies—early on, for example, exchanging rice in return for slaves. The merchants would take a cut, usually 10 percent of the rice being sold; from that they would have to pay an import duty on the slaves and wages for the slave ship's crew while it was docked. Profits were enormous.[5] "The streets swarmed with blacks as slave-traders brought in cargo after cargo before the import duties increased. Fabulous fortunes were reaped from black cargoes by merchants like [Henry] Laurens, who sometimes negotiated the sale of more than 700 slaves in one year."[6] The slave merchants knew that planters who bought slaves in Charles Town preferred certain African tribes and certain characteristics: as Fraser notes, more than a third of the 338 recorded cargoes that arrived in Charles Town from Africa during the colonial period were brought in from either Gambia or Angola.[7] As the merchants built their businesses, they evolved into their own social class; families intermarried and sons acquired the slave businesses of their fathers.

The slavery statistics are staggering. Peter Wood's in-depth study, *Black Majority, Negroes in Colonial South Carolina from 1670 Through the Stono Rebellion* (1974), provides a grim ledger of numbers for the early 18th century alone. In 1706, among some 68 vessels 24 slaves were offloaded. By 1714, the number of ships had nearly doubled (121), while the corresponding number of slaves had increased seventeen-fold to 419. The total number of slaves entering by 1723 was 4,503, from the visits of 1,919 vessels. Over the next 15 years the delivery of slaves continued unabated. The increase in the number of slaves brought into the colony was stimulated by the opening of two other ports of entry: one at Port Royal to the south of Charleston, and the other at Georgetown to the north. But Charleston remained the primary port for a majority of the slave trade ships. In 1726, 146 ships brought in some 1,728 slaves. Seven years later, in 1733, 222 ships offloaded 2,792 Africans. In 1735, some 248 ships and 2,907 slaves came. Between 1706 and 1739, as Wood accounts, some 32,233 negroes came to the colony, as 4,843 ships called on the area's ports. The merchants of this bleak trade at times sound like reputable businessmen: J. Wragg & Co., Jenys & Baker, Montaigut & Curry, and Cleland & Wallace. One active merchant had a more deserving moniker: B. Savage & Co.[8]

The size of each of their cargoes conveys the crowded and hideous environment of the enslavement. In April 1735, the vessel *Morning Star* dropped off 334 Angolan slaves for the Charleston market, of whom 269 were adults and 65 children. A month later the *London*, also bearing captures from Angola, unloaded 378 slaves—324 adults and 54 children. In August 1736, the *Bonetta* dropped off 382 Angolans—340 adults and 42 children. Later that same month, the *Garlington* unloaded 289 slaves from the Gold Coast and Angola—259 adults and 30 children. Some ship manifests were complicated, involving groups of slaves from several different companies. For instance, the *Savannah* dropped off a total of 341 slaves gathered by four different companies, the smallest contingents being 79 slaves from the Cattell & Austin traders, with 75 adults and 4 children, as well as one slave each from the companies B. Cross and T. Shubrick. The largest shipment noted in Wood's list was aboard the *Levant*, which in December 1739 offloaded 442 slaves—375 adults and 67 children. Perhaps the most appalling of this census is the March 1738 arrival of the ironically named *Shepherd*, with her flock of 354 Angolan slaves—179 adults and 175 children.[9]

As the slave trade business grew, so too did the need for a better supporting infrastructure. By the 1750s slave imports were disembarking at numerous points other than Sullivan's Island along the coastline, creating a chaotic—and, for slave merchants, inefficient—system. One such merchant, Christopher Gadsden, saw in this situation a business opportunity. He invested in the construction of a large wharf complex, begun in 1767 and eventually completed by 1774. This project, built by slave labor, was massive. Gadsden purchased large amounts of materials, including long and short pine logs and piles of oyster shells.[10]

The construction of what became known as Gadsden's Wharf is documented in a number of newspaper advertisements published between January 1767 and the spring of 1774. In some of the advertisements, Captain Gadsden requested the delivery of construction materials to his waterfront site. Over the years, for example, he advertised to purchase a total of 3,650 pine piles (20 to 40 feet long), 1,100 cords of pine logs (four feet long), and 64,000 bushels of oyster shells. Gadsden drove the long pine piles into the mud to outline the frame of his planned wharf, dumped the cords of wood on the marsh within his frame, and then used the oyster shells to build causeways so carts could roll in from the high land, across the marsh, to the new wharf.

Gadsden, ever the astute businessman, advertised frequent updates for potential customers on the status and availability of his wharf. By December 1767, when he undertook the effort, he announced that the southern end of his new wharf was ready for a single ship at a time. Barely three months later, his wharf could moor three ships. By October 1770, some

3. Charleston the Slave Port

400 feet of the wharf had been completed. And by January 1774, eight years after it had begun, the wharf was completed. At its heyday the wharf, the largest in North America, stretched some 840 feet along the Cooper riverfront and was capable of docking six ships and handling over 1,000 slaves. On a modern map of Charleston, it would span from Calhoun to Laurens streets, and from the harbor to East Bay Street.

The Revolutionary War disrupted the slave trade business. Charleston itself was besieged and a major portion of the battle occurred on Sullivan's Island itself. Slaves often defected to the British on the promise of freedom, some helping the British fleet navigate the waters around the harbor.

After the war, the grim mathematics of the slave trade multiplied through the remaining years of the 18th century and the first decade of the 19th century. It was during this period that the greatest numbers of slaves arrived in America. Charleston continued to fulfill its role as the primary port of entry for slaves. Some historians even labeled the city as "the Capital of Southern Slavery."[11] During the first decade of the 1800s, rice growing and cotton growing expanded rapidly, fueled by high demand and high prices, and some 40,000 slaves were brought into Charleston.[12] Eli Whitney's cotton gin revolutionized the cotton industry, and cotton quickly became the major export for the city's port. The cotton and rice markets went through boom-and-bust cycles and the port profited and then suffered accordingly.

The gyrations in the business were exacerbated by fluctuating legal regulations. The South Carolina legislature banned slave imports for three years beginning in March 1787; it later extended the ban until 1803. After that slave merchants exploited the pent-up demand for slaves: some 14,000 arrived between December 1803 and the end of 1805. Gadsden's Wharf quickly began advertising slave sales the following year. Gadsden had friends in positions of political power. As a result, a city ordinance of February 1806 directed that all slave ships had to disembark their human cargoes at his massive wharf. For the remaining years when slave imports were still permitted, perhaps the busiest years in Charleston's grim history of slave importation, Gadsden's Wharf was the single point of entry.[13]

That brief boom in international slave commerce came to a very rapid end. Towards the end of the first decade of the 19th century, slave trading was outlawed as the result of legislation in England and the U.S. In 1807, the British Parliament formally ended England's participation in the business; that same year the U.S. Congress passed an act prohibiting the importation of slaves.[14] By the 1820s and 1830s, the only slaves appearing on many ship manifests were the personal servants of their owners who were undertaking local voyages; their numbers rarely exceeded more than four or five persons.[15] Illegal shipments and marketing in slaves continued throughout the first half of the 19th century, but the peak of the slave trade business had passed. Although "legal" slave trading withered, its legacy, slavery as an institution, remained. By 1860, the slave population in the United States numbered some four million, of whom 400,000 resided in South Carolina.

Prior to Sullivan's Island becoming a destination for vacationers, Gadsden's Wharf passed into relative obscurity. It became the target of Union bombardments throughout the siege of Charleston during the Civil War. In July 1875, a massive fire destroyed about 50 buildings in the area and burned up some 20,000 barrels of naval stores. The great earthquake of 1886 also took a toll on the wharf. By the 20th century its original structures were mostly gone; in the 1940s the area was used for public housing projects. In 1989 Hurricane Hugo added further destruction. A section was temporarily condemned when it was found to be polluted by a coal gasification plant. Following a cleanup, a recreational park was built; it often fills with parents and their children.[16]

Along the Cooper River, the slave ships have been replaced by houseboats and cruise liners. Now the area awaits a special tenant: the International African American Museum. The museum's goal is to inform people about the significance of Gadsden's Wharf, the slave trade and the people who suffered as a result of that trade.

Former Charleston mayor Joe Riley announced the museum project at his 2000 swearing-in ceremony. "The museum will be nationally and internationally significant," he said. "It will help us to honor those brought here against their will, and to try to understand that experience as well as what their life here was like, for decades after that, up to modern times. We have a duty here to do that." Riley, who retired as mayor in 2016, has continued to work to raise $75 million for the project. "It will help people to understand history, to understand how some of the descendants of people who landed at that wharf became great leaders."[17] Michelle Obama, the former first lady, and 15 million other African Americans have ancestors who arrived as slaves in Charleston, Riley noted.

Gadsden's Wharf, like Sullivan's Island, is a link to that past that will forever remain, regardless of any modern constructions. The museum will offer a center for family history to assist those who wish to dig deep into

3. Charleston the Slave Port

their past and uncover their own journey to that spot. Harvard professor and historian Henry Louis Gates, Jr., speaking in support of the museum's funding program, noted that "forty-eight percent of all the African slaves that came to the United States entered this country through Charleston. So, blackness, black culture, the African experience, the African American experience, slavery—however you want to slice it—this is ground zero. I think it's very important that a great city in the South be the home of a great museum celebrating the achievements, the history and the culture of persons of African descent. And I can think of no place more ideal, no place more perfect, no place more appropriate than Charleston."[18]

In June 2018, the Charleston City Council issued a formal apology for the city's role in the slave trade. The resolution, debated and signed in the city hall built by slaves, confessed that Charleston had directly profited from the business of slave trading and that numerous wrongs—including Jim Crow laws—had been perpetrated against African Americans throughout the city's history. The resolution stated that "fundamental to the economy of colonial and antebellum Charleston was slave labor, Charleston prospering as it did due to the expertise, ingenuity and hard labor of enslaved Africans who were forced to endure inhumane working conditions that produced wealth for many, but which was denied to them." The council pledged to develop cooperative ventures with local businesses and organizations to further foster racial equality. This was a landmark moment in the city's history, a history that unfortunately included two centuries as a slave port.[19]

In March 2019, Kenny Riley stood at Gadsden's Wharf and reflected on the fate of the slaves who once arrived there. "The feeling is hard to describe," he said. "Those of us who are here today, we owe a lot to the strength of our ancestors—not just the ones who made it, but also think of the ones who didn't make it. I'm sure some of them didn't make it off this site."

"I travel to West Africa a lot," Riley said. "I see men and women there, and I think to myself, 'They could have grabbed this guy, or they could have grabbed this woman.' When I think of all that our ancestors endured, it is surreal to think that we could be able to memorialize that in this city."[20]

4

A City Is Born: It Grows on the Backs of Slaves

In 1670 the first black man, an African slave, arrived in what would become Charleston Harbor.

No one knew then that all the African Americans who followed would play a critical role in the history of the colony and the state of South Carolina, the city of Charleston, and that city's port. They would be forced to plant and harvest the crops, first rice and then cotton and indigo; they would mine the phosphate. They would travel and fish the rivers; they would bring harvests and catches to market. They would work the waterfront, loading ships with good and products to be sold elsewhere. They would pilot ships navigating the perilous harbor channels. They would build the fortifications that protected the region's livelihood. Defining their place in this economic and social system would trigger a war that resulted in the deaths of as many as 750,000 Americans and the redefinition of the United States and that, in some ways, is still being fought today.

Europe began probing what would become South Carolina in the 16th century. Spanish explorers visited Winyah Bay (Georgetown) in 1526 and French Huguenots followed at Port Royal in 1562. Neither attempt succeeded at establishing a permanent settlement. But the safe waters of the harbor remained enticing.[1]

The arrival of the English in 1670 marked a turning point in the harbor's history. Their ship, the *Carolina*, which had come from the West Indies colony of Barbados, sailed up past the current-day site of the two Ashley River bridges and came ashore on high ground at what is now called Charles Towne Landing, some five miles from the sea. To honor

4. A City Is Born: It Grows on the Backs of Slaves

their monarch, King Charles II of England, they named their new home Charles Town.

Those disembarking onto the coastal land would have been a curious sight. They brought with them a class-structured society, with the first grim hints of a future economy dependent on enslavement. The practice of slavery was not new to them; it was already flourishing on several Caribbean islands. Of the 92 who came ashore, a third was clearly of a higher class, better dressed and known as "masters." The ship manifest also included 63 indentured servants who, to pay for their passage to the New World, owed their "masters" two to seven years of labor on a 100-acre plot of land. Amongst them was at least one black slave.

Slavery had arrived in the colony and future state of South Carolina. It would flourish there for another 195 years.[2] Agriculture became deeply implanted as a way of life and as the life blood for the entire region. Often, agriculture was enabled by slave labor. Charleston's port would feed the enterprise. It would import the goods and the laborers and slaves needed to work the economy. It would export the harvests and end products, as well as slaves.

The landing site offered several advantages. It was easily fortified and defensible on the land side, and a magnificent deep-sea harbor spread out before its waterfront. Charleston's economy would eventually grow to match those of other port cities with similar characteristics, including Boston, New York, Philadelphia and Baltimore, as well as French Quebec and Spanish St. Augustine.

By 1680 Charleston's population had grown to around 1,000. The masters and their indentured servants eventually settled on a money crop—not cotton, and not tobacco either, but rice. Soon the arrangement expanded into other commodities, to include cotton, tobacco, indigo, hemp, sugar, lumber, and animal skins. Interaction with Indian tribes increased the offerings: corn, peas, and wheat as well as animal stock—cattle, chickens, hogs and sheep.[3]

Laborers, particularly laborers with experience in the rice fields, were needed. And slaves, many of whom had prior knowledge of working a rice crop, came with the cargoes. They came via London, Barbados, and even New York. They had mixed African roots—mostly West African, but some came from as far away as Angola.

Some local Indians were also taken as slaves. Charleston's port business grew, not just by importing slaves from abroad, but also by exporting Indian slaves to buyers up and down the East Coast as well as to markets in the West Indies. The port quickly became the main entry point for slaves being shipped to America. Of the approximately 450,000 slaves brought to North America over the next decades, about 40 percent came through Sullivan's Island, located near the mouth of Charleston Harbor.[4]

In 1696, Carolina passed its first slave law, addressing how the slave population would be controlled. Borrowing heavily from the Barbados slave codes, the law established guidelines for policing the slave population and for conducting trials of slaves accused of crimes.

The pine forests in the surrounding landscape helped to transform the early shipbuilding industries of the port. The area provided lumber for ships, pine and tar to seal the hulls, and animal skins for trade. This enterprise required skilled workmen, and slaves who demonstrated a penchant for such handiwork moved from the fields to the harbor area. They became carpenters, shipwrights and dockworkers. The historical predecessors of future longshoremen were already at the wharves and docks of young Charleston in the early 18th century.[5]

Peter W. Wood, in his detailed history *Black Majority: Negroes in Colonial South Carolina from 1670 Through the Stono Rebellion*, offers several telling examples: "Often slaves mastered their trade so thoroughly that their owners sold them, along with their tools, as accomplished artisans. In December 1742 Elizabeth Bampfield offered to sell 'A Fine young Negro Man, born in this Country ... brought up to the Ship Carpenter's Trade, and can Caulk very well,' and two weeks later another white woman named Anne Lorey advertised 'A likely Negro Fellow to be Sold ... a Ship Carpenter and Wheelwright by trade.'"[6]

In the early 18th century, Wood tells us, "fishing Negroes" were plentiful in the area, enterprising and resourceful on the local waters, dexterous with nets and boats of all sizes. More than just fisherman, these men "literally provided the backbone of the lowland transportation system during most of the colonial era, moving plantation goods to market and ferrying, and guiding whites from one landing to another."[7] Wood describes these early shore men: "Young men were often advertised in terms of their abilities on the water: 'a very good Sailor, and used for 5 years to row in Boats, ... a Lad chiefly used to row in Boats,' 'a fine strong Negro Man, that has been used to the Sea, which he is very fit for.'"[8]

A flotilla of boats, all shapes and sizes, manned by slaves and free African Americans, serviced the harbor and rivers. The ships' workers moved goods from the plantations to the wharves; they carried finished products from the docked ships to the city and inland customers. They

4. A City Is Born: It Grows on the Backs of Slaves

transported the slaves. And they provided a taxi service for the white communities. By 1708, the colony's population was 9,580, of whom 4,100 were African American slaves, 3,960 were free whites, 120 were white servants, and 1,400 were Indian slaves. At this point, South Carolina was unique among the North American colonies because it had a population that was more black than white.[9] (By the time of the 2010 census, South Carolina's population was 28 percent black, fifth among the states.)

Despite the inviting port, Charleston's location was far from ideal. Nature continually took a toll on the town, its inhabitants, and the surrounding lands. Disease thinned the ranks of the city folk and the local Indian tribes: over time, disease and wars would virtually annihilate the tribes. Earthquakes, hurricanes, fires and floods hit hard, and with frequency. Pirates made appearances; raids by the French and Spanish continued. Rebuilding became a constant chore.

The town's fortifications needed to be bolstered. The original settlers had built some rudimentary defenses, but these had faced inland in order to address the potential threats from the Indian tribes. Now came the time to look to dangers from the sea, not just from pirates, but more significantly from England's 18th-century enemies, the French and the Spanish. The Caribbean would be a battleground between England and those nations. For England, Charleston needed to be a fortress and a depot for its military.[10] As early as 1704 improvements were being made along the Cooper River. "Parapets, sally ports, gates and drawbridges"[11] were erected. Slave laborers as well as white men worked on these. Artillery batteries, bastions and entrenchments gradually encircled the town itself. Charleston became a walled city.

Initially, there was an inland threat from hostile Indian tribes that raided the colony. In 1715 war broke out with the Yamasees. Because white manpower was so meager, blacks were mobilized to fill the ranks. A small army was put together to protect the settlements and their valuable crops. The army was composed of 600 whites and 400 Negros.[12]

The British navy established a presence, placing demands on the nascent but booming shipbuilding industry. A dedicated naval-support effort emerged. Slave and free carpenters and artisans filled the woodworking and rigging needs of warships. These workers provided ropes, casks for storage, sails and sail repair, armaments—all the bits and pieces that made the ship and its crew a viable naval force. The British Empire needed Charleston.[13]

As Charleston emerged, the physical, economic, and social devel-

Kenny Riley and Black Union Labor Power

In this 1768 view of Charleston Harbor, some of the smaller craft are pilot boats, operated by slaves who would board the larger ships and maneuver them past obstacles to the wharves (Library of Congress).

opments along the waterfront and in the surrounding countryside established the city as a key hub of the American colonies. Charleston served as the capital for the Carolina colony. In 1712, the British Crown divided the colony into two parts, North and South. The number of African Americans increased. By the end of the decade, blacks outnumbered whites 2 to 1; by some estimates approximately 10,000 West Africans had been imported and offered for sale.[14] A 1720 census of Kenny Riley's home parish, St. Andrews, reported there were over 2,400 slaves and over 1,000 "free" people.[15] Skilled black laborers, proficient at rice production or naval-related work, became a much sought-after class. As the number of slaves increased, so did their level of resistance: some ran south to Spanish Florida or west to Indian country, and rumors of arson or poisoning by slaves circulated.[16]

Charleston's port expanded in correlation with the mercantile networks of supply and demand. Where a half century before a mere three ships sailed, soon there were hundreds. The port expanded from two

4. A City Is Born: It Grows on the Backs of Slaves

wharves in 1704 to at least eight by 1739, with eleven accompanying warehouses and a market area for selling and buying goods, including human cargoes of slaves. Robert Rosen in *A Short History of Charleston* notes: "The port of Charleston was trading heavily with English cities by 1742. As a matter of fact, trade with England was six times greater than that with other American ports. There was regular passenger and shipping service between Charleston and New York after 1728, but little direct trade with Boston."[17]

Wharf building became a busy industry that fostered spin-off work. Business offices and housing sprang up nearby as the city stretched along both sides of the point. The demand for skilled slaves continued to increase. Black ship carpenters, caulkers, wheelwrights, smiths, and soap makers were coveted and sold for a high price.[18]

Slaves were initially landed at Sullivan's Island for quarantine and then brought to slave markets for sale either to the local plantations or to buyers in the North or Europe. Throughout the course of the 18th century, by some estimates, Charleston could claim the dubious title of being the point of entry for over 20 percent to 40 percent of the slaves imported into America.[19]

Slaves, subject to all manners of cruelty, seemed occasionally to accept their fate, but their resentment smoldered and regularly surfaced. The first reports of unrest amongst the slave population appeared; in both 1720 and 1721, so-called conspiracies that threatened the overthrow of white rule emerged and prompted punishments including burning, hanging and banishment, as well as white street patrols.[20] The darker side of the town's success was festering. In 1739 South Carolina experienced the bloodiest slave revolt of the pre–Civil War era—the Stono Rebellion. A group of slaves broke for Spanish Florida and freedom, killing a dozen-plus whites and destroying properties. Eventually they were apprehended and tried; some were punished brutally, some hung.

Authorities feared further rebellions and became concerned about the size of the black population in the colony. In 1740, extremely high import duties on slaves were passed by the government assembly. A year later a "New Negro Act" was instituted. It would stand as the core of the slave code for South Carolina until the Civil War. Slaves were forbidden to meet in large groups; even their very movement through the town's streets and beyond was regulated. They were not permitted to purchase alcohol. Teaching slaves to read or write was banned. And the assembly reserved for itself the power to grant freedom to a slave.[21]

Yet, after an enormous fire in November 1740, slaves were once again conscripted in large numbers to help rebuild the wharves and fortifications. A similar phenomenon occurred in 1753, when a hurricane devastated the city, destroying property and killing young and old, white and black. Slaves once more shouldered much of the work, rebuilding Charleston proper and its port facilities.[22]

Internationally, Europe's historic conflicts now also encompassed the North American continent, and many of the European powers coveted and quarreled over its domains and riches. The British American colonies were squeezed between the Atlantic, the burgeoning French colonies to their west, and Spain's presence in Florida. All sides rushed to claim land and build forts and settlements. Both Spain and France coveted Charleston and its harbor. To add to this tinderbox, various trading companies desired the lucrative profits offered in the New World. Frontier raids by Indian tribes encouraged by Britain's enemies exacerbated the situation. The various powers were clearly on a collision course. In 1754, they collided in the French and Indian War.[23]

Although the fighting in South Carolina and Charleston mostly provided a sideshow compared to the battles fought in the northern colonies and along the western frontiers, the area was not untouched by the war. Three fronts raised concerns. From the sea, French and Spanish ships might any day descend on the harbor and attack. On the frontier, relations with the Indians, particularly the Cherokee, were tenuous and fragile. Internally, slavery always created opportunities for uprisings.[24] In 1757 Colonel George Washington was ordered to send a contingent of 200 men under his regiment's second-in-command, Lieutenant Colonel Adam Stephen, to Charleston, not to fend off a French attack, or to counter Indian incursions, but rather to deter a slave rebellion.[25] A regiment of freed slaves was formed to support the British army; in addition, a slave labor force of some 2,000 slaves was raised in Jamaica.[26]

Charleston was now the fourth largest city in Britain's colonies. Its population boomed from 2,500 in 1685 to 6,800 in 1742, with over half of those numbers being slaves.[27] It needed to be protected. South Carolina's royal governor, James Glen, initiated a widespread upgrade of the city's and the colony's fortifications, both seaward and inland. Once again, the slave community provided much of the muscle for this undertaking. The improvements to the fortifications were completed by May 1756. Black artisans also helped to construct a new, lavish state house.[28]

Meanwhile, the British naval presence in the harbor grew, so that by

4. A City Is Born: It Grows on the Backs of Slaves

1757 over 1,700 soldiers were camped in the city. Their demands for supplies, including a need for slaves, boomed. In 1760, Charleston suffered another tragedy when a devastating smallpox epidemic arrived, possibly from a nearby Indian village.[29] The magnitude of the infestation was horrific: hundreds of townspeople died. More blacks succumbed than whites. At the "Negro Burying Ground" just beyond the city limits there were 12 to 18 burials a day. By the time the disease subsided in June of that year, over 730 blacks and whites had perished, some 9 percent of the city's population.[30]

During this same period, relations with the Cherokee soured to the extent that tribal members attacked the colony. This fed rumors that the slaves were simultaneously planning to rebel. Governor William Bull, Jr., authorized military action, which eventually resulted in the slaughter of a large portion of the tribe. A peace treaty signed in 1761 with the Cherokee Chief, Little Carpenter, included a provision for the return of slaves captured by the Indians during the conflict. It marked the end of South Carolina's and Charleston's principal involvement in events associated with the French and Indian War.[31]

Afterwards, the city flourished. In particular, the indigo industry thrived, not surprisingly on the backs of the slave population who worked the abhorrent job of "boiling, fermenting, and of processing the crop, which gave off a horrible smell."[32] Indigo rivaled both the rice and cotton crops as the paramount agricultural export of the colony. However, the principal export remained slaves. Demand for slaves grew after the war and Charleston obliged the market demand accordingly.

As the economy expanded, inequalities intensified competition for jobs. Waves of poor white people flooded the port, only to find that black slaves already occupied many key port jobs. In fact, by the late 1760s, a dedicated, almost formal system to provide for slave labor had evolved. Slaves were issued "tickets," which verified that they could be employed. Most of their wages—minus expenses for food and clothing—were then given to their masters. The scope of this labor force is telling, for it reflects the further evolution of skilled black labor in the city. Skilled black coopers, carpenters, wheelwrights, boatmen, and fishermen were hired out, as were "house wenches" and a few male domestics like the "very orderly negro man that understands how to wait on a gentleman." Slave "porters" were rented out for heavy physical "labour in ships at the wharves." Some slaves sought out skilled jobs on their own initiative; even runaways were welcomed in some enterprises desperate for cheap labor.[33]

The earliest black union activities have roots during this very same period. Skilled black apprentices as well as common laborers at times united to fix their proffered wages, one of the earliest union-like movements in the Americas. "Venturesome black apprentice chimney sweeps, slave porters and black common laborers sought to manipulate the local economy by combining to fix the pay for their services during the 1760s. These were some of the first such labor actions in North America." In some cases, local officials even complained that blacks set the prices for seafood sold in the city.[34]

The impact of these developments on the white labor force did not go unnoticed. Some of the wealthy class raised concerns about blacks infringing on the labor market and squeezing out white workers. In the Assembly, some legislators sought to update the Negro Act, which aimed at restricting black slaves from taking work away from whites. However, this broached a clear conflict of interest among legislators who themselves profited from hiring out their own skilled slaves. Protecting the welfare of poorer whites garnered little support when matched against the influx of monies from ticket-holding slaves.[35]

This plaque in downtown Charleston commemorates Colonel William Rhett, who successfully defended Charleston against a Spanish attack in 1706 (Jeff Siner).

4. A City Is Born: It Grows on the Backs of Slaves

Charleston's wealth also attracted attention in London. How to pay for the debts incurred by the French and Indian War? The obvious answer was for the Crown to tax the colonies. Charleston was subject to the same royal tax impositions that were laid on the rest of the colonies. The slave trade was already taxed heavily. The Stamp Act of 1765 cut into the profit margins of the merchants and also stung and eventually radicalized the poorer white workers. Large mobs protested in the streets. The Stamp Act was quickly repealed. It was followed by the Townshend Acts, which imposed duties on imports. The duties represented the first time local coastal shipping faced regulations that sucked off profits. They too were eventually repealed but a tax on tea was left in place. Charleston joined its Boston cohorts and boycotted the import of tea. Carolina society was polarizing, mimicking a trend across colonial America.[36]

Christopher Gadsden, owner and builder of Gadsden's Wharf in Charleston, was one wealthy merchant who eventually became an agitator for independence. He and other Charlestonians began attending meetings with other colonists angered by the Crown's heavy-handedness. Gadsden was one of five South Carolina delegates who attended the First Continental Congress in Philadelphia in 1774.[37] The following year, the Battles of Lexington and Concord would light the flame of revolution in the North, but in 1774 the South remained divided on what steps should be taken. The majority preferred some kind of peaceful resolution with Britain rather than any form of separation. Families split openly. At the Second Continental Congress, held in Philadelphia in 1775, the South Carolina delegation opposed Thomas Jefferson's first draft of the Declaration of Independence. A section of the draft blamed the king for slavery and the slave trade, but its inclusion caused problems for the southern attendees.

The problem facing the South Carolina delegates was that while one might blame the king for the onset and existence of the slave trade, one could not avoid the fact that the colonists willingly supported it. Indeed, they had grown dependent on it. To accuse the king of this misdeed meant also accusing those who currently participated in it, who prospered because of it, and who wished to preserve it. The state's delegates succeeded in removing this paragraph from the text. This deletion marked a momentous step towards the Civil War.

It would also predetermine the course of Kenny Riley's heritage and the nature of his life in the 21st century.

5

The War for Freedom Leaves Many Enslaved

The American Revolution is known as one of history's greatest struggles for freedom and independence, but it had little impact on the status of African Americans in Charleston. Many, in fact, had trouble deciding which side they should fight for.

By the time of the Revolution, South Carolina, Charleston, its port and dockside wharves, its harbor islands, the ships and boats and goods that moved through there, and the surrounding countryside of plantations and farms were inextricably linked to slavery and the slave trade. The institution was visible everywhere, inescapable. The size of the slave population was outpacing the free white population.[1] Samuel Dyssli, writing to his family in 1737, noted that "Carolina looks more like a Negro country than like a country settled by white people."[2]

One South Carolina delegate to the Second Continental Congress was Henry Laurens, a millionaire merchant, rice planter and slave trader, who succeeded John Hancock as President of the Congress. He owned over 300 slaves, yet at the same time voiced concerns about the dichotomy between slavery and the movement for independence. His situation typified the plight of those caught between the precepts of Enlightenment thinking, the bounds of religious and moral suasion, and the purse-stuffing necessities of economic reality.[3]

With import duties looming, the numbers of slaves brought into the city increased quickly. Between 1772 and 1773, over 10,000 black slaves on some 65 vessels passed through the port. Slave auctions multiplied.[4] Slave merchants became even more selective about the qualities and origins of new arrivals, demanding "the very best kind of slaves ... free from blemishes, young & well grown, the more Men the better, but not old. None sell better than Gambia Slaves."[5] The city's elite

5. The War for Freedom Leaves Many Enslaved

families, including Laurens's family, grew wealthier and politically more powerful.

There was no monopoly on slave ownership. Even the less well-off artisans owned slaves. One shipwright accumulated enough money to own his own shipyard. A cabinet builder had seven slaves. Serving as assistants and helpers, some slaves became experts in their own right.[6] Slaves became "carpenters, masons, coopers, sawyers, and blacksmiths." They worked the forests and lumber industry, preparing tar and building boats

The Pink House is one of the oldest surviving buildings in Charleston. In its earliest days it hosted a tavern and bordello, frequented by sailors from the visiting ships (Jeff Siner).

and houses. They fished, weaved and made baskets.[7] By 1775 South Carolina was populated by approximately 110,000 slaves and barely 90,000 whites.[8] With all of the social disparity came frequent rumors and whispers of slave conspiracies and potential insurrections.[9]

The blend of slaves from diverse African tribes also contributed to the development of a distinct culture, particularly in the fields and lowlands of the Carolina and Georgia coastal areas. Most notably slaves developed their own language—Gullah—so that they could communicate. The origin of Gullah is debated; one theory is that it is a mutation of "Angola" or perhaps of the "Gola" or "Gora" tribes of the Sierra Leone area of coastal Africa.[10]

With the onset of open hostilities between the British and the revolutionaries, London soon turned its eyes to Charleston. By capturing the city, the Crown hoped to sever the southern colonies from the northern ones and restore the four Loyalist governors who had been booted out. (Loyalists were American colonists who remained loyal to the Crown.) Once they held this base of operations, the army and fleet would be able to turn next on the northern colonies and restore Crown rule. Lord William Campbell, the Crown governor of South Carolina exiled to "rule" from a British ship offshore, wrote that "Charles Town is the fountainhead from which all the violence flows. Stop that and the rebellion in this part of the colonies will, I trust, soon be at an end."[11] In 1775, the British sent a large fleet to Charleston. It had 50 ships with over 100 guns, while the Charleston defenses could mount only 21 guns at the harbor entrance.[12] Great Britain had a tremendous advantage, not only in its military might, but also in its population, around 8 million people compared with the colonies' 2.5 million, of whom 500,000 were black slaves and another 500,000 were Loyalists.[13]

The Continental Congress was already sensitized to the possibility of a British threat to the South, in particular to the port of Charleston. The Crown's fleet was at work blockading the entire coast of colonial America, seeking to shut down commerce and to prevent any military aid from France and Spain from being delivered. Congress authorized an increase in the colony's home-grown force from 12 to 14 regiments. Charleston's City Council directed that "all able-bodied negro men be taken into the public service" to work on the city's defenses: Masters who hired out their slaves to the city were compensated.[14] A palmetto-tree-log fort was built on Sullivan's Island, with two of those South Carolina regiments posted there. Militia units also filed into the city, raising the colonial force to over 6,500 men.[15]

5. The War for Freedom Leaves Many Enslaved

During this same period in 1775, Loyalists began spreading rumors that the British intended to provide arms to blacks, Catholics, and Indians to forestall any move towards independence. The perpetrators of that hoax were tarred and feathered by a Charleston mob.[16] A number of blacks were also imprisoned by the provincial authorities, suspected of planning a revolt. They were found innocent and released except for one, Thomas Jeremiah. A free black, Jeremiah was a successful property owner with slaves of his own and known as "one of the best" licensed harbor pilots and fishermen in Charleston. Jeremiah was an accomplished businessman as well. He built boats; his reputation as a firefighter was renowned; his personal wealth made him perhaps the richest African American in all of the colonies. His success unfortunately served to condemn him. Henry Laurens, who was involved in the subsequent trial, openly complained that Jeremiah was "a forward fellow, puffed up by prosperity, ruined by Luxury & debauchery & grown to amazing pitch of vanity & ambition."[17] Jeremiah was found guilty and hanged, even though a key witness retracted her testimony.

The fear of a black slave insurrection was further fueled by the famous proclamation of November 7, 1775, by the Earl of Dunmore, Royal Governor of the Virginia colony. He announced that "all indentured Servants, Negroes or others, (appertaining to Rebels) free, that are able and willing to bear Arms, they joining his MAJESTY'S Troops as soon as may be."[18] This backfired among many Loyalists who were slave owners and not happy to see their "property" run off to the British army. Much scholarly debate exists concerning the extent of support offered by runaway slaves to the British army. Dunmore's proclamation brought in only about 300 slaves to the British cause. Morrill argues that blacks who took up arms were more likely to do so in support of the British army: "Few saw service in combat, but slaves were especially helpful as laborers, teamsters, carpenters, blacksmiths, foragers, naval pilots, spies, informers, guides, and the like."[19] But the sentiment among some blacks was that the Crown's cause was a potential path to freedom. A private in the Continental Army, Joseph Plumb Martin, observed this belief firsthand: "The man of the house where I was quartered had a smart looking negro man, a great politician. I chanced one day to go into the barn where he was threshing. He quickly began to upbraid me with my opposition to the British. The king of England was a very powerful prince, he said—a very powerful prince; and it was a great pity that the colonists had fallen out with him; but as we had, we must abide by the consequences.... He ran away from his master, before I left there, and went to Long Island to assist King George."[20] At the same time, South Carolina's leaders refused to obey recommendations by the Continental Congress to form military units of slaves. The city did continue to use gangs of slave laborers to work on the fortifications, but slaves were never issued arms or uniforms as soldiers. Tensions throughout the South were high.[21]

The British fleet arrived off Charleston in May 1776 and commenced its attack on June 28. It hired black harbor pilots to help navigate through the harbor. But the pilots, fearing running aground, balked at approaching as close to shore as the British wished in order to outflank Fort Sullivan. Consequently, the British plan of attack miscarried. Its bombardment, while heavy, did little damage to the fort. Several ships were seriously damaged. The fleet was forced to withdraw and celebrations broke out.[22]

But the British were not done. Rather, fueled by a military stalemate in the northern and central colonies, they developed a new southern strategy with the hope of defeating the rebellion once and for all. In December 1778, they attacked and captured Savannah. Then they marched and sailed on Charleston. By March 1780, they had laid siege to the city. Employing classic 18th-century tactics, they bombarded it relentlessly and forced its surrender, a horrendous defeat for the Patriot cause. The Royal Navy occupied the harbor and took over its port facilities; redcoats once again marched through the streets of Charleston.[23]

The British then turned on the South Carolina backcountry with the aim of subduing the entire colony. Their army, with Tory assistance, ravaged the state; they took to "destroying furniture, breaking windows, etc. taking all their horned cattle, horses, mules, sheep, fowls, etc. and their Negroes to drive them." To the horror of some of the population, the redcoats sometimes "had several armed Negroes with them, who threatened and abused" the white colonists.[24] There were retaliations against Tory colonists.

As the Crown's forces occupied the colony, runaway slaves poured into Charleston seeking the British promise of freedom. Others attached themselves to the marching Royal columns, expecting the same reward. The British often abused them with little remorse. In the city, they were once again put to work repairing fortifications and were housed in squalid conditions.[25] The British commander, Cornwallis, while using them in building his defensive lines at Yorktown, had limited supplies and could not feed them. Their ranks became infected with smallpox.[26] Private Plumb Martin describes the consequences: "During the siege, we saw in

5. The War for Freedom Leaves Many Enslaved

the woods herds of Negroes which lord Cornwallis (after he had inveigled them from their proprietors) in love and pity to them, had turned adrift, with no other recompense for their confidence in his humanity, then the small pox for their bounty and starvation and death for their wages. They might be seen scattered in every direction, dead and dying.... After the siege was ended many of the owners of these deluded creatures, came to our camp and engaged some of our men to take them up, generally offering a guinea a head for them."[27]

The conclusion of the Revolutionary War brought chaos to the South. When the British army evacuated Savannah in early 1782, 2,000 Tories and 5,000 slaves departed with it. Anticipating a similar flight in South Carolina, authorities moved to preclude it. Light Horse Harry Lee, a confidant of George Washington and father of Confederate general Robert E. Lee, noted that a formal agreement was reached in October 1782 on the return of slaves. The agreement was between the colonial governor on one side, with the British commander Leslie and his Loyalist representatives on the other.

"That all the slaves of the citizens of South Carolina now in the power of the honorable Major-General Leslie shall be restored to their former owners as far as is practicable; except such slaves as may have rendered themselves particularly obnoxious on account of their attachment and services to the British troops, and such as had specific promises of freedom.... That no slaves, restored to their former owners by virtue of this agreement, shall be punished by the authority of the state for having left their masters and attached themselves to the British troops; and it will be particularly recommended to their respective owners to forgive them for the same."[28]

Regardless of the promissory wording of that agreement and its somewhat benign clauses, by December 1782, the same fate befell the white Tories of Charleston as had impacted their counterparts in Savannah. By one account nearly 10,000 left South Carolina, taking with them almost 7,000 slaves.[29] Even during the departure of the Loyalists and British units, there were disagreements over the disposition of accompanying slaves. When 200 slaves were seen embarking on the ships, colonial authorities argued that this constituted an "infraction of the compromise" and requested "permission to restore this small part to their owners."[30] The Revolution had brought independence to the colonies, but slaves remained slaves.

6

South Carolina Declares War on the United States

On April 12, 1861, the American Civil War began when South Carolina forces opened fire on a United States military post, Fort Sumter, located in Charleston Harbor. By that time the institution of slavery had become totally embedded in southern society and resonated as the most important issue of American national politics. In 1861, it split the country in two.

With the conclusion of the Revolutionary War, many of South Carolina's elites viewed the colony as an independent state to be ruled as a democracy; however, it would be a democracy controlled primarily by the colony's aristocrats. Political steps were taken to construct a government reflecting that inclination. Charleston for the first time instituted a municipal authority with a mayor and a city council empowered to make laws affecting the "harbor, streets, lanes, public buildings, work-houses, markets, wharves, public houses, carriages, wagons, carts, drays, pups, buckets, fire engines ... seamen or disorderly people [and] negroes."[1]

The city's social structure had evolved into five distinct classes. The big backcountry plantation owners were rivaled by the city's wealthy merchant class; those constituted the top two classes. John Lambert, an Englishman who sailed to Charleston aboard the ship *Calliope* in 1808, sarcastically described the wealthy plantation owners: "Unlike the farmer and merchant of the northern states, who are themselves indefatigably employed from morning to night, the Carolinian lolls at his ease under the shady piazza before his house, smoking segurs [*sic*] and drinking sangoree; while his numerous slaves and overseers are cultivating a rice swamp or cotton field with the sweat of their brow, the produce of which

6. South Carolina Declares War on the United States

is to furnish their luxurious master with the means of figuring away for a few months in the city or an excursion northward."[2] Next down this social pyramid, the third class, were the white merchants and "mechanics," who were tradesmen and workers, many of them white immigrants. Fourth were the free African Americans, who had amassed their fortunes by acquiring skills and creating small economic ventures. Classes being classes, free blacks viewed themselves as socially superior to slaves; some were slaveholders themselves. Lambert observed, "Free blacks are also a step above those who are in bondage, and nothing offends them more than to call them negroes."[3]

Finally, at the bottom were the slaves, some living with their owners, others living apart and hiring out their work time.[4] Margaret Hunter Hall, visiting a plantation outside the city with her British husband, Basil Hall, in 1828, described what she felt was a typical scene in a letter to her sister: "The slaves on this plantation are I believe as well used as any that we could see. They have a doctor to attend them when they are ill, and tho' not sumptuously fed and clothed, they have both food, clothing, and weather-tight houses, but still it makes one melancholy to see them even at their best. There was no laughing or talking in the field, no sign whatever of merriment or happiness; they seemed to work on mechanically, aware that the slightest relaxation was watched by the driver and would be followed by the infliction of his cart whip."[5] Those that lived apart worked in the city streets, as stevedores at the docks, firemen, fishermen and so on.[6] Some of the work was backbreaking: three-hundred-pound cotton bales would be piled up by the black stevedores to be loaded onto ocean-going ships headed for northern and European markets.

Charlestonians were active in the debates and negotiations to create a new national government for the United States. Their political philosophies contained an intellectual element, but were encumbered by an unyielding commitment to slavery. Charlestonians generally favored replacing the Articles of Confederation with a stronger central government. However, they made it clear that their support for a strong central government would not come at the expense of the institution of slavery.

When slavery was addressed at the Constitutional Convention in Philadelphia in 1787, the four South Carolina delegates rallied in force to defend it. In particular, General Charles Cotesworth Pinckney, a Revolutionary War hero from Charleston, spoke out strongly. He had already announced his views in a dispute in the South Carolina legislature regarding a failed attempt to end the importation of slaves. He claimed the state's economy needed a constant influx of new slaves.[7] At the convention, General Pinckney and Charles Pinckney, a cousin, raised similar arguments. James Madison's convention notes cited Charles Pinckney's argument. "If slavery be wrong, it is justified by the example of all the world. He cited the case of Greece, Rome and other ancient States; the sanction given by France, England, Holland and other modern States. In all ages half of mankind have been slaves.... An attempt to take away the right as proposed will produce serious objections to the Constitution."[8]

General Pinckney was even more direct. "He contended that the importation of slaves would be for the interest of the whole Union. The more slaves, the more produce to employ the carrying trade; the more consumption also, and the more of this, the more of revenue for the common treasury."[9]

The South Carolina delegates managed to have a pro-slavery clause inserted into the final draft of the Constitution: "No Person held to Service or Labor in one State, under the Laws thereof, escaping into another, shall, in Consequence of any Law or Regulation therein, be discharged from such Service or Labor, but shall be delivered up on Claim of the Party to whom such Service or Labour may be due."[10]

This provision formed the legal basis for the passage of the Fugitive Slave Act in 1850, requiring the return of runaway slaves to their masters. There it would remain, in force, until the Thirteenth Amendment abolishing slavery was passed in 1865.

Between 1803 and 1807 over 39,000 slaves debarked in Charleston, passing through quarantine on Sullivan's Island and then landing at Gadsden's Wharf. Slave auctions multiplied, concentrated in the area bounded by Broad, East Bay, Queen and Meeting streets.[11] An estimated 24,000 of those new arrivals were sold to buyers from other southern states.[12] The rest remained in South Carolina, which, like other southern states, devised legalities to restrict their freedom. For instance, new ordinances prohibited large groups of slaves from assembling, while slaves engaged in selling anything were subjected to stricter licensing rules.[13]

With the Napoleonic Wars raging in Europe, Congress sought to reinforce U.S. neutrality by passing the Trade Embargo Act of 1807. This measure prohibited all trade with Britain and France, impacting much of the South's normal economic commerce as well as the slave trade business. The slave trade was further diminished in March 1807 when Congress, prompted by President Thomas Jefferson, approved the Act Prohibiting Importation of Slaves. The act stated that no new slaves could be imported

6. South Carolina Declares War on the United States

The Charleston slave mart, where slave auctions were once held, has been converted into a museum (Jeff Siner).

into the United States. It took effect in 1808, the earliest date permitted by the Constitution.[14]

The War of 1812, when the colonies again battled Great Britain, brought another Royal Navy blockade of Charleston. During the hostilities, the British were able to entice slaves to run away, some 600 in one instance. Later, after the Battle of Baltimore (September 1814), some 2,000 slaves left with the invaders.[15] Other runaways turned to various means to acquire counterfeit freedom, as one Charleston newspaper reported, by attempting "to pass by forged papers as free."[16]

Once the slave trade was banned, Charleston experienced a leveling off in the slave population, while the white population increased. The city's population in 1820 was 10,663 whites and 12,652 slaves. In 1860, there were 23,376 whites, 13,909 slaves and 3,237 free blacks.[17] Free blacks worked in a range of enterprises. They were seamstresses, mantua makers (an early term for dressmakers), barbers, cooks, cabinet makers and bricklayers. Although they were not slaves, free blacks were still subject to laws and regulations that relegated them to a lower-class status. They could be whipped for many simple transgressions, such as "whooping or halloing [sic] anywhere in the city."[18] In 1822, South Carolina passed the "Negro Seaman's Act," which made it illegal for free black seamen to leave their ships to enter the city.[19]

Even though no major slave revolt ever materialized in Charleston, the nagging fear of such a possibility never subsided. In June 1822, a slave artisan who had bought his own freedom, Denmark Vesey, and a number of other conspirators were accused of plotting rebellion, tried, convicted, and executed, in spite of professing their innocence. White newspapers claimed that they had planned to create a rebel army of plantation slaves who would seize weapons from local arsenals and then capture Charleston.[20]

Stung by continual threats from the sea, including the British naval blockade during the War of 1812, the city invested in a major fort to protect the ocean approaches. Planning began in 1837. Actual construction started two years later and dragged on for decades, delayed and troubled by legal fights and management arguments. Laborers from the city and masons from as far away as Baltimore worked under severe conditions, battling the sea, the tides and yellow fever. That fort, named after Revolutionary War hero, Thomas Sumter, would be forever linked to the history of Charleston. By 1860, Fort Sumter was still considered incomplete.[21]

The national debate over slavery continued to involve loud voices from South Carolina politicians. John C. Calhoun was perhaps the loudest, an advocate of "nullification," later known as "states' rights." The theory was that each state was a sovereign nation before joining the United States and hence reserved the legal right to nullify any federal law that might be averse to its interests.

6. South Carolina Declares War on the United States

Through the many events that led up to the Civil War—the Missouri Debates and the arguments over whether the territories acquired during the Mexican War should be slave or free, the Wilmot Proviso, the Fugitive Slave Act and Compromise of 1850, the Kansas-Nebraska Act of 1854, "Bleeding Kansas," the Dred Scott Decision of 1857, John Brown's raid at Harpers Ferry, and the election of Abraham Lincoln in 1860—Charleston and South Carolina remained steadfast in defending slavery. They maintained a deep sense of fear and resentment and distrust. A "Charleston Vigilance Association" was created in 1859 to keep watch not just on slave activities, but also on free blacks and whites who might be advocating anti-slavery thoughts and deeds.[22]

On December 17, 1860, Charleston's elites met with other representatives in the state capital of Columbia to discuss secession. Because of a smallpox contagion, the session moved to Charleston, where on December 20 the ordinance to secede was passed. South Carolina was no longer a part of the United States.[23]

In response to the growing threat, federal troops stationed at various military posts around the harbor withdrew to Fort Sumter. Free blacks in the hundreds fled the city; as many as a thousand were gone within a year. Slaves, too, began to sneak away, seeking out the Union lines.[24] Those who stayed were put to work in support of the Confederate cause. General P. T. Beauregard, commander of the secessionist forces in and around Charleston, mobilized a large gang of slaves from the plantations and put them to work strengthening the harbor's fortifications. While they dug and built, Beauregard's troops were free to drill and prepare to operate the artillery positions.[25] Plantation owners complained of the practice of forcibly taking their slaves to work on the defenses. The slave population diminished so that by the spring of 1863 Beauregard would lament that "the want of [a] sufficient number of negroes ... has materially crippled the artificial defenses of Charleston."[26]

On April 12, 1861, South Carolina attacked the United States. Confederate batteries fired on Fort Sumter. South Carolina soldiers occupied a score of fortified posts that had, over some 200 years, been built by slaves, free blacks, and whites to protect the harbor. These posts included batteries at Morris Island, Stevens, Cummings Point, James Island, Sullivan's Island, Fort Moultrie and Mount Pleasant. Crowds of civilians swarmed the wharves along the waterfront and filled rooftops to watch the spectacle. Some hired slaves to row them out into the harbor for a better look at the action.[27]

Kenny Riley and Black Union Labor Power

After the surrender of Fort Sumter, four more slave states joined the original seven that had seceded from the United States. Those 11 states formed the Confederate States of America. In response, Lincoln ordered a blockade of southern ports on April 19. On May 11, the first Union blockader, the USS *Niagara*, arrived off Charleston Harbor. The Confederates moved quickly to rebuild the shattered Fort Sumter. Gangs of 300 to 400 slaves were transported day and night, back and forth to and from Sumter, under the control of engineers overseeing the reconstruction. African Americans—unskilled black laborers as well as free black carpenters—were also used to construct the fledgling Confederate Navy.[28]

The North seized a position on Morris Island and began firing on Fort Sumter and other Confederate positions. The almost constant cannonade (which at one point went on for 587 consecutive days) would not cease until 1865. In November 1861, a flotilla of Union ships descended on the South Carolina coast. The blockade's squeeze on Charleston's port grew dramatically. To support the fleet and strain the Confederate defenses, some 13,000 Union troops seized nearby islands and set up land batteries. The Union Army launched a dedicated effort to recruit slaves, many of whom had been freed during federal raids into South Carolina, Florida and Georgia.

One famous incident in May 1862 highlighted the degree to which some slaves would go to achieve freedom. Robert Smalls, a slave in his early twenties who worked as a harbor pilot and navigator for years before the outbreak of the war, took matters into his own hands. When the white crew of the Confederate steamer *Planter* left him with the ship's eight black crewmen, he snuck his family on board. Then he steamed the *Planter* towards the Union blockading fleet and ran up a white flag. Not only was he given a monetary award for bringing over the vessel, Smalls was later commissioned as an officer in the 33rd Regiment of the United States Colored Troops. He was able to provide the Union force with important information on the harbor and its defenses.

By the time of the 1863 campaign, the North had four African American regiments: the 1st, 2nd, and 3rd South Carolina Volunteer Infantry and the now-famous 54th Massachusetts Volunteer Infantry. The Union Navy also recruited African Americans for onboard service. Initially former slaves as well as free blacks were assigned unskilled tasks, such as heaving coal. But that policy changed in December 1862 when black sailors were given the right to be promoted and to be paid the same as white sailors. By 1865 some 15 percent of the Union Navy enlistees were African Amer-

6. South Carolina Declares War on the United States

icans, about 19,000 men. For example, the crew of one of the Union ironclads blockading Charleston, the famous *New Ironsides*, was 6.9 percent black in April 1863, and then over 12 percent by January 1865.[29]

Confederate authorities responded by issuing proclamations declaring that free blacks and their white officers were considered outlaws and insurrectionists who would either be returned to slavery or executed.[30] They tightened restrictions on slaves, denying them the right to fish in parts of the harbor where they might attempt to defect to the Yankee fleet. A strict curfew was imposed.

Yet at the same time, many free blacks and slaves provided valuable support to the Confederate war effort. They continued to labor in the shipyards and

A plaque in downtown Charleston commemorates the May 1862 exploits of Robert Smalls, a slave harbor pilot who commandeered a Confederate steamer and escaped with its crew and his family to the blockading Union fleet (Jeff Siner).

various machine shops. Some worked as crewmen aboard Rebel quartermaster ships and a few even served on the Confederate Navy's ironclads defending the harbor. Free blacks could enlist; slaves could serve only with their masters' consent. Like their Union counterparts, they generally worked as coal heavers, officers' stewards or, as was the case in Charleston Harbor, as tidewater pilots. In general, the Confederate Navy strictly enforced the guideline of keeping the number of African Americans at no more than 5 percent of a unit's total personnel ranks.

Confederate naval shipbuilding and maintenance efforts, which employed whites and blacks, were plagued with problems. Funding was erratic; consequently, suppliers would refuse to provide requested goods. All the workers suffered through irregular payments, and wage rates inflated grossly as the value of Confederate money tumbled. Working conditions deteriorated: shift and Sunday work were instituted to squeeze out more results. Slaves, as well as skilled free blacks, were employed extensively by the Navy. Many of the skilled carpenters in the Charleston Navy Yard were blacks. By the end of the war in 1865, the number of blacks working in ordnance factories across the South roughly equaled the number of white workers.[31]

Charleston suffered heavily throughout the war. A massive fire on December 11, 1862, destroyed a large portion of the city. With much of the city's white male population away to fight in the Confederate Army, free blacks constituted the main firefighting force and saved portions of the old town. A free-black fire brigade gained notoriety for its determined battles against the fires started by the Union bombardment.

On January 1, 1863, Lincoln issued the Emancipation Proclamation, freeing all slaves in 10 of the secessionist states. Thousands of blacks and whites in the Union-controlled coastal areas of South Carolina held tumultuous celebrations. The former slaves in the Beaufort District were elated. The 1st South Carolina Regiment of African American soldiers cheered wildly when the Emancipation announcement was read to their ranks. Charleston itself, however, remained mute. The slaves of Charleston, in spite of the American president's proclamation, continued to live as slaves.[32]

In April 1863, a strengthened Union Navy featuring ironclads and an armored frigate tried again with a fearsome bombardment to force a surrender in Charleston, but it failed. In July 1863, the African American 54th Massachusetts Volunteer Infantry regiment attempted to storm battery Wagner. It also failed.

As this military and naval noose tightened, the port went idle. Wharves emptied of goods; ships sat immobile at anchor. The number of blockade runners slipping through the stranglehold dropped. The devastation of the 1862 fire was compounded by the Union cannonade; streets were strewn with rubble and bordered by empty shells of destroyed houses and buildings.[33] Confederate soldiers looted the empty ruins. "Our own soldiers are doing us more damage than the shells," wrote one native.[34]

Charleston's eventual fall came about not as a result of the relentless Union attacks from the sea, but rather as a result of the collapse of the

6. South Carolina Declares War on the United States

Rebel defenses on land. The city's fate was sealed by Sherman's capture of Atlanta, his march to the sea and the subsequent fall of Savannah in December 1864. As his troops moved on Charleston's southern approaches, panic spread. Fires broke out. On February 17, 1865, Confederate forces evacuated Fort Sumter. The city's elites departed with them. The next day Union soldiers arrived in the city. Some of them looted. What followed would have been impossible and shocking to Charleston's residents in 1861.

Much of the city was a ghost town, mostly in ruins, with houses and buildings destroyed by artillery and the fires. The harbor was ravaged, its

On April 14, 1865, the Union flag was once again hoisted over Fort Sumter. Hundreds of former slaves, now freed, attended this ceremony (Library of Congress).

shore facilities wrecked and its channels littered with Union blocking ships, other sunken vessels and Confederate mines.[35] Fort Sumter, the focus of so much attention and celebration at the start of the war, was reduced to a pile of rubble. The dream of secession had turned to a nightmare.

The Union command had several African American regiments march through the city. Thousands of slaves flooded the streets, joyously cheering the occupying army. The victors mustered groups of blacks to fight fires and clear debris. Food distribution points were quickly overwhelmed by lines of hungry blacks and whites. Union forces commemorated their victory on February 19 with gun salutes. Army commanders set up headquarters in some of the houses evacuated by the city's elites. On March 29, a massive parade to celebrate emancipation included the 21st Regiment of "Colored" Troops as well as marching groups of over 4,000 black artisans and tradesmen—tailors, coopers, firemen, sailors, butchers—and 1,800 schoolchildren. A coffin proclaiming the death of slavery was one highlight. Not surprisingly, few whites attended.[36]

On April 14, 1865, a ceremony marked the official reoccupation of Fort Sumter. Robert Anderson, the Union commander who had surrendered the fort in 1861, returned and raised the original flag of his garrison. Over 3,000 blacks attended. Various VIPs joined him. The fleet and batteries fired yet another salute. When a lavish ball followed that evening, the news that President Lincoln had been assassinated had yet to arrive. When it did, Anderson's flag was lowered to half-mast.[37] A great man had died. A great city had been leveled, but it would rise again.

7

Ex-Slaves Form a Labor Union and It Folds

The Civil War ended in April 1865. Within months African Americans in South Carolina were dominating statewide elections. Subsequently, Charleston's black longshoremen felt sufficiently empowered to walk off their jobs in protest of low wages. In 1868 they organized a labor union, the Longshoremen's Protective Union Association (LPUA). The union became powerful, but only briefly. Like most signs of black progress that occurred in the postwar South, it withered and died once Reconstruction ended in 1877.

In the immediate aftermath of the war, the port of Charleston, which had flourished before the war began, largely ceased to exist. "By 1865, the city and its docks were in ruins, and most of its ships had been captured, sunk or damaged beyond repair," reads the port's official history. "The Union had blocked the shipping channel with sunken ships, and the harbor was filled with defensive mines and torpedoes. The Golden Years had given way to the depths of despair."[1]

Nevertheless, once the Confederacy collapsed, newly freed blacks from throughout coastal South Carolina made their way to Charleston. The streets of the city morphed into an entirely new world. Armed black troops were everywhere; black slaves from the plantations and free blacks mingled where before they had been forbidden to walk. The Freedmen's Bureau, established by Congress in 1865, sought to alleviate the South's economic crisis by distributing food and clothing to the poor, white and black alike, and also by organizing educational opportunities for illiterate ex-slaves.

Many Charleston whites were fearful and angry about the gains black

Kenny Riley and Black Union Labor Power

people had made. "Some whites deeply resented the educational opportunities the federal government provided the illiterate ex-slave through the local Freedmen's Bureau." They did not like seeing blacks walking on the city's Battery, a place reserved for whites before the war, and they complained regularly. "Negroes shoving white persons off the walk," observed one resident, whose family, he bemoaned, felt "a dreadful state of apprehension of insurrection." As white resentment festered, the derogatory term "n*****" came to be used more commonly.[2] The seething hatred was compounded by the severe economic losses that the city's elite had sustained.

From the day that Charleston fell until 1877, the North maintained a military presence in the city. The occupation forces sought to clean up

A view down Meeting Street shows the devastating aftermath of the Civil War. Much of the rebuilding of Charleston was done by freed slaves. (Library of Congress)

7. Ex-Slaves Form a Labor Union and It Folds

Charleston and to police its volatile racial mix. During 1865, visitors to postwar Charleston included General William Sherman in May and General Ulysses S. Grant in December. Sherman was struck by the extent of the destruction, while Grant found the city's whites welcoming. But, later, one of Grant's aides commented that white women had made faces at the general's party, perhaps reflecting the population's true thoughts about northern occupation. In July 1865, "when riots erupted between black troops and local whites, weapons were seized and white soldiers armed with clubs were detailed to keep order among the Afro-American troops."[3]

In September, Major General Daniel Edgar Sickles was named South Carolina's military commander. Sickles was at first accommodating to white Charlestonians. When he allowed municipal elections, white Charlestonians voted in an all-white city council and a former Confederate Army colonel as mayor. In statewide elections, South Carolinians elected an all-white state legislature. In both locations, the governments set out to restore prewar race relations, establishing laws that maintained black inequality. Sickles' cooperative approach was tempered by his desire to protect the rights of freedmen and to curb disloyalty to the federal government. In 1866, he declared South Carolina's restrictive "Black Code" null and void. The state legislature responded by modifying parts of the code.[4]

The situation in South Carolina mirrored the split personality of the national political establishment. The white people of the South, who had lost the Civil War, had an ally in the White House. President Andrew Johnson, a native of Raleigh, North Carolina, was governor of Tennessee before being elected one of the state's U.S. senators and then vice president on Abraham Lincoln's 1864 national unity ticket. He became president when Lincoln was assassinated. After the war, he expressed sympathy for the southern states and sought to hasten their return to the Union and to quickly reduce the North's military presence. But northern military presence was the only way to guarantee blacks' right to vote.

Blacks had the support of Congress. They and many northern whites believed that the provisions of the Emancipation Proclamation should be enforced in the postwar South. In April 1866, Congress passed the Civil Rights Act over Johnson's veto. The act declared that all persons born in the United States were citizens, without regard to race, color or previous condition. In 1867, Congress gave black males in the South the right to vote and prohibited whites who had supported the Confederacy from voting. Military commanders were appointed to oversee the Reconstruction of the South, and Sickles was appointed commander of North and South Carolina. His headquarters were in Charleston.

Progress continued in 1868, when the Fourteenth Amendment to the Constitution was ratified by the states. Initially, most of the former Confederate states refused to approve it, which led Congress to establish the military governments. The Fourteenth Amendment addresses citizenship rights and is considered one of the most important amendments. It stipulates "equal protection of the laws," which it applies to all citizens, and it includes a due process clause that prohibits state and local governments from depriving people of their rights without fair procedures. The Fifteenth Amendment, adopted in 1870, establishes that all men—including black men—have the right to vote. In the short term, it led to an extraordinary period of black empowerment in the South, particularly in South Carolina. Between 1867 and 1876, blacks had more political clout in South Carolina than in any other southern state: during those years, they won 52 percent of all elections in the state, and served as speaker of the house, lieutenant governor and secretary of state.[5]

Despite all of its promise, Reconstruction did not last long and is now viewed as a massive failure. Although it was effective while in place, it was abandoned in 1877, in the face of relentless opposition from white southerners, weariness in the South and a compromise in Congress that enabled the Republican Rutherford B. Hayes to become president with the backing of segregationist Democrats. The compromise ended military intervention in the South and led to the reestablishment of Jim Crow laws and to an ugly, decades-long period of armed and largely unrestrained Ku Klux Klan–led terrorism against unarmed black people. The rise and fall of the Longshoremen's Protective Union Association must be viewed in the context of the rise and fall of strong black institutions that occurred throughout the South during the same period.

Under Reconstruction and with a military occupation in place, Charleston fitfully worked its way back to life. In 1866 an effort began to rebuild the burnt and damaged sections of the city. Markets struggled to fill demand. Theaters reopened. The land and sea-trade routes were resurrected and the port came back to life. The rail line to Savannah, destroyed by Sherman's troops, was slowly being repaired.

A black middle class sought to establish itself in Charleston. "A remarkable group of educated and articulate Afro-American leaders" converged on the city, wrote Walter Fraser. He cites a half dozen examples, including a Presbyterian minister who returned to the city of his birth to

7. Ex-Slaves Form a Labor Union and It Folds

help establish schools; two ministers who left Philadelphia "to minister to Charleston freedmen"; and a Methodist minister educated at Oberlin who "came south as chaplain to the 26th Colored Infantry." Meanwhile "Major Martin Delany, one of the few Afro-Americans to receive a commission," was stationed in Charleston with the U.S. Army and became a nationally known figure. Before the war he had attended Harvard Medical School. The new arrivals joined resident black leaders, such as "the young tailor, Robert C. DeLarge, the city's most enthusiastic and ambitious black politician," in seeking to alter the repressive conditions that had existed before the war. In November, the Colored Peoples' Convention of South Carolina opened at the Zion Presbyterian Church. The convention issued a letter asking for the vote, the right to testify in court and repeal of the Black Code. It was ignored by the state legislature and the white press.[6]

In 1867, Charleston observed an early demonstration of black power, as a successful protest ended segregation of the city's street cars. In March, "about 2,000 Afro-Americans gathered on the Citadel green to organize a local Republican party, the party of Lincoln and emancipation. As the meeting ended, dozens of black men, inspired by speakers who urged them to unite and to demand equal rights, boarded the horse drawn streetcars of the Charleston City Railway Corporation, whose unwritten company rules prohibited blacks from riding inside the cars. The black riders were arrested and removed by local police and federal troops, but following a second 'sit-down' on April 1, the president of the railway company ended the white-only policy."[7]

On the waterfront, black labor activism found an inviting environment. Even before the onset of the Civil War, black laborers, both free and enslaved, had dominated the backbreaking and sometimes deadly work of loading and unloading ships along the city's dock area. Whites viewed the stevedore work as socially demeaning and generally avoided it.[8] Thus, the labor-intensive, cargo-handling sector of the longshore industry remained predominantly African American, even as the less numerous, semi-white-collar record-keeping positions, known as "checkers," continued to be held by whites.[9]

Former slaves who worked on the docks, likely heartened by South Carolina's Reconstructionist government, gained the opportunity to make independent decisions. In 1867, they walked off their jobs in protest of low wages. They demanded a daily 50-cent increase in pay. After four days, shipping companies conceded. In January 1868, 200 to 300 longshoremen again walked off the job and demanded an additional 50 cents a day;

after failed efforts to break the strike, shipping companies again increased wages.[10]

The next year, emboldened by successful strikes and a sympathetic government, the workers organized the LPUA. The union was formally chartered by the South Carolina General Assembly on March 19, 1869. It developed a vocal, aggressive personality, regularly staging protests and work stoppages. "With each successful protest, the LPUA grew bolder, and its profile in the community through newspapers and word of mouth heightened," Eli Poliakoff wrote. "In September 1869, the LPUA announced new wage rates and hours. When most of the shippers did not adhere to the new conditions, the longshoremen again walked off the docks." Within a week, the shipping lines conceded, increasing wages and overtime pay and designating specific working hours. LPUA leaders scored another victory when the shipping lines agreed to a closed shop, where all dockworkers had to be union members. This gave the union a monopoly on waterfront labor after only six months of official existence.[11]

As time passed, the LPUA grew increasingly aggressive in confronting the waterfront business community. Soon after the 1869 walkout, union leaders announced that members would be fined for working with non-union stevedores, who did essentially the same work loading and unloading ships. This forced the non-union stevedores to join the LPUA. Without protest, shipping lines met cotton longshoremen's demand for a 50-cent daily raise and regular laborers' demand for a 75-cent daily raise.[12] In 1873, LPUA protestors staged a strike, blocking all entrances to a wharf whose shipping line paid below the union wage scale.

Charleston's Democratic mayor then convinced the shipping line to offer union-scale wages, one more indication of LPUA strength.[13] At its height in the late 1860s and early 1870s, the LPUA—with 800 to 1,000 members—spurred Charleston's labor movement: its visibility and success steeled the resolve of other labor organizations. In 1869, a biracial tailors' union and a painters' group both went on strike. In 1873, labor leaders sought unsuccessfully to stage a citywide strike that potentially would have involved nearly all of the phosphate, rice and sawmill work in the Charleston area.[14]

But in the emerging phosphate industry, labor failed to gain a toehold, despite Reconstruction and the emergence of labor rights. Phosphate workers were doomed to work under extremely harsh conditions.

Mining on phosphate plantations began in late 1867. Black-owned mining companies competed with white-owned enterprises. Young black

7. Ex-Slaves Form a Labor Union and It Folds

males, in their twenties and thirties, toiling in deep mud and a blazing sun with shovels and picks, dug through the top soil to reach the phosphate layer. Rocks had to be lugged to small railroads, then hauled to the river to be processed, and then shipped by boat to Charleston's dockyards. In a little more than a decade, over 1,600 men were at this work, earning $1.75 a day. Freedmen also took to dredging along the riverbeds for phosphate deposits. By the 1890s some 5,200 men were employed in the phosphate industry. Working conditions were horrendous. The workers, white and black alike, had no union to represent them. In fact, most freedmen phosphate miners preferred their status. Like slaves picking cotton, they were paid based on the amount of material they mined. A set wage could cut into their pay. This was a tough obstacle for the union to overcome and it hindered efforts to organize the miners.[15]

Despite such challenges, the LPUA was a forceful presence in Charleston politics. It had the support not only of the Republican Party, but also of C. H. Simonton, a conservative white Democratic state legislator from Charleston. Simonton was the legal advisor to the union. He led legislative efforts to obtain the charter for the LPUA in 1869.[16]

On the Fourth of July in 1875, the union showed off, with more than 500 of its 800 members parading through Charleston. It was a joyous occasion, but at the same time black people in Charleston realized that the political winds were no longer behind them. While the parade was applauded by black Charleston, whites were demonstrably unhappy. The day was viewed as "a holiday that white southerners scorned as a black celebration."[17] The *News and Courier* in December 1875 called the LPUA "the most powerful organization of the colored laboring class in South Carolina."[18]

In fact, Reconstruction would last just two more years. Conservative political and business leaders were working to persuade poor whites to join the movement to re-create a white-led government. Beginning in the 1870s, the Ku Klux Klan roamed the backcountry of South Carolina, instigating violence. Blacks sought to fight back. They recognized the threat and sought to preempt it before the survival of their newly won freedoms and power was compromised.

In South Carolina, the showdown with the conservative movement came during the 1876 campaign for the governorship. Democrats nominated a former Confederate general, Wade Hampton, to run against the Republican incumbent, Governor Daniel Chamberlain. A white paramilitary group known as "Hampton's Red Shirts" marched through Charleston

A five-generation family portrait, from Smith's Plantation near Beaufort, S.C., includes young children who would grow up as freed men and women (Library of Congress).

city to intimidate blacks and keep them from voting. September brought rioting and gun fights that pitted blacks against whites. Chamberlain was victorious in the Charleston area, but the statewide vote appeared equal. Both sides claimed victory. Chamberlain stayed in office, but Democrats refused to accept his claim and formed their own state legislature with Hampton as governor. Hampton would eventually prevail.[19]

7. Ex-Slaves Form a Labor Union and It Folds

The reimposition of white supremacist racial politics, coupled with economic hardship, brought the downfall of the LPUA: "In the 1870s, northern economic interests pressured the national Republican Party to make the South better for business; this necessitated reducing the influence of labor. At the same time the national GOP tried to become more competitive among southern whites by shedding its image as a black party. Both trends were evident in the attitude of Charleston's Republican-led city government in the mid–1870s. In 1874 union officials pressured a group of dockworkers against accepting lower wages until the city stepped in and assured the men protection from intimidation. Later that year, Charleston's Republican mayor and police chief arrested waterfront union members who prevented non-union laborers from working."[20]

"With the return of Democratic rule in 1876, blacks ceased to be a political factor except as a scapegoat and the LPUA suffered from the lack of political influence and attention," Poliakoff wrote. "South Carolina's state constitution effectively disenfranchised black citizens and relegated them to the political periphery for decades. Through either lack of legislative support or initiative, the LPUA's charter was not renewed in 1900. Soon after, the Port of Charleston fell into serious disrepair and the LPUA faded from significance."[21]

8

Charleston Rots and Then Rebounds

In the latter years of the nineteenth century and the early years of the twentieth century, the Port of Charleston seemed stuck in a rut. The city was plagued not only by the aftermath of a lost war but also by natural disasters. But "even during these dark days, the precursors of the modern port of Charleston were forming," according to the port's official history.[1] Railroads were built, and the federal government built the Charleston Navy Yard, which brought particular benefit because it responded to allocations in the national defense budget rather than to the whims of the overall economy. "For more than 50 years after the war, little change occurred in South Carolina ports," the port history says. "Charleston Harbor remained a shambles, and its once extensive network of private wharves was generally neglected and left to rot. The Southern economy struggled to recover from the war and produced relatively little for export. Contributing to difficult times were four wharf fires in the last quarter of the 19th century; major hurricanes in 1871, 1873, 1885, 1893, and 1991, and the Great Earthquake of 1886."[2]

While railroads boosted access, they also posed a problem. Charleston's port was partially owned by the same railroad company that controlled the Savannah port system. Since the company had closer financial ties to the railroads serving Savannah, it deliberately pushed business towards the Georgia port.[3] In Charleston, piers deteriorated, warehouses crumbled and the waterfront came to be viewed as a disgrace. Falling prices for cotton and rice further reduced commercial traffic. Higher freight rates and poor rail connections in the South Carolina low country made Charleston's port an increasingly unattractive shipping destination.[4]

Still, a superior port such as Charleston's could not help but hold promise, hidden as it was. In 1880, the city's chamber of commerce sought

8. Charleston Rots and Then Rebounds

to publicize the region's attractions with the release of a glowing report on its prospects.

The study had elements of prescience. It underscored the bright future of a major ocean port in a region that would one day burgeon, even though it obviously could not foresee the circumstances that would enable that scenario. The study focused on "the advantages of the city of Charleston as a port of import and export for the trade and commerce of the Northwestern states of the United States and of Central and South America, the West Indies, and Europe."[5] It highlighted the benefits of the port's geographic location and its extensive inland infrastructure, particularly roads, railroads and waterways. The committee recommended that an elaborate map be published, "showing the railroad lines, built or projected, from Charleston to every part of the United States, and the position of this port in relation to trade of the West Indies and South America. With this will be given a plan of Charleston and its surroundings, showing its water front and wharf accommodations, its proximity to the ocean, the capacity of the harbor and the depth of the water, the adjacent towns and islands, the lines of the Ashley and Cooper Rivers and of the Canal which is to connect them, the location of the truck and vegetable farms, and the line of the national jetties now under construction."[6]

By 1883, three years after the report was issued, Charleston's economy was experiencing a boom. Some 273 business enterprises employed over 8,000 people in and around Charleston. That year the phosphate mining industry produced some 350,000 tons, bringing in $14 million. Processing plants, sawmills, bagging and cotton presses, printing shops, a cigar factory, various shipyard works—all were bustling enterprises.[7]

While black and white laborers jointly profited from the work and wages provided by these industries, on a personal level their domestic lives became more stratified and segregated. Neighborhoods were populated along strict racial divides, with blacks stuck in decadent and declining lands around the city rim. Elite whites lived in the lower wards, with the richest south of Broad Street. Other forms of prejudice emerged: when cutbacks in budgets occurred, inevitably it would be blacks who were fired first.[8]

Charleston could not escape natural disaster. Fires, hurricanes and earthquakes scarred the city time and time again, with four hurricanes between 1871 and 1893. The hurricane of 1885 was followed by a massive earthquake in 1886. On August 25, 1885, a 125-mile-per-hour hurricane smashed into the city, tearing homes and buildings and even portions of the railroad to pieces. The accompanying tidal surge devastated a portion of the waterfront; wharves, piers, and ships were pulverized.[9] A year later, on August 31, 1886, the earthquake struck. The battery seawall was severely damaged and the waterfront area suffered grievously. Warehouses were gutted. At the gas works only the smokestack remained standing. About one-quarter of the entire city's property value was wiped out.[10]

If there was a positive side to the destruction, it came in the form of wage inflation for all the black and white laborers doing repair work. For example, bricklayer and carpenter pay quickly jumped from $3.00 to $3.50 a day, then to $5, then $8, topping off in October at $10 a day.[11] Within a year, the city had swiftly cleaned away many signs of the earthquake's devastation.[12]

Another hurricane struck in 1893. It put much of the lower peninsula and western city sections under several feet of water. The rice planta-

This 1900 view of downtown Charleston, looking towards the harbor, includes a modern high-rise building (Library of Congress).

8. Charleston Rots and Then Rebounds

tions were effectively destroyed. Charleston's economy stagnated and the port deteriorated, unused. Businessmen shifted operations to Savannah.[13] Falling prices for cotton and rice further reduced commercial traffic. Higher freight rates and poor rail connections in the South Carolina low country made the Charleston port an increasingly unattractive shipping destination.[14]

As has happened throughout history, economic despair heightened the appeal of extreme racist politicians. Rural and working-class whites grew to detest the city's "aristocrats" and turned to leaders such as Benjamin Tillman and Coleman Blease. Ardent prohibitionists, anti-intellectuals and haters of both blacks and the old Confederate ruling class, they condemned Charleston, accusing the city of fomenting its own woes and decline.[15] Tillman was governor from 1890 to 1918 and a U.S. senator from 1895 to 1918, while Blease was governor from 1911 to 1915 and a U.S. senator from 1925 to 1931. As they and their supporters ascended, Charleston lost its political clout in the state. The dominance of reactionary sentiment during the final years of the 19th century and the first years of the 20th meant that South Carolina passed severe laws segregating railroads, streetcars, steamboats, ferries, restaurants, restrooms, schools, hotels, drinking fountains, playgrounds and parks. Blacks were virtually disenfranchised.

Yet even Tillman brought some benefit. As a member of the Senate naval committee, Tillman put aside some of his hatred for Charleston and successfully lobbied to have a new naval facility built in the port. In 1901 the Charleston Navy Yard was created; this move proved to be a significant development in the economic life of Charleston.[16] The new yard fostered a turnaround. As it expanded to meet the Navy's growth, it created more and more jobs. Dry-dock, ship-repair, and ship-building structures went up. Clothing shops to supply uniforms appeared. Soon over 5,000 civilians worked in the yard, hosting some 7,300 Navy personnel.[17] With the U.S. entry into World War I in April 1917, a flood of over 25,000 naval recruits passed through the base. By 1930 the Yard had assembled 21 destroyers. The yard made numerous contributions to the war effort.[18]

With the surge of new economic opportunities provided by the Navy Yard came pressure from the black community for a fair share of its benefits. By 1906 the city's population had reached 55,807, including some 24,238 whites.[19] The Charleston branch of the National Association for the Advancement of Colored People (NAACP) was founded on February 23, 1917, eight years after the biracial civil rights organization was formed in New York with a goal of advancing justice for African Americans. Its early focus was on litigation to overturn black disenfranchisement, particularly in the southern states.[20] In Charleston, its demands secured Navy Yard jobs in the naval clothing factory for 1,000 women, 300 of whom were African Americans.[21]

After World War I, Charleston's economy, like the rest of the nation's, began to deteriorate. The stock market crashed in 1929. As northern markets closed down, bulk-cargo movement dropped precipitously. Financial support to black programs, such as orphanages and senior citizen homes and even hospital aid, dried up. Large numbers of southern blacks began migrating to the northern cities.

> The Depression lasted for a decade. Wages stagnated; food prices rose. After President Roosevelt appealed to clergymen nationwide on September 24, 1935, for recommendations on how to alleviate the economic crisis, he received over 30,000 letters. A pastor in a congregation near Beaufort, South Carolina, A.D. Prentiss, replied three days after the President's request, telling Roosevelt
> "...I have been in the ministry nearly 18 years. We have here in Beaufort county, S.C., about 10 to 1, negro to white population. I think for a few whites and nearly all negros we need better living conditions, better homes, schools, farms, living wages, new administration to administer to the real needs of our people here. Labor wages here is from 50 to 75 cents per day, carpenters and other skilled labor receive 20 cents per hour. In the name of God and human fairness how can these people live, with advancing food prices, common white meat 25 cents per pound, with no time of their own to help themselves? How can you or any one lead out to better times if living conditions remain like the above named?"[22]

In Charleston many black laborers, in particular unskilled ones, moved from job to job, at times barely making a living. Black journeyman Benjamin J. Rivers, accused of killing a Charleston police officer (a crime for which he was eventually convicted and executed), testified at his trial in September 1936 that he had worked, in succession, as a stevedore for the Clyde Line, then putting up posts and running wire for Southern Bell Telephone Company, then helping in a shop for the Wagener Company, then returning to harbor work on the buoy tender *Cyprus* as a fireman and mess boy—a job he was able to keep for thirteen years.[23]

Much of this human drama was captured in the famous and controversial story *Porgy and Bess*, written by Dubose Heyward and made famous by George Gershwin's musical version in 1935 and often criticized because of racial stereotypes. Taking place in a fictional black tenement located along the Charleston waterfront, it features black stevedores and fishermen and working women, a white detective and lawyer, crime and

8. Charleston Rots and Then Rebounds

poverty. The tale flows back and forth between hopelessness and hope, the characters yearning for a better future.[24] Catfish Row, the scene of the story, mirrored reality.

The presence of the Charleston Navy Yard served to counteract harsh Depression-era conditions.[25] But the yard generally benefited whites as many new white immigrants from the North sought employment. Although Navy yard employment fell to prewar levels, with the production workforce dropping to a paltry 241 laborers, the facility provided security for those longshoremen who worked for the government.

The yard had an ardent friend and supporter in Franklin D. Roosevelt. From 1913 to 1920, when he was Assistant Secretary of the Navy, Roosevelt championed modernizing the U.S. Navy and the country's coastal defenses. Even after Roosevelt stepped aside to run for vice president in 1920, federal money continued to flow to Charleston. In the 1930s, Congress mandated a new cruiser-building program, centered on Charleston. The Yard became active in repairing, altering, converting and building vessels. Coast Guard cutters and tugs, Navy destroyers and a gunboat were built.

During his presidency, which began in 1932, Roosevelt visited Charleston twice to check on the Yard's modernization. Charleston came to be known as "the Navy's youngest and fastest growing yard."[26] Employment soared with over 2,000 ship production workers; contracts for additional destroyers and destroyer tenders brought in more monies.[27] These build-

In 1935 and 1936, the Theater Guild performed *Porgy and Bess* in New York. The play takes place along Charleston's waterfront (Library of Congress).

ups were supplemented with help from national programs designed to combat the Depression. Between 1933 and 1939, New Deal agencies spent $35 million in Charleston and the surrounding county: They spent an additional $6.6 million on the Navy Yard.[28]

Navy Yard programs grew exponentially during World War II. At the time of the Pearl Harbor attack in December 1941, the destroyer USS *Sterrett* had been commissioned, three more destroyers were approaching completion, and contracts for an additional two had been signed. Employment at the yard reached the unheard-of level of 25,948 in July 1943. Over the next two years, keels for two even larger destroyer tenders were laid. The yard worked at a breakneck pace right up to the end of the war.[29]

The peace brought a different sort of work. A submarine overhaul yard was built and capacity was expanded. In the late 1940s, 132 ships were overhauled and the workforce had settled around 5,000 civilians. The Korean War in June 1950 stoked demand; the shipyard's ranks grew to 8,000, and 44 ships were activated there.[30]

The Navy Yard remained an integral part of Charleston's economy until it closed in 1996, a victim of a Congressional effort to reduce the cost of military bases following the conclusion of the Cold War. Anticipation that the closure would harm the city was concerning, but turned out not to be warranted. Over the next quarter century, the three-mile-long site by the Cooper River was populated by a mix of government agencies, non-profits, academic institutions and private companies. By 2019, the *Post and Courier* estimated, between 4,000 and 5,000 people were employed on the site.[31]

While Charleston's economy weathered the Navy Yard's shutdown with limited long-term disruption, the minimal impact belied the occasional periods during the yard's 90-year-history when the facility seemed indispensable, as the growth of the port's commercial side followed a rocky path that included recovery from a war, harsh natural events and a gyrating economy. In fact, throughout the 20th century, the port could almost be said to have displayed the characteristics of a split personality. The commercial portion, with its wharves, piers, and docks loaded with arriving and departing market goods, depended on volatile exogenous factors. The Navy Yard—funded by a generally committed Congress—expanded and generated jobs, at times even jobs for black people.

For decades following the Civil War, competition from the Port of Savannah had seemed an intractable challenge to the port's commercial operations. This issue was front and center in Charleston's 1919 mayoral

8. Charleston Rots and Then Rebounds

race. Eventual winner John Grace's campaign argued that Charleston Terminal Company's franchise should be discontinued and that the city itself should take over the operations of the commercial waterfront.[32] In March 1920 Grace succeeded in getting an act passed in the South Carolina Senate "allowing municipalities of at least 50,000 residents to acquire, own or operate public port facilities."[33] Subsequently the privately held terminal company lost its franchise rights and the city purchased its docks for $1.5 million. A Port Utilities Commission (PUC) was established; the dollar value of cargo flowing through Charleston quickly doubled.[34]

However, the Depression "dealt a near lethal blow to the port and to the Port Utilities Commission," according to the port's official history. "Traffic and revenue dropped sharply and by 1941 the public port facilities were in virtually the same shape as they had been in 1921."[35]

During World War II, it became clear that the city and the PUC "did not have the resources to build and maintain a port that could serve the whole state, and competition from other state-supported ports was intense."[36] In 1942, the state legislature created the South Carolina State Ports Authority (SCPA), which presided over the port's expansion into the container cargo business. That was accompanied by the emergence of a powerful labor union.

9

George Washington German Brings the Union Back

The economic recovery that followed the Depression triggered a resurgence of the labor movement. Unions flexed their muscles during a series of strikes in the landmark year of 1934. The following year, Congress approved the labor-friendly Wagner Act. Subsequently, wages rose and union membership increased. In Charleston, black longshoremen found a leader in George Washington German, a grandson of slaves, who led the effort to charter a new local and then headed it for more than three decades.

During his 33 years at the helm of one of South Carolina's few powerful black organizations, German was an influential figure in Charleston and an early advocate for black participation in electoral politics. His efforts were reinforced as the civil rights movement emerged, especially in Charleston, where a smattering of. progressive white leaders made unique contributions. However, German's influence waned when the civil rights movement spotlight shifted to Charleston for the 1969 hospital strike, a long-overlooked landmark event that celebrated its 50th anniversary in 2019. The strike seemed to mark the moment when German's leadership style—strong yet sometimes reticent to overstep—fell behind the pace of a rapidly changing society.

In 1934, four major strikes demonstrated labor's ability to publicly insist that working people were entitled to better lives. The strikes took place in diversified locations throughout the country. They included a textile workers' strike involving mills in the Carolinas and New England; a San Francisco general strike, led by longshoremen; the Toledo Auto-Lite strike; and the Minneapolis Teamsters strike. In the case of the textile workers, the United Textile Workers declared a nationwide strike in Sep-

9. George Washington German Brings the Union Back

tember. About 400,000 textile workers stayed home, including about 65,000 in North Carolina and 43,000 in South Carolina.¹

Labor's influence in South Carolina may have reached its height in 1934, when Olin D. Johnson, a pro-labor, pro–Roosevelt Democrat, was elected governor in the aftermath of the textile workers' strike. Johnson was the rare South Carolina legislator who had a genuine connection with organized labor. "He grew up in a mill village," said Eli Poliakoff. "His base was white male labor guys. When he was campaigning, he would walk through the mills and shake hands with everyone. He could even fix a loom."² Johnson was from Honea Path, a small town in northwest South Carolina that was the site of a violent confrontation during the 1934 uprising. In the confrontation, factory guards killed six picketers and injured 20 more.³ After serving as governor from 1935 to 1939 and again from 1943 to 1945, Johnson spent 20 years in the U.S. Senate. "People say South Carolina is historically unfriendly to unions," Poliakoff said. "The only exceptions are Olin Johnson and Kenny Riley."⁴

In Charleston in the 1930s, economic expansion at the port combined with growing labor strength to enable the rebirth of organized dockside labor for the first time since the LPUA collapsed around the end of the 19th century. German had returned home to work on the waterfront after serving in the military during World War I. In selecting a trade, he followed the examples of his father, who had worked the docks in various capacities (including boatman), and his grandfather, a former McClellanville slave who worked as a rice-boat navigator after the Civil War. In fact, German's grandfather had been involved in the 1869 effort to incorporate the LPUA. "For 15 years, George German labored without a union," Poliakoff wrote. "By the 1930s, increased labor union activity in South Carolina and the revival of the Port of Charleston led to renewed union interest along the docks."⁵

At the time, the two longshoremen's unions, the ILA and the International Longshore and Warehouse Union (ILWU), battled for jurisdiction in Charleston, just as they were doing in nearly all Southeast ports. ILA leaders were especially fearful that shippers would forgo unionized ports in the North for the lower-cost, non-unionized ports of the South. In 1935 the ILA set out to organize southern dockworkers, beginning with Tampa and moving to Jacksonville, Miami, Savannah and finally to Charleston in 1936.⁶ Charleston longshoremen leaned towards the ILA because the federal government had designated that union as the official longshoremen representative during World War I.

Kenny Riley and Black Union Labor Power

German cast his lot with the ILA. In September 1936, just months after Local 1422 won its charter and made German its first president, Charleston dockworkers struck over low wages. At the offices of the A. E. Holleman Stevedoring Company, 300 dockworkers protested, demanding pay restitution. Charleston police broke up the crowd, but work stoppages and more street protests continued. By the end of the year, the port companies gave in and acknowledged Local 1422 as the official spokesman and negotiator for the dockworkers.[7]

Although the economy worked to German's benefit, South Carolina racism was a constant barrier. Charleston, at the time, presented a conflicting picture on the exclusion of blacks from commerce and politics. On the one hand, the region was firmly committed to segregation. On the other, as the civil rights movement began its postwar emergence, a U.S. District Court judge from Charleston realized that the segregationist legal system of the post–Reconstruction South violated equal rights provisions of the U.S. Constitution. That judge was Julius Waties Waring. His seminal

This plaque portrays the four presidents of Charleston ILA Local 1422. George German, wearing a hat, is at the left; Samuel Simmons, Sr., is at the top; Benjamin Flowers is at the right; and Walter Bankhead is at the bottom (ILA Local 1422).

9. George Washington German Brings the Union Back

role in the civil rights movement gained renewed attention in 2019 with the publication of the book, *The Blinding of Sgt. Isaac Woodard and the Awakening of President Harry S. Truman and Judge J. Waties Waring,* by Richard Gergel, a U.S. District Court judge in Charleston.

In 1944 the United States Supreme Court ruled in *Smith v. Allwright* that states could not "exclude African Americans from voting in primary elections."[8] In response, South Carolina legislators moved to amend the state constitution to make the Democratic Party a private club that could exclude black voters. However, in 1947 Waring ruled the private primary unconstitutional.[9] In his ruling, the eighth-generation Charlestonian declared that "private clubs ... do not vote and elect a president (or) Senators and members of the House of Representatives." He concluded, "It is time for South Carolina to rejoin the union ... [and] adopt the American way of conducting elections." In response, black leaders were jubilant, but many whites in South Carolina were angry. Some suggested dropping the Democratic Party altogether while others advocated for keeping it white.[10]

The 1947 ruling was an early example of an emerging pattern of independent, principled rulings Waring was to issue; those rulings became a touchstone for white southerners seeking change in the region's racist legal landscape. In his book, Gergel focuses on Waring's role in a 1946 case involving the vicious blinding of a returning black veteran, Isaac Woodard, by the white police chief of Batesburg, a small South Carolina town west of Columbia. The police chief was acquitted by an all-white jury. Waring was deeply affected by the outcome, which he felt was unjust. The Woodard case attracted the attention of President Harry S. Truman, who reacted by becoming a firm advocate for civil rights. In 1948, Truman issued an executive order that abolished discrimination, including racial discrimination, in the United States Armed Forces. In 1951, Waring issued a famous dissent when a three-judge panel upheld school segregation in the case of *Briggs v. Elliot.* That dissent was consolidated into *Brown v. Board of Education,* which eventually led to school desegregation in the South. Waring is a key figure in the story of how some white Charlestonians helped to lead the South out of its unseemly past: Longtime Charleston mayor Joe Riley continued that same tradition.

German, of course, was fully cognizant of South Carolina's political climate. He understood that he needed to position himself so that he could benefit from the Warings of the world, and from the slow winds of change they embodied, while not threatening the state's racist power structure. He also realized that for the Port of Charleston to function smoothly, he and his members would necessarily have an alliance with the white power structure within Charleston, even if more insular, more segregationist segments of South Carolina abhorred him. In general, German tread a thin line, not only between the two sides in South Carolina, but also within a union that was more focused on the New York waterfront than on the Charleston waterfront.

German understood that a vocal black presence in Charleston would provide an easy scapegoat for the state's opportunistic race-baiting politicians. So he tried to work quietly and behind the scenes. "Worst thing he could have done was get in the media," recalled his daughter Isabel Liggins, as such attention could only distract from wage and hour issues.[11] German "advised all his men to participate in the civil rights movement ... but he didn't put the union in front," recalls veteran longshoreman Marion Turner, who worked under German for nine years. German didn't oppose the civil rights movement, Turner said, but he "didn't want to go but so far."[12]

During German's tenure as local president, "the later part of which coincided with the post-war civil rights movement, the ILA exercised a quiet influence amidst an incendiary racial atmosphere."[13] German focused on education and on economic objectives that could be achieved through private negotiations with shippers. "As far as German was concerned, the outside world need never have known that the ILA was predominantly African American. His daughter cannot recall German marching in any civil rights demonstration. A grandson of slaves, he urged members to learn to read and write before pursuing grander ambitions."[14]

It would be wrong to say that Local 1422 abstained entirely from political involvement, but its involvement was subtle. It exercised political power through strategic relationships, indirect involvement and quiet coercion. The local's strength lay in its ability to mobilize a large, registered, cohesive block of voters. German even required potential members to register to vote before they could join the union. The registrations became important once Waring ordered the primary opened to blacks in 1948. More importantly, local politicians understood the grip that Local 1422 had over port business, and they responded accordingly to demands. Liggins recalled that local police would occasionally pick up union members for alleged public drunkenness and detain them at the station. German would call the police to ask why the police chief was stalling port business by preventing longshoremen from working. He would quietly make it known that he had the power to slow port work.[15]

9. George Washington German Brings the Union Back

Local 1422 had the ear of longtime Charleston mayor William Morrison, who served from 1947 to 1959. As city politics evolved along with an emerging civil rights struggle, Morrison was the first mayor in decades to court black votes by appointing African Americans to the police force and other city jobs. The hallmark of his first term in office was the extension of sewer lines into black neighborhoods and the renewal of slums with Federal Housing Administration projects. Morrison also championed the Port of Charleston, encouraging a massive mid–1950s expansion project that added waterfront property, piers, docks and railway extensions. Morrison had personal and professional connections to the Charleston ILA. His grandfather had owned George Washington German's grandfather until freeing him in 1861. Liggins believed this relationship affected Morrison's conscience and encouraged a sympathetic attitude towards German and the ILA. When German needed a lawyer for the young organization, he turned to Morrison, who would fill the role for the next 33 years. German's wife was a caregiver for Morrison's children, and the mayor helped German's daughter gain employment in Washington, D.C., Liggins said.[16]

Local 1422's nonconfrontational approach extended beyond its response to Jim Crow. "German's low profile and economic emphasis carried over to the policies of the union," Poliakoff wrote. "German disliked work stoppages, especially when called by the New York headquarters and not involving Charleston events. This often set German and Local 1422 against the international leaders. In October 1959 ILA leadership called a strike along the Atlantic and Gulf Coast ports. Local 1422, however, broke the strike early by unloading banana boats waiting in the port."[17]

The rivalry between the ILA and ILWU resurfaced during the 1959 strike. Once again, the ILWU expressed interest in Charleston, hoping to exploit local antipathy toward the ILA's national headquarters.[18] But, once again, the ILA prevailed, even though the San Francisco–based union generally took a far more aggressive approach to racial inequality than ILA did and offered far more support to the emerging civil rights movement. Thirty years later, this division would become important in Charleston when the ILWU seemed more committed to supporting Kenny Riley and his black longshoremen than his own union was. The ILWU's egalitarian ideals sprang from the Communist inclinations of its San Francisco founders, who had split from the more conservative ILA. Reflecting its political conservatism, ILA leadership was more committed to local autonomy, which enabled segregation in some locals. Ironically, their segregationist approach also provided a rare opportunity for black leadership.

Kenny Riley and Black Union Labor Power

ILA workers load stocks of bananas onto trucks in the early 1950s, after the bananas were unloaded from ships (ILA Local 1422).

In 1962, German once again refused to go along with a strike called by the union's international leadership, which wanted East Coast workers to stay home over disagreements with shippers. Three days into the strike, the front page of the Charleston *News and Courier* announced in large type "Local Longshoremen Defy Union Mandate." German had agreed to unload potatoes and bananas from New York. William Bradley, the New York–based president of the ILA, voiced displeasure with the Charleston Local and threatened to revoke 1422's charter. (Bradley never acted on the

9. George Washington German Brings the Union Back

threat.) Recalling the incident, a newspaper profile of German suggested, "It has been said that [he] has a knack of getting lost when a strike call was expected, so that there would be 'nobody around with authority to issue orders, and the men could continue working.' As a result, German had 'few, if any disagreements with stevedoring contractors.'"[19]

German's affinity for quiet maneuvering came face to face with a new reality in 1969, when it was challenged by the merger of the civil rights movement and the labor movement during the Charleston hospital workers' strike. Tragically, the year before the Charleston action, the same civil rights/labor movement alliance provided the backdrop for the assassination of Martin Luther King, Jr. King had traveled to Memphis to back a strike by black sanitation workers. As tragic as it was, King's assassination only strengthened the resolve of the Charleston hospital workers.

In the summer of 1969, the predominantly African American and female support staff struck at the Medical College of South Carolina (MCSC) Hospital. More than 400 workers walked off their jobs at two MCSC hospitals for more than three months, seeking equal pay for blacks and whites, courtesy titles and union recognition. As a state agency, the Medical College was in a similar legal position to that of the State Ports Authority, which accepted unionization, but it claimed that state laws prevented the unionization of its employees. The conflict took on racial tones, with opponents of the strike citing the nurses' lack of formal education while advertisements in the News and Courier linked anti-union sentiment to racism, involved the Ku Klux Klan and instructed supporters not to "Tom" for state politicians who opposed the strike.[20]

Jack Bass, who at the time was Columbia bureau chief for the Charlotte Observer, said the college president was a doctor who had little understanding of how to respond to the strike and its steadily growing support. "There was resistance to doing anything," Bass said. But numerous marches, backed by national civil rights organizations, drew attention and motivated strikers. King's top lieutenants got involved. Andrew Young, Southern Christian Leadership Conference (SCLC) vice president, served as a chief tactician for the struggle and, along with SCLC president Ralph David Abernathy, attracted national media attention to the strikers. Bass recalls attending a march that was led by Coretta Scott King. "Andrew Young was there," Bass said. "You'd see people on their porches, and he would wave to them and say: 'Come down and join us.' The size of the march kept expanding and growing." Bass said the strike got national attention, which put pressure on state government officials in South Carolina.[21]

When the strike was settled in June, the strikers had secured all of their demands except for union recognition. Seen as a successful challenge by a previously voiceless group against a powerful oppressor, the event empowered the black community. The black community "learned from the strike that when effectively organized, they could accomplish a great deal," recalled former South Carolina state senator Arthur Ravenal. "It gave them a realization of the strength they had politically."[22] The hospital strike came in the aftermath of the passage of the Voting Rights Act of 1965, signed into law by President Lyndon Johnson, which sought to overcome legal barriers at the state and local levels that prevented African Americans from exercising their right to vote as guaranteed under the Fourteenth and Fifteenth amendments to the U.S. Constitution.[23] In 1968, over 200,000 black South Carolinians registered to vote for the first time. The strike's impact was that even more African Americans became involved in Charleston politics and registered to vote. In the 1970s, Charleston Democrats increasingly recognized that Local 1422 provided a path to black support. Before that, "politicians never came to the union to count votes," said Isabel Liggins.[24] It was a sign that once again, for the first time since Reconstruction, Charleston longshoremen were in the middle of the city's political world.

Fifty years later, former Charleston mayor Joe Riley called the strike "a seminal event" in the city's history. "It was a very important time because the strike was about black hospital workers, who did the same work as white hospital workers but got paid less, which had been an accepted practice in the South," Riley said. "What happened in Charleston was fortunate in that the strike had good leadership in Bill Saunders, a wonderful man who represented workers and helped bring both sides together, and the city had a police chief, John Conroy, whom the African American community trusted. It was a difficult controversy that was resolved without violence." Riley had been elected to the South Carolina House of Representatives in 1968. In his second speech on the floor, he said, "I spoke about how some people were lumping all black people together as radical trouble makers. I deflected that in a reasoned way."[25] Riley served three terms in the legislature. In 1975, he was elected mayor of Charleston, a post he held until 2016.

Kenny Riley's brother Leonard also recalled the hospital strike. At the time, Leonard Riley was 16 and Kenny Riley was 15. The brothers

9. George Washington German Brings the Union Back

both recollect their awareness of nighttime curfews and their mother's admonition not to get arrested as a result of some engagement on the perimeter of the strikers' activism. "I remember the city being in chaos then, with curfews and people wanting higher wages and being arrested," Leonard said. "Mom didn't want us to march with them, didn't want us to go out after curfews. She didn't want us to get arrested for anything. But we identified with the workers wanting more for their labors. I remember I felt offended that they were being arrested and that all of us were being impacted. By then we had started to grow our beards and wear our Afros, and we had a sense of right and wrong. We were raised in a believing, Christian family, and our sense of right and wrong was embodied in that belief."[26]

Although Local 1422 provided financial aid and other support to the strikers, George German did not believe the strike was any of his business and did not get involved. The national ILA leadership, however, took an entirely different tack, threatening a strike at the Port of Charleston in order to show solidarity with the workers. "ILA national wanted to weigh in and shut down the port," Kenny Riley said.[27] Jack Bass said the ILA's threat played a major role in forcing a settlement. And German, who declared his opposition to the idea, realized that times had changed. Immediately following the strike, Local 1422's first president stepped down after 33 years of leadership.

Afterwards, Local 1422 gradually took on a more vocal and aggressive persona, reminiscent of the LPUA of the 1860s. Just as Reconstruction had created a climate that strengthened the 19th-century union, the civil rights movement created a welcoming environment for the Local. As German's influence faded, a new public image developed, one that projected assertiveness, a desire for publicity and political involvement. By the late 1990s a new generation of leadership had restored the Local's political voice into one that was prominent within the South Carolina labor community.

Nationally, black labor leaders were becoming more vocal within the AFL-CIO. The national labor federation's refusal to endorse either George McGovern or Richard Nixon in the 1972 presidential election enraged black leaders, who disliked Nixon's policies regarding the poor. African American labor officials believed this demonstrated racial insensitivity on the part of AFL-CIO leadership. In 1972, they organized the Coalition of Black Trade Unionists (CBTU). By 1974, one third of all working African Americans belonged to a labor union, yet many of the AFL-CIO's member unions maintained segregated policies. CBTU leaders tended to be younger, more outspoken, and more willing to challenge tradition and convention. By the mid–1990s, the CBTU developed state organizations. The organizer of the South Carolina/Georgia chapter of the CBTU was a youthful Kenny Riley.[28]

10

On the Waterfront

Kenny Riley had graduated from college, but going to work on the docks, he started at the bottom—literally, the bottom of a ship's hold—and he learned lessons that are not taught in school. For instance, some work is better than other work. Some co-workers are better than other co-workers. Sometimes, if you get hurt, you should keep your mouth shut. Stacking isn't just stacking; you must employ your brain as well as your muscles. Workers don't have to be treated badly, not if they have a labor union. But even labor unions can be improved.

In the late 1970s, Charleston was still largely a bulk port, rather than a container port, which meant that much of the work involved moving goods and parcels—weighing as much as several hundred pounds—to and from the ship's holds. The work was hard but the pay was good, close to $8 an hour to start. When Riley was in college, working occasionally on the docks, he bought his first vehicle, a 1971 Ford sports custom pickup truck. He named it "Mad Dog" and painted a growling dog on the tailgate. His monthly payment was $93. "My dad would say you can work one day a month and make your truck payment for the whole month," Riley recalled. After graduation, he was offered textile industry jobs paying about $17,000 annually in Richmond and Greensboro. He loved Charleston, however, and he recalled thinking,

> Heck, I'm in college and I'm already making half of that working part-time, just pinch-hitting. Why pick up and go? I said, "I want to go to work on the docks." And after about two months, I was full time. There was no need for anyone to ever call me for any job in the corporate world because I had found my place.
>
> On the docks, I was home. We had the beauty of the waterfront, and I could be my own man. I could determine when I was going to work—days or nights. I didn't have to accept going to the same place every day. I didn't have to tell anybody when I was coming, and I didn't have to work nine to five. We didn't go to the same terminal every day and we didn't work the same commodity every day. Some days were hard; some days were easy. But I had never shied away from hard work.

Kenny Riley and Black Union Labor Power

As a kid, I worked in packing sheds, I worked raising hogs, I worked on the dump with my grandmother and I worked at all the other different kinds of jobs I did for my dad.

On the docks, I started out as a common laborer. In teams of two, we might be lifting sacks that weighed 250 pounds. Or we might be rolling 700-pound bales or pulling timber. In those days, containerization was just starting to come to Charleston. Containers were maybe 10 percent of it and you had to be a very senior guy to get that work, which was much easier than the break-bulk work. If you got a job on the container side, you were in heaven. You might operate a crane, picking up containers, or you might drive a truck, flagging those loads—either way, it was great to get out of the ships' holds.

On the break-bulk side, we had cargos like cowhides, fishmeal, and glue. Any cargo we had, we lifted by hand. Two men would pick up the bags. When you got to the docks, guys would team up. Maybe you would be on the barges, loading flour, which was in bags you couldn't handle by yourself. The guy you worked with, you called him your "breaster"; your breaster could make or break you. Quite a bit of the time, I worked with my brother. The risk was always that you would be paired up with someone that couldn't or wouldn't do their share. One time, it was on a Sunday, my brother wasn't there and everyone was paired up and I was left by myself. The older guys, the most seasoned guys, were not going to work with a new guy like myself. So I was left alone with this skinny old guy who drank a lot. All day long, I could smell the alcohol coming from him, and he wasn't willing to lift much. It nearly killed me. I was very sore from doing all that hard work. But

A Port of Charleston crane maneuvers a container between a ship and a truck as two longshoremen talk (Jeff Siner).

10. On the Waterfront

then, when Wednesday came, I saw the check. It was like a reward for having stuck it out.[1]

Among the products shipped through Charleston, in a form that resembled lentils and collected into large bags, was something called "guar gum." Extracted from guar beans, guar gum is a thickener and stabilizer that is used in both food products and hydraulic fracking. "Anytime you would hear the words 'guar gum,' most people would try to go the opposite way," Riley said.

It was shipped in 250-pound bags. It was better to load flour, shipped in bags that weighed 100 pounds or 150 pounds. Desert sand was another product shipped in bags; they were too much for one man but not enough for two. Also, we shipped out a lot of peanut oil—the U.S. gave it away to countries we helped with food aid. It came in little square boxes. You had to pick them up and stack them all day.

Another product was huge bales of polyester-type fiber, synthetic fiber from the Dupont plant in Charleston, which were going to Asia. You can imagine working all day, 80 to 100 feet deep in a ship's hold, and you are loading 600- or 700-pound bales of fiber all day, all night, nonstop, week after week, month after month. You had to use a bale hook to handle them. Eighteen or 20 men would work in one ship hold for a week, trying to squeeze the bales in.

Coming into Charleston, we had commodities like plywood coming from Korea. Then we had steel. We both imported steel and exported steel. Steel beams would be 60 feet long and the hatch opening was only 40 feet long. You had to hook them up to the chains on the cranes at an angle to get them into the ship. Guys would be running to get out of the way. Some guys got killed that way. My first injury I ever had on the docks was to my thumb. I was hooking a steel beam to a chain—you had to hold the hook on the chain in one hand, get slack on the chain as best you could, then throw it under the beam, which was supported on a piece of lumber. I went to throw the hook in there. One day, it bounced back and it pinned my thumb against the steel beam. After that my thumb was killing me. I made it to the bathroom and pulled my glove off and all you could see was open flesh and blood. I tore off a piece of my undershirt, wrapped it tight around my thumb and pulled my glove back on. I didn't tell anybody about it. If you told the foreman you had gotten hurt, he might think you were too young to do that kind of work. Sometimes those foremen got safety bonuses, and one thing you didn't want to do was to lose their safety bonus for them. If somebody got hurt and claimed workmen's comp, the foreman's safety bonus would be taken away. So if you got hurt, you tried to hide it. It took me years before that thumb and fingernail looked normal again.

Another time I had a forklift run over my toe on my left foot. I never said a word. Finally, about six years ago, I had surgery on it. The big toe was all messed up and all those years I was overcompensating, which caused problems with the bones in my second toe. I loved to walk for exercise and I would walk in a way that took the pressure off the big toe and shifted the weight towards the middle and the left side of my foot. Over time it caused severe pain at the ball of my foot and at the base of my second toe. They had to put an artificial joint in the big toe and shorten the second toe. Once they did that, I could once again balance my weight equally.

My dad was a big help to my brother and me. When I started in 1971, he was just a worker for Southeastern, a stevedoring company. But in 1978, the same year I decided to go to the docks full time, Southeastern decided they needed a new foreman for a new shipping company that was coming to town. At the time, Dad was in line to become a foreman. Each foreman had his own gang of workers, maybe six men for each foreman. When Southeastern had work, they would call one of the foremen. At first my dad didn't want all that responsibility, but my brother and I convinced him to do it. We told him that if he got to be a foreman, then we could be in his gang and we could get better jobs. Once he took it, we worked in his gang when we could. The only time we could get container work was when our dad got a call. On the other days, we had to take what we could get, especially when we were starting out. Eventually, we both became crane operators for my dad's gangs. Those jobs were like heaven on earth compared with working in the hold.

One thing working break bulk on the waterfront did, it taught you how to think. You would always be trying to figure out how in the world are you going to get all that cargo, all the different shapes and sizes, into the space you had. Containers can get boring; the work is the same routine every day; you just stack them on top of the ships. But when you're handling different commodities, you have to consider what is called the "stow factor." If you're in one hatch and I'm in the other, and I get one and a half times more cargo in my hatch than you got in yours, then I had a higher stow factor. It requires a lot of thought. If you ordered the wrong piece of cargo in first, you cannot get everything you need in there. At UPS, when I worked there, they taught us to "build a wall every five feet." When you were sorting boxes that were coming at you on a conveyor belt, you had to think quickly. It was the same at the port. When we are doing work for the military, putting tanks and jeeps and tractor equipment and sometimes mine-resistant machines and folding bridges on the ships, our stow-factor percentage was in the low 90s. Charleston had and still has one of the highest stow factors for any military port. Some other ports do well to get to 65 percent or 70 percent stow factor.[2]

Gradually, Riley came to see that a path existed that might enable him to improve not only his own work life, but also those of his co-workers.

Riley had joined ILA Local 1422 in 1975, when he was working on the docks part time. Once he started working full time, it didn't take him long to decide to run for office. One day in 1978, he went to his first monthly union meeting. "When I got there, I saw total chaos," he said. "Guys were yelling and screaming. One guy was cussing the president [Walter Bankhead] and he jumped up and a gun fell from his clothing. Forget Roberts' Rules of Order; I didn't know if World War III would break out. And these guys were huge. I don't mean fat and huge, I mean built. There was not a

10. On the Waterfront

front four of any NFL team that wouldn't be worn down if they had to go to war against these guys."

At the time, Riley and his brother Leonard were still living at home. "We had twin beds; we would talk at night," he said. "Leonard said, 'How was the meeting?' and I said, 'You don't want to know.' We had already realized how great a job we had, earning a good day's pay, but we realized that the union could be better than it was. I said, 'Listen, man, we're going to get involved.' There was a union election coming up. I decided I would run for one of the five board seats. I started campaigning and guys would come up to me and say, 'You just got here. You went to college but you are still green around the edges. Get away from me.' I took a step back. I started thinking about how I could win. I knew I could get a solid block of votes from the younger guys, and I knew there were some older guys, friends of my family, who might support me. My campaign was tied to the name Riley—we had Dick Riley, who was governor of South Carolina, and Joe Riley, who was mayor of Charleston. So I drew a picture and I went to a print shop and got it copied on a little business card."[3] The picture showed a triangle, the heads of the two white men on the bottom and the head of a black man with an Afro on the top. The layout did not escape notice in a union that was nearly all black.

Once elected, Riley became the local's youngest board member. Two years later, he and Leonard were elected to posts on the three-man contract committee. The assignment meant frequent travel to other ports—including Morehead City, Wilmington, Jacksonville and Tampa—where Local 1422 had contracts to negotiate or enforce. Forty years later, Riley still serves on the contract committee, and he still negotiates the same contracts. He has become one of the country's most knowledgeable authorities on ILA contracts.

As a rising young power in the union, Riley aligned himself with Benjamin Flowers. Flowers lost the 1978 presidential election to Walter Bankhead, but challenged the results because Bankhead had allowed retirees to vote. Eventually, 18 months later, a rerun election was ordered, and Riley decided that he would run for recording secretary, one of the top five jobs in the local.

"By that time, I had won the confidence of some older guys because I was a standup guy," Riley said. "I knew the contract, and if I saw anybody violating the contract, I would say, 'There's no way I can sit here as a board member working this gang and allow you to do this.' Some of the foremen didn't like it." The contract included a provision ensuring that a crew could not be split up until its work was completed. That way, every man would

Kenny Riley and Black Union Labor Power

Kenny Riley talks with the driver of a port truck that transports containers between a ship and the container yard, where containers are moved to and from over-the-road trucks (Jeff Siner).

be paid for every hour allocated to a job. Some foremen would evade the provision, making deals with individual stevedore companies that allowed a few workers to go on to the next job before the previous work was completed. "Let's say our crew had to work two hatches one day, and each hatch would take 12 or 13 hours," Riley said. "Sometimes they would split the crew, and send a few guys to open the hatch on the second job. That would cut the time it would have taken if we had stayed together. It might cut two or three hours. That violates the contract. But it saves money for the stevedoring company, which would give some money to the foreman while the rest of us would lose a few hours. I couldn't turn a blind eye. I wanted it to be honest. After I raised the issue,13 of the foremen decided to teach me a lesson and not let me work for them. I even had a conflict with my own father. I would not get hired for anything except backbreaking break-bulk work."

In the rerun election of 1980, Riley ran for recording secretary while supporting Flowers for president, as did his brother. This pitted the two sons against their father, Leonard Riley, Sr. "My father was upset," Kenny

10. On the Waterfront

Riley said. "My father said, 'How can you oppose the guy who brought you into the union?' He said, 'You are in my gang right now. When I go to work you go to work. Had it not been for Walter Bankhead I would not have that gang.'" But Riley told his father that Flowers was the better candidate, causing a rift with his father and several of his father's close associates. "Our relationship fell apart," Riley said. "I had a strong sense of what was right and what was wrong and my father didn't agree with it."[4]

As Riley continued his political ascent, he learned the ins and outs of union politics and of union work. In 1988 he ran for vice president and lost. In 1991, running on a ticket with Flowers, he won. In 1994, he would lose again. During his tenure as vice president, he ran the union's day-to-day activities and also served as head of the grievance committee. In three years, he filed about 50 grievances. Some concerned cases where employers had sought to pay workers for less time than a job required under the contract. "I came out of one grievance that I won, and the employers had to pay 90 individuals eight hours of pay each," he said. But the majority of cases involved protecting union jurisdiction when non-union seafarers, who worked on foreign-registered ships that called on Charleston, sought to do union work. "Securing and lashing down containers is within our jurisdiction," Riley said. "Ships that didn't want to pay us would have seamen drop those lashes."

Meanwhile, the alliance between Riley and Flowers was fraying as the two men increasingly found themselves on opposite sides of generational, cultural and political divides. Walter Bankhead was a Mississippi native two generations older than Riley—old enough to be his grandfather. For Riley, 1980 "was Flowers's time; he was younger than Bankhead, he had a vision for that time, and we hitched our wagon to him." But in the 1990s, differences emerged. "At first, Flowers was much more progressive than Bankhead had been, but that changed," Riley said. For Riley's dad, Flowers's failure to meet his son's expectations was an affirmation, and the two Rileys again drew close. "Dad always saw Flowers for what he was," Kenny Riley said.[5]

While Riley could argue that Flowers had never embraced societal change and had backed away from strong union advocacy, he could not argue that Flowers's tenure had been without accomplishments. "ILA Local 1422 thrived under Flowers' tenure, and with its more than 700 members, it remains one of the strongest forces on the Charleston waterfront," the *Post and Courier* reported in a 1997 story. "The union's pension fund ballooned into one of the state's largest private pension funds, with assets of about $200 million [and] the work force also developed a solid reputation for high productivity."[6]

One highly visible symbol of union strength, the 1984 construction of a larger union hall—which replaced a cramped facility—occurred on Flowers's watch. "We left the old storefront that had become the union hall, which was a sign of success," Riley said.[7] One day in 1984, union members staged a march from the old building to the new building, marking a festive, dramatic day in the Local's history. In 2001, the building was displaced by the construction of the Arthur Ravenal Bridge, and the Local moved again to an expansive building on Morrison Drive.

Flowers was responsive to the membership in terms of his advocacy for respecting seniority in hiring and, as the port became more containerized, he was more aggressive in asserting union rights than Bankhead had been. At some ports under ILA contracts, such as the Port of New York, every aspect of port operations is conducted under union jurisdiction; at others, at ports in Charleston and Savannah that are in right-to-work states, the port authority fills jobs that would be union jobs elsewhere. "At the time, we did not have jurisdiction to run the cranes because Bankhead had allowed the port authority to get jurisdiction," Riley said. "Flowers was the first one to try to tackle it. He didn't succeed, but he made a valiant effort."[8]

Nevertheless, the relationship between Flowers and Riley completely broke down in 1993. Riley was on the union's 10-member executive board, but he and a handful of board allies could not get Flowers to call monthly meetings with the board or with members. "The guy was operating like a dictator," said Riley, who responded by filing a charge against Flowers with the ILA. The union struck back in a duplicitous manner: It put the Local under a trusteeship, but named Flowers to be the trustee. This was the first in a long series of events in which Riley and the union's national leadership were at odds. "When they named Flowers as trustee, we decided that we had to fight," Riley said. "I was vice president, and everybody was looking at me to initiate the challenge. But when I filed charges with the international, the response was, 'OK, Riley, you guys are on a mission and you proved your point, so we will put you in a trusteeship, and now you don't really have to have any meetings at all.' And they told Flowers, 'Try to work with these guys, but now you can fire anyone you want, since you are the trustee.'"[9]

After effectively losing their internal appeal regarding the scheduling of meetings, Riley and his supporters decided to move their case out of the

10. On the Waterfront

union judicial system and into the federal court system. This led them to the office of Charleston attorney Armand Derfner, the type of lawyer who had decided to accept only those cases that he personally supported. He had moved to Charleston after marrying a local resident. Over the next quarter century, he would be among Riley's key allies.

Born in Paris in 1936, Derfner fled to New York with his parents in 1938, two years ahead of the Nazi invasion. A graduate of Princeton University and Yale Law School, he became engaged in the civil rights movement, moving to Mississippi in the 1960s to work as a lawyer seeking to register black voters. In 1968, he recalled, a judge ordered him arrested on a charge of practicing law without a license during a court hearing in Holly Springs, Miss. The charge was later dismissed, Derfner said, because federal law allows attorneys to practice in state court, without a license in the state, if no local attorneys are available. At the time, he said, "homegrown lawyers wouldn't take civil rights cases."[10]

Derfner had argued half a dozen voting rights cases in the Supreme Court. Perhaps the most notable was the 1968 case *Allen vs. (the Mississippi) State Board of Elections*. The case represented an early test of the 1965 Voting Rights Act, one of the signature achievements of the civil rights movement. The act was intended to discourage efforts by southern states to prevent blacks from voting. A key portion of the act was Section 5, which explicitly prohibits states from making legal changes that affect voting without preclearance from the U.S. Attorney General or the U.S. District Court for the District of Columbia. In the *Allen* case, Mississippi's board of election sought to make such a change and was challenged by a group of black citizens. In a 7–2 vote, the Supreme Court upheld Section 5.

The protections of the Voting Rights Act were severely diminished in a 2013 Supreme Court ruling, *Shelby County (Alabama) vs. Holder*, when the court ruled by a 5–4 vote that Section 4(b) of the act was unconstitutional because it used 40-year-old data to establish which jurisdictions should be covered. Without such data, Section 5 no longer covered any jurisdictions. "Over the years, the Justice Department blocked more than 1,000 changes," by the states, Derfner said. "When the Supreme Court threw out (Section 4), that was the Supreme Court saying 'we know better.'" In a sense, *Shelby vs. Holder* seemed to threaten much of the work Derfner had done throughout his life. Asked in 2018 whether he should try another line of work, he responded, "It's just a question of patience."

Derfner was immediately impressed by Riley. "My first impression was that he was the kind of person who is a leader," Derfner said. "He knew what made sense and what didn't make sense. He knew how to get things done, and he had a broad vision of what the union needed and what leadership meant." Additionally, it seemed to Derfner, Riley had a broad awareness of the labor movement because of his father's involvement and a broad sense of the civil rights movement because of his own life, coming of age in Charleston in the 1960s.

In his early representation of Riley, Derfner was disturbed by the conduct of the national union. But he could not convince the court to agree that Flowers's administration had not informed members of meetings or that the trusteeship had not resolved the Local's representational issues. "My recollection is the decision was that there had been adequate notice, based on some passing statements that were made that we didn't think added up to notice, and that international unions have a huge degree of leeway in imposing trusteeships," Derfner said. "It is hard for a local to fight that. It was an uphill battle and we lost it."[11] Moreover, legal battles—even legal battles in a righteous cause—cost money. The international union had more financial resources than Riley and his band of about ten union dissidents. The group eventually spent around $50,000, which they allocated from their royalty checks and, later, from their holiday and vacation checks. The ILA attorneys continuously filed motions; counter-motions consumed the group's financial resources even before the case got to a court hearing.

The trusteeship ended after 18 months with the approach of the 1994 election. That year, Riley lost his run for the vice presidency by 30 votes; his campaign came under attack because he had sued the union. He returned to dock work, but tore his rotator cuff and underwent two surgeries. Each was followed by six months of recovery time, during which Riley remained involved in union activities, including negotiating for various East Coast ports and attending conventions. He began to think seriously about running for president in 1997.

11

Containers Take Over the World

During the period when Kenny Riley advanced from low-level dockworker to leader of ILA Local 1422, the Port of Charleston was emerging as one of the East Coast's most important container shipping ports.

The transformation of global ocean shipping from a bulk-cargo business to a container business began in the 1960s. The Port of Charleston and the ILA were transformed along with it. In fact, the Port of Charleston played a key role in the transition, which in the United States was largely the result of the work of a single man, Malcolm McLean, a onetime North Carolina trucking-company executive whose 1965 visit to Charleston came in the very early days of the shift to containers.

"Containerization began right before I started on the port in 1971, when I was still in high school," Riley said. "The shift was taking place at a pace that meant that in the 1980s containers became the dominant cargo in Charleston. Automation and containerization caused huge changes. In the 1970s, it was almost all manual labor. It was not uncommon to have as many as 18 men in one crew in the bottom of the ship hold. When you have loose cargo, it might take two hours to load 40 tons into a ship hold. But when you lift one container with a crane, you can lift 40 tons in a minute. That's the impact of automation. And as that was happening in Charleston, the need for the level of manning we once had diminished. For instance, the port served two large paper manufacturers: one in Charleston and one in Georgetown. They would put huge rolls of paper onto railroad cars to the terminal, and then we would lift them off the cars and lay them down and then load them into the wings of the ship. The crews would work round the clock. Now that paper is stuffed in containers. You have a crane operator, he picks it off a truck and it's in the ship in a minute to a minute and a half, depending on where it goes in the ship."[1]

Kenny Riley and Black Union Labor Power

One day in March 1965 two executives from Elizabeth, N.J.–based Sea-Land called on Capers Barr, a retired Navy captain who had become general manager of the S.C. State Ports Authority. One of the executives was McLean, who is described in his *Washington Post* obituary as "a former North Carolina truck driver whose deceptively simple idea transformed the world's commerce and economy." McLean, who died at 87 in May 2001, became "the father of containerization" when he acted on his concept for lifting the container portion of a truck into the hold of a ship, onto the flatbed of a train or even into a cargo airplane. The traditional method of freight transfer, known as break-bulk shipping, "had not really changed in theory from almost prehistoric times, and many thought there was no reason to change it at all."[2]

Kenny Riley presides over the Port of Charleston, the fourth busiest container port on the East Coast and the ninth busiest in the United States (Jeff Siner).

In an important historic footnote, McLean's visit to Barr led not only to the rebirth of the Port of Charleston but also to a diminution of the importance of North Carolina's ports. As a native Tarheel, born in Maxton, N.C., which is near the South Carolina border about 110 miles south of Durham, McLean wanted to stimulate the growth of the Port of Wilmington, N.C. But the Carolinas' port authorities responded differently to his 1965 visits, during which McLean was accompanied by Ken Younger, a longtime Sea-Land executive whose long career in shipping included a stint on the N.C. State Ports Authority from 1994 to 1998.

By 1965, Sea-Land had assembled a fleet of six converted military ships. Each could carry 226 containers, a tenth of what today's ships carry, and each carried a small crane to lift the containers. The firm was rapidly attracting shippers, who no longer had to pack cargo into crates, and McLean had begun buying old petroleum tankers to convert to container

11. Containers Take Over the World

carriers. To create even more space, he took the cranes off the ships and asked ports to install shore cranes. In the early to mid–1960s, principal U.S. and European ports began adding cranes.

Sea-Land also wanted a mid–Atlantic port: McLean and Younger both favored Wilmington. They traveled south from their New Jersey headquarters to visit the region's ports. Sea-Land's strategy was to have ports finance the cranes and build private dock areas, then to pay the cost with user fees. "We told the port director at Wilmington what we wanted, which included a crane, our own section of the port and a private entrance," said Younger in 2000, when he and McLean spoke about the trip in interviews with the *Charlotte Observer*. "He told us he had to ask his board, and he said that, really, we should go to Morehead City. We said Morehead City isn't big enough, and we want to go to Wilmington. That evening, we went to Charleston and had dinner with Captain Barr and told him what we wanted. He said, 'Why don't we have lunch tomorrow, and we'll have an answer for you by then. But first, we'll drive around tomorrow morning and I'll show you what we can do.' The thing that impressed us was that they had a master plan to expand into North Charleston, and they told us that as we grew, they would make more space available for us," Younger said. At lunch, Barr told McLean and Younger that he thought they could make a deal.

McLean "felt you could move freight cheaper on a ship than over the road," Younger told the newspaper. "This thing was faster, more efficient and cheaper than the competition. We could see it had an application in Europe and everywhere else in the world. The comment we made to the Port of Charleston was that our business, the container business, will change world trade."[3] In response, "Captain Barr said, 'I know it. That's why we're doing this,'" recalled McLean. "But the people in Wilmington never grasped what the future was."[4] Today, while the Port of Charleston is among the world's leading container ports, the North Carolina ports still struggle to find their way.

Negotiations continued into the next month. According to the port's official history, "The authority was enthusiastic about the prospect and in April told Barr that the space and the office could be made available, but that the crane was a problem. With the crane's cost estimated at $850,000, the authority told Sea-Land that it hoped it could make other arrangements for the crane. In May, Sea-Land informed the authority that it could indeed make other arrangements in Savannah, where the Georgia Ports Authority had indicated its willingness to have Sea-Land located if Charleston could not provide the facilities it needed."[5]

Kenny Riley and Black Union Labor Power

The threat convinced the Port of Charleston to move ahead. Sea-Land, meanwhile, was liking Charleston more and more. "After our meeting, we told Barr we'd think about it, and we waited a few weeks," Younger said. "We called Wilmington a few times. But we never got an answer."[6] The crane was installed in Charleston and on March 12, 1966, the Sea-Land Gateway City became the first container ship to call on Charleston.[7]

Besides McLean, the other giant in the transformation of the shipping business was Teddy Gleason, president of the ILA from 1963 to 1987. Gleason's story, described in an obituary in *Joc.com*, which covers global trade, "is the story of the waterfront in America": "When the man who would lead the International Longshoremen's Association for 24 years first joined the union in 1915, longshoremen were numerous, but poorly paid," the obituary said. "When he died five years after his 1987 retirement, the longshore rolls in New York had fallen from tens of thousands of men to only a few thousand. But those remaining were among the best paid workers in the nation."[8]

Born in New York in 1900, Gleason became active in the ILA at a time when several New York unions were predominantly Irish and led by forceful personalities whose exploits, particularly in the strikes they led, were extensively covered by New York's nine newspapers. Gleason was a contemporary of the New York labor icon Mike Quill, who was born in Ireland in 1905. Quill fought for the Irish Republican Army, immigrated to New York in 1926 and went to work for the IRT, then an independent subway line. In 1934, a year of intense labor activism throughout the country, Quill co-founded the Transport Workers Union, which primarily represented New York subway workers. He was a top labor leader until his death in 1966. Gleason, meanwhile, left school after the seventh grade and went to work on the docks. In 1931, as wages were falling due to the Depression, he was involved in a work stoppage. In retaliation, he was barred from dock work for several years. But he returned as the economy improved, joined the ILA, worked his way up, and was elected president in 1963. A third major labor leader to emerge from Irish New York was John Sweeney, who was born in the Bronx to Irish immigrants in 1934. Sweeney rose to prominence as a leader of Services Employees International Union and served as president of the AFL-CIO from 1995 to 2009.

Harold Daggett, who became the ninth president of the ILA in 2011, lived in the same Irish enclave in Greenwich Village as Gleason's family did. "I met Teddy Gleason when I was a young kid," said Daggett, who was

11. Containers Take Over the World

born in 1946. "My father and Teddy grew up together." Gleason "was a super family guy" who had 10 children, many grandchildren and a home in the resort town of Greenwood Lake, just north of New York City, where his family could gather, Gleason also owned a nearby boxers' training camp, Brown's training camp. Gleason "worked his way up through the ranks," Daggett said. "He was general organizer, then president. He had a rough time. For a while, another union was trying to take over the ILA. He fought hard, it was brother against brother, but he won and the ILA won."

The New York/New Jersey area had a half dozen separate ports, including not only Midtown New York and Brooklyn but also Newark, Port Elizabeth and Bayonne in New Jersey. At the time, the busiest ports were on Manhattan's West Side, although break-bulk cargos included large amounts of lumber that moved through Port Newark. The advent of containerization not only meant a reduction in jobs, but also it led the New Jersey ports to become dominant because the midtown area lacked storage space for containers. "In Manhattan, there was no room to park these containers, so all the work started to go to Port Elizabeth and Newark," Daggett said. "My father went out there to Port Newark; he worked for Sea-Land at Shed 190. Today, the only work in Manhattan and Brooklyn is passenger ships."

As containerization began its assault on the New York harbor in the 1960s, Gleason "saw that the future would be the end of break bulk and the end of a lot of longshoremen and he saw that his men would be out of work, so he fought the companies tooth and nail," Daggett said. The result of Gleason's vision was an agreement to provide a guaranteed annual income (GAI) to longshoremen who showed up at the hiring hall, even if they could not actually find work loading and unloading ships. First implemented in 1964, the GAI enabled hundreds of longshoremen who lost jobs to containerization to collect as much as $32,000 a year even if they did not work.

"It was 40 hours a week, as long as they badged in at the hiring hall at the end of the week," Daggett said. "That way, they could support their families. This went on for years and years, into the eighties." Eventually, the workers who were protected aged out of the workforce, but the GAI was replaced by container royalties, which compensate the remaining workers for cargo movements through their ports. "I still marvel at the fact that this guy had so much insight and was able to get this done," Daggett said. "No other dockworkers' union anywhere in the world negotiated a container royalty."[9]

Gleason hired Jim McNamara, then a reporter for the *Irish Echo* newspaper, to be the ILA director of public relations in 1981. McNamara, still on the job in 2018, became a repository of ILA history. When McNamara was hired, Gleason was an elder statesman of the labor movement, nearing the end of a 24-year-run as ILA president that began in 1963 and ended in 1987. He was referred to as "labor secretary of state" by Lane Kirkland, president of the AFL-CIO from 1979 to 1995. Gleason "was regarded as a tough man," McNamara recalled. "He wasn't tall, but he had broad shoulders. He looked like a linebacker or a fullback; you can imagine him with a leather helmet in the early days of football. He was mild-mannered in most of his daily doings, but when he got into negotiations, he became a totally different animal, very ferocious and caustic with management, very impatient with bad offers."

Most importantly, McNamara said, "He could really see the future, and he had this ability to see what effect his actions would have on the future. Faced with containerization, he saw a tremendous loss of ILA jobs, a loss of revenue not only for ILA members but for the ILA itself, and he was able to conceive a program that would allow for a reduction of manpower but would protect the ILA men that were still there and (later) protect the container royalty fund."[10]

Though it might appear as a setback for employers, who paid out as much as $75 million a year for the GAI, the deal with Gleason ensured the steady operation of ports and helped to replace an inefficient system where men would have to bid for jobs each morning, sometimes securing them due to kickbacks and violence. The GAI "gradually went away because the men who were protected retired or passed away," McNamara said. "The last guy retired in the 1990s." Meanwhile, as global shipping increased, employers became vast beneficiaries, with ever-growing quantities of cargo handled by ever-diminishing numbers of workers. "Teddy Gleason understood that employers were gaining tremendously on the amount of cargo handled with a smaller workforce, so he instituted a container royalty fund, basically a tax on each container based on the weight of the container," McNamara said. "What it meant was that as tonnage increased, so would revenue for the member and the international." One result, McNamara said, is that ILA health-care benefits would continue at a high level. On the West Coast, meanwhile, the International Longshore and Warehouse Union took a different tack, providing existing workers with enhanced retirement and pension benefits rather than a royalty fund.

When Kenny Riley was first elected to his local's contract committee

11. Containers Take Over the World

in 1978, he gained a chance to watch Gleason in action. "I started traveling on a contract committee and I thank God I had the opportunity to sit under Teddy Gleason and to watch him negotiate and see how strong he was and how he was able to use every advantage available to him," Riley said. "He is a hero. He negotiated container royalties, something that no other union in the world has. His concept was that containers will cut my manpower, cut earnings, and cut dues, so I want to tax containers. We negotiated a tax of $3 per ton: it is now $5. This started in the early 1970s. We collected royalties for each container, provided we did not load the cargo into the container or remove it from the container. If a truck comes into Charleston with 40 tons of cargo in a container, it would take a few minutes to put that load on a ship with a crane, whereas if we had loaded it pallet by pallet by pallet, it might take 18 men an hour or so. Currently we collect $5 per ton for each of these containers. Of that, $2 goes into a local container royalty fund. At the end of the year those funds are distributed to all of the men and women who qualified by working 700 or more hours on the docks in the previous year. The other $3 subsidizes the cost of our national health care, the container freight stations and the training programs. The royalties paid to the workers all qualify as lost-wage supplements for lost work due to automation, and Teddy Gleason negotiated that. He was brilliant."[11]

By 2018, for Local 1422 members, the average annual distribution of container royalties amounted to nearly $24,000 for a full-time worker However, the transition to containerization meant a reduction in membership to a 2018 total of about 800, about half the 1980 total. Nationally, while about 65,000 longshoremen worked on the nation's waterfront in 1974, according to figures from the U.S. Maritime Association, the number declined to about 25,000 in 1997. On the plus side, the remaining workers went from unskilled to skilled workers, often operating giant cranes and earning an average of around $120,000 annually, up from $60,000 or $70,000 in the 1980s.

Despite containerization and the associated higher salaries, the early 1980s were not a good time for the Port of Charleston or for Riley personally. In 1982, unemployment reached 10.8 percent, the highest level since the Depression, and the prime interest rate reached 21.5 percent as the Federal Reserve sought to battle inflation by raising rates. "By 1982, the bottom had fallen out of the economy and work on the docks was scarce," Riley said. "I had been doing well and I had bought a Corvette, but all of a sudden I had to let the Corvette go back. I lost everything except my home. I had work when my dad's gang was called, but that was happening maybe only once a week."

One thing that did not change with containerization was the racial separation associated with the port's work. As has been the case since before the Civil War, the manual work was—and continues to be—done by blacks: they comprise the vast majority of Local 1422. The clerical work of tracking cargo is performed by a few dozen white workers; they comprise Local 1771. Meanwhile, Local 1422A, which is largely black, performs maintenance work. Riley recalled that in the 1940s, in the classified sections of the newspapers, ads would appear seeking "colored longshoremen" to apply at a certain pier. "Throughout the South, in every port, the majority of the longshoremen would be African American," he said. "They were needed to do the lifting. 'Bring the people with strong backs,' they would say. The clerical people were white. When the maintenance guys came in, the majority of them were black too."[12]

In a 2000 story in the Charleston *Post and Courier*, published 10 days before the Charleston Five showdown drew worldwide attention, reporter Tony Bartelme set the stage for the coming encounter by writing a story about the port's labor history, including the racial component, as the industry moved to containerization. The story, entitled, "Behind Battle

A giant crane towers over containers stacked at the Port of Charleston (Jeff Siner).

11. Containers Take Over the World

Lines: ILA vs. Non-Union Labor," focused on labor activities in 1953, 1966 and 1997.

Describing events that took place in the spring of 1953, Bartelme wrote, "The waterfront is a much different place than it is today. When a ship arrives, hundreds of burly longshoremen swarm over the vessel, hoisting pallets of cotton, bananas and other goods with forklifts and muscle. Like much of the South, it is a segregated place. The longshoremen are generally black and the stevedores—the companies that hire the longshoremen—are white. Tensions are high, but not because of race."

That year, ILA members shut down the port for two weeks to protest their inability to secure union recognition and higher wages for employees of the SCPA. "South Carolina's right-to-work laws have made it difficult for labor groups to organize, and the SPA [another abbreviation used for SCPA] has strongly resisted any attempts by the ILA to organize its workers," Bartelme wrote. "But the ILA has grown in strength over the years, winning concessions from shipping lines. Where the men once worked for a pittance, now they earn good wages." The strike ended with port workers remaining non-union "and everyone on the waterfront shaken up."

Thirteen years later, in 1966, Sea-Land's *Gateway City* became the first container ship to call on Charleston. Dockworkers "use cranes to hoist 35 rectangular containers packed with flashlight batteries and textiles," Bartelme wrote. "It marks the beginning of what will be a radical transformation of the maritime industry." By the 1990s, the waterfront has changed dramatically. "The smaller breakbulk vessels that hauled the pallets of cotton and bananas have been replaced by giant containerships stacked high with standard-sized 20- and 40-foot containers," the story said, and Charleston had become the fourth busiest container port in the country. (In 2018, Charleston was the fourth largest container port on the East Coast, behind New York, Savannah and the four ports that form the Port of Virginia, and ninth in the country.)

The port remained largely segregated in 1966, Bartelme wrote. "Members of ILA Local 1422, the longshoremen who load and unload containers, are nearly all black, while members of ILA Local 1771 Clerks and Checkers are mostly white, as are the bosses and the stevedores," he said. "But for the most part, it's a stable place where most everyone gets along. Despite automation, which has dramatically cut the number of workers needed to load ships, longshoremen make good wages, and ILA Local 1422, the largest chapter, has nearly 800 members. The union has built up a local pension fund with more than $300 million in assets. A union member with seniority and overtime can make more than $100,000 a year. At the fortress-like union hall on Morrison Drive, it's not uncommon to find a parking lot full of luxury cars. Along with healthy wages and benefits, the union has created a respected and highly trained work force. The union requires members to take random drug tests and safety classes. Some members, dubbed the A-Team, have been trained to load and unload the military's M1 tanks and other vehicles." Bartelme asked Benjamin Flowers whether the segregation mirrored "the plantation system of the Old South," and Flowers responded, "Slaves don't make $100,000."

While the workforce was largely union, the port authority continued to employ non-union crane operators. The port functioned smoothly. But in 1997, when a newly created non-union company sought to load and unload ships hauling frozen chicken to Russia, Local 1422 staged protests. "It's a peaceful protest, but an ominous sign of what's to come," Bartelme wrote.[13]

12

A Sixties Kid Takes Over Local 1422

For Local 1422, the Kenny Riley era began in February 1997, when Riley took office as president after ousting onetime mentor Benjamin Flowers in an overwhelming election victory a few weeks earlier.

On election day, Riley supporters set up a heated tent outside the union hall and served barbecue, fried fish, steamed oysters and red rice. The paper ballots were counted overnight during a 12-hour stretch that began at 7 p.m. "A New Leader Found on the Waterfront," proclaimed the headline in the *Post and Courier* on February 8, 1997. "As the International Longshoremen Association [ILA] faces more challenges, voting members of 1422 decided it was time for a change," the subhead said.[1] Riley ousted Flowers, a 16-year incumbent, in a landslide, getting about 70 percent of the 500 votes that were cast.

At 44, Riley was a symbol of a new generation of black leaders, a 1960s kid with an Afro who had lived through the start of the unraveling of the segregated South and had graduated from college, one more place where he was in the vanguard of integration. In his view, union leadership was a continuation of a role that had chosen him. He saw Local 1422 as an untapped resource for the civil rights movement in Charleston.

"I had come out of college, where I was involved in the movement," Riley said. "We had brought Dick Gregory and other civil rights icons to campus." As a business management major, Riley had written a paper on management's social responsibility. Out in the working world, he perceived the local's leadership to be largely indifferent to the concept that it might have any such responsibility. The union was insular, always looking in rather than out, eschewing community involvement and public displays of pride or solidarity.

"Here was this black institution, with union workers who had the right to stand up and say no and who were being paid more money than I had ever dreamed of," Riley said.

> But growing up, with my father a longshoreman, I never saw high visibility. I thought our history was something to celebrate, not something to hide. I wanted the local to be something everybody knew, someplace that when you needed a contribution or support, you could come to us. I felt that we in management had a social responsibility to the community in which we operated, and I brought that to the ILA.
>
> The labor movement is much more than a group of guys who come to the union hall, get a job, make money and go home. We wanted to be part of the community. We wanted to be like Teddy Gleason, a progressive thinker. The question for us in Charleston was, "What could we, at the port, do differently?"[2]

During the 1980s, Riley seized on opportunities to distribute union-themed apparel. The local began by selling patches that could be sewn onto shirt sleeves, then added shirts and caps. "In other cities I would see guys with ILA shirts and ILA license plates, but in Charleston no one had anything like that," he said. "I decided to design some patches for our coveralls to boost ILA pride. None of the union veterans would purchase them. They wanted to hide it. They said, 'We don't want to identify with it, we already live in style,' and I said, 'No, we are much more than that. We are a lot of good decent people, and this is something we should be proud of, something we should be promoting.'"

Four issues formed the basis for Riley's 1996–1997 presidential campaign. One was a proposal to enhance the container royalties that Teddy Gleason had devised. In recent negotiations, Charleston stevedores had agreed to cap their annual royalties at $15,000, in line with a national cap implemented by the ILA and the employers. But the average annual royalty in Charleston had reached around $16,900, so the national cap represented a pay cut for Charleston longshoremen. "It was crazy that we would have to take less," said Riley, who pledged to seek an increase. "I said, 'Cap us where we are.' Others have room to grow and we do not." Soon after his election, the parties resumed negotiations on the cap. The outcome, advocated by the national ILA, was to raise the cap for the entire country to $16,500. Royalties have continued to rise. In 2018, Charleston's royalty totaled about $25,000 for a worker with at least 700 hours in the previous three years, and no Local had a royalty cap.

A second pledge Riley made was to establish a strike fund. Members could elect to designate a portion of their income to go into the fund; every three years, the money would be returned to the members. Riley said his strike fund had reached as high as $58,000. "The strike

12. A Sixties Kid Takes Over Local 1422

fund was a struggle, but during my first term we got one," Riley said. "I still pay into it."

Additionally, Riley pledged to set up an additional pension for members working more than a minimum number of hours required for a pension credit. At the time, members received the same pensions whether they worked 800 hours a year or 3,000 hours a year. "That was not right," Riley said. "I wanted pension dollars for every hour we worked."[3]

Seniority hiring also remained an issue. Despite efforts by Flowers to make a change, hiring for the day's work was still done by foreman's fiat. Senior workers began pushing for a provision to include seniority in the criteria for hiring, a chaotic process that occurred in the union hall. "You would pick the foreman who gave you your best shot, the guy you thought you had the best chance of working with, and then you would get in a circle around him, and you would be saying, 'Pick my card, pick my card.'" Riley said. "He may be hiring 20 individuals, and when he gets to that total, he holds up his hand and says, 'That's it.' If you didn't get picked, you would have sealed your fate for the entire day. Leonard and I were new guys, but we said, 'Okay, even though what we have now works for us, we will support the seniority proposal because one day we will be senior guys.'"[4]

"All of the things that I ran on, I was able to accomplish in a very short period of time," Riley said. "I fulfilled all of my promises." Unfortunately, Riley's relationship with Flowers continued to deteriorate after the election. "We didn't get along afterwards," Riley said. The older man returned to work as a line handler, a high-skill job that involved tying up ships that docked and then releasing them, and also retained his jobs as a district and international union official.

Contract improvements were important: It was also important that Riley brought to the local the consciousness and social awareness of his generation. The transition is discussed in the 2008 book *On the Global Waterfront: The Fight to Free the Charleston 5* by the husband and wife team of Suzan Erem and E. Paul Durrenberger. They captured the changing mood of the organization as Local 1422 members gathered at the union hall on January 19, 2000, the night of the Charleston Five incident:

> In the crowd were men Riley had grown up with, men who had supported him in his battle to reform the local. But also in the crowd were some of the old guard, supporters of the previous administration of Ben Flowers, who had served as president for almost twenty years. The new leaders thought Flowers would sacrifice the best interests of the union and the men to avoid any confrontations. He had gone

along to get along, and members had paid the price for his compliance. Riley was convinced the old-timers had nothing like he and the men shared—a brotherhood that comes from taking risks together and building something better than their fathers had. The new leadership had changed the role of the union and taken it beyond the waterfront, into the community.

These new leaders, all of whom had graduated from college, set an example so that more longshoremen would send their children to college and buy their own homes, instead of spending their paychecks partying every week. The new slate didn't drink, didn't smoke, and didn't curse, and banned all activity unrelated to the union from the hall's parking lot. Now, on payday, a time that always flushed the community with cash, the women looking for their men, the small businessmen, and the fellow partyers who used to cruise the lot, had to find a new place to hook up with the newly paid longshoremen; the union hall was off-limits. The last three years had raised longshoremen's self-esteem and their image in the community, but it hadn't been easy to change old habits. Supporters of the old leadership could sabotage what these new guys had done.[5]

Another cause Riley embraced was filling the void in ILA leadership of African American leaders. Two decades later, in 2018, he believes that he has only partially succeeded and that the next generation of African American leaders will have to continue that battle after he retires.

From the start, Riley strove to ensure that black dockworkers in a majority black union could be fairly represented within the union's leadership. An early step in those efforts came at a 1999 district meeting in Savannah. Among the attendees was Eddie McBride, president of Savannah ILA Local 1414, another all-black longshoremen's union. McBride was a natural ally. Born in Savannah on October 29, 1947, he was six years older than Riley and could serve as a mentor. McBride had also attended college; he was similarly impassioned by the civil rights struggle, and he wore an Afro. Riley "was sort of like me," McBride said in a 2019 interview. "He was a fighter. We weren't going to go along with things in the industry (where) everything was controlled by whites."[6] McBride was well aware of the discrepancies that made whites leaders and blacks followers in the leadership, while in the workforce whites were "checkers," filing forms and keeping time, while blacks were laborers. Working together, McBride said, he and Riley battled for change, at a time when change was not welcome in the union, and they made progress. McBride, who retired as union president in 2017, still resides in Savannah. He is often surprised, he said, at the number of people who recognize him.

Riley said McBride was a strong influence. "If you think I'm radical, you should talk to Eddie McBride," he said in 2018. "Eddie McBride and I were not satisfied with the way blacks were being treated in the ILA.

12. A Sixties Kid Takes Over Local 1422

The membership was about 55 percent African American and we thought that top leadership should be more reflective of the population. We controlled Charleston and Savannah, and we felt that with two progressive presidents leading, we could compete. We knew that if we could not be in a position to direct how we spend capital, we could not have real leverage."

Although he had become acquainted with McBride before his election as president, the Savannah meeting represented "one of the most powerful days I ever spent," Riley recalled. "So many people in the union were frustrated. Individually we felt like we were considered the scum of the earth. But at that meeting we came together as brothers—white, black and Puerto Rican." Riley quickly realized that to succeed he needed to organize the union's black membership into a group that could coherently wield power. He wrote letters to local leaders around the country, gaining support for an insurgent organization that came to be called the Longshore Workers Coalition (LWC), and cementing his reputation as a troublesome rebel. He and McBride advocated for a one-man, one-vote election of national leadership, rather than representational voting where local union leaders selected national officers. "The rallying cry for the LWC was one man, one vote," Riley said.[7]

Additionally, Riley moved quickly to take a stand in the continuing battle over the use of non-union workers in Charleston Harbor. He had taken office at a critical time for the ILA, which faced challenges, both nationally and locally, from membership reductions that accompanied containerization as well as from a continuing effort by non-union waterfront companies to chip away at its jurisdictions and to pay dockworkers less.

In June 1997, Local 1422 set up a picket—the first demonstration of labor unrest on the Charleston waterfront in more than two decades—as the non-union company Carolina Marine Handling loaded frozen chickens onto a Russia-bound ship. The company was loading a freighter called Green Glacier for NOCS Group, a New Orleans–based cargo-management firm. The arrangement violated a previous agreement with NOCS, which had said it would use union workers for at least two years if workers agreed to accept wages that were below the contract rate. Local 1422's concession meant the union agreed to take $4 an hour below the standard rate and also loosened other work rules. But that wasn't enough for NOCS. Chicken ships became a critical battleground because, "unlike container ships, which can be loaded with 20 or 30 people in a few hours, chicken ships require 100 people over four or five days," and because they represented a growth business, the *Post and Courier* reported. "When the

117

A Local 1422 longshoreman checks containers as they are loaded onto a ship (Jeff Siner).

Soviet Union dissolved, U.S. poultry producers discovered that they had a huge new market," the newspaper said. "Americans generally prefer white meat, but people in Eastern Bloc countries generally prefer dark meat. So poultry producers such as Arkansas-based Hudson Foods started shipping huge volumes of dark meat to Russia. In late 1994, Hudson Foods began shipping frozen chicken out of Charleston, using NOCS Group to store the chicken and a union stevedore to load the ships."[8]

The demonstrations lasted for about a week, after which the Green Glacier steamed off with 4,000 tons of frozen chicken. They drew attention, but the problem of allowing non-union workers to load and unload ships continued.

Two and a half years later in December 1999, a similar battle erupted when non-union crews unloaded the 440-foot *Schackenborg*, operated by the Danish company Nordana. The ship was sailing between Houston, Charleston and Baltimore: in Charleston, Nordana employed a non-union stevedore, even though Local 1422 had offered contract concessions. "Chanting 'No union, no peace,' about 75 ILA members blocked the entrance road to the SPA's Columbus Street Terminal for about 15 minutes," the *Post and Courier* reported. "Charleston police watched but didn't

12. A Sixties Kid Takes Over Local 1422

move in on the protesters. Officers gave them a 'reasonable amount of time' to demonstrate and then asked them to leave, Police Chief Reuben Greenberg said [adding,] 'We know they are going to move because they are honorable men.' Moments later, the crowd dispersed and the gates re-opened. No one was arrested."[9] Despite that first demonstration, Nordana ships continued to arrive in port, non-union longshoremen continued to load and unload them, and members of Local 1422 continued to stage peaceful protests. Eventually, a not-so-peaceful protest in January 2000 would draw the world's attention.

13

A World Beyond Charleston

As union president, Kenny Riley ascended to roles on stages he had not previously known. Rather quickly, when he was in his mid–40s, these stages came to include the Supreme Court—where a Local 1422 member was pursuing a case—and South Carolina state politics, where the governor appointed Riley to the state ports commission, then withdrew the appointment after a round of hysteria because a labor union member was to join a state commission. The governor told Riley to say he had withdrawn—which he would not do.

Then, at the end of 2000, the Charleston Five incident thrust Riley into a role as an international labor leader, one who influenced global events. He had to travel widely to raise support for a cause that reverberated because it had both labor/management and black/white dimensions. Still later, starting in 2004, Riley would assume a place in a national political primary structure that allowed him to help pick the Democratic presidential candidate. In every case, Riley found himself in settings that were unfamiliar to him. He came to realize that he was comfortable in all of them.

"My world was opening up when I was in my 40s," Riley said. "It was a time when we started looking at the whole movement, not just the ILA [International Longshoremen's Association] network. When I became president, I found out that there were organizations like the A. Phillip Randolph Institute and the Coalition of Black Trade Unionists, which I had never heard of, that catered to black trade unionists. My world just opened up. And then there was so much exposure, so much greater than what we had ever experienced, that came about through the Charleston Five."[1]

Riley first sat down in the Local 1422 president's office on Monday, February 17, 1997. During his first week on the job, an attorney came to

13. A World Beyond Charleston

see him about Ceasar Wright, a Local 1422 member, who had suffered a serious workplace injury five years earlier. Wright had fallen from a slick shipping container, shattering his right heel and hurting his back. He had received a $250,000 settlement plus continuing disability payments. Then his injury subsided, his payments ceased, and he wanted to go back to work. The stevedore companies of Charleston, however, didn't want him back. They reasoned that they had paid Wright a large settlement and that he had consented to the end of his career.

"Ceasar Wright had been locked out of the industry for two or three years," Riley said. "He had suffered an injury, quit work and gotten compensation. He got a big settlement, and he was not supposed to work anymore. He had a bone that was protruding from his foot. Then, miraculously, that bone started to recede. He could now function. He could go back to work. That ended his disability pension, because Social Security decided he was no longer disabled. But the stevedores all decided that no one would hire him. They said he was disabled, he had gotten a big settlement, and he couldn't work. At the same time, the ILA pension fund said he couldn't collect a pension because he could work. So Ceasar Wright was trapped."

The case was already winding its way through the courts, headed for the Supreme Court, but Wright's attorney envisioned pursuing it on a second track through the union/management grievance process. "This was a case that had never gone through the grievance process," Riley said. "Two days after I took office, an attorney who represented Ceasar Wright came to see me. He wanted me to review the case. He said my predecessor assumed that Ceasar Wright had already lost and had said, 'We are not going to touch this case.' But I looked it over. I burned the midnight oil for two or three days, reading all the paperwork. Then I decided I am going to pursue this. I decided the only way to resuscitate the case would be to send Ceasar Wright back to work. Then, when they wouldn't let him work, I would file a grievance."[2]

The reason Riley knew that the stevedore firms wouldn't let Wright return to work was because Wright had tried to go back to work in January 1996 and was sent home after a little more than a week on the job. The result was exactly the same when Riley sent Wright back to work a year later; he worked for 11 days before he was sent home. When that happened, Riley filed a grievance. It was heard first in Charleston—where the port grievance committee deadlocked—and then by a district panel in Atlanta, which sent it to arbitration.

Meanwhile, the court system was eyeing the case from a different perspective. The issue for the courts was whether an employee is required to use the grievance procedure, which can lead to arbitration, or if there also was an option to use the court system by filing a discrimination lawsuit under the American with Disabilities Act (ADA). The Supreme Court heard the case, *Wright vs. Universal Maritime Service*, on October 7, 1998, and ruled on November 16 that Wright had the option to pursue his case in court and that his right to file a case under the ADA cannot be waived.

In a unanimous opinion written by Justice Antonin Scalia, the court reviewed Wright's actions after he was sent home from work in January 1996. It noted that, rather than pursuing a union grievance, Wright hired a lawyer and filed cases with both the Equal Employment Opportunity Commission and the South Carolina State Human Affairs Commission, alleging that the stevedoring companies had violated the ADA by refusing him work. Then he went into the court system, where a U.S. District Court dismissed the case, saying it lacked jurisdiction because Wright had not filed a grievance, and an Appeals Court backed the District Court.

"The cause of action Wright asserts arises not out of contract, but out of the ADA, and is distinct from any right conferred by the collective-bargaining agreement," said the court, which concluded, "We hold that the collective-bargaining agreement in this case does not contain a clear and unmistakable waiver of the covered employees' rights to a judicial forum for federal claims of employment discrimination. We do not reach the question whether such a waiver would be enforceable. The judgment of the Fourth Circuit is vacated, and the case is remanded for further proceedings consistent with this opinion."[3]

The ruling was applauded by Riley, the National Association for the Advancement of Colored People and the labor community. The headline in the *Post and Courier* read "Dockworker Wins in Supreme Court Discrimination Actions"; the subhead read "The ruling allows union employees to file some lawsuits against companies despite arbitration clauses in contracts."[4]

A week before the Supreme Court hearing, Riley and Armand Derfner went to Washington for preparations that included a mock trial at the headquarters of the AFL-CIO. "The case was very important to the AFL-CIO, and it was widely watched," Riley said. "Folks came from Europe to study that case. I don't know that it specifically helped the Local that much, but it was important to the labor movement. It meant that a union

13. A World Beyond Charleston

worker does not have to take every claim through arbitration, but also has the option to go to court." [5]

Ultimately, as a result of the Supreme Court ruling, the stevedore companies owed Wright for the four years he had been kept from working. Riley said the payout was several hundred thousand dollars. Not only did the companies owe Wright money; the union container royalty fund owed him money too. Riley went to the container royalty fund to argue on Wright's behalf, and the fund agreed to a $78,000 payout. "I was excited," Riley recalled. "I called Ceasar Wright and I said 'Get your pickup truck and come to the fund office, because you just got another truckload of money.'"[6]

Riley's involvement in a 1999 statewide controversy did not reach such a happy conclusion. That year, South Carolina governor Jim Hodges nominated Riley to become one of the nine members of the SCPA, which operates the Port of Charleston. The appointment would have made him the second African American and the first labor leader and waterfront representative to serve on the board. "Membership on the ports authority board is one of the most significant positions within state government," Riley said.[7] But he never got there. Rather, Hodges backed down, deciding—in the face of strong opposition from the South Carolina Chamber of Commerce and other business leaders—that perhaps he had overreached by nominating Riley.

In the 1998 South Carolina gubernatorial campaign, Riley had backed Hodges, who became an upset winner. "Sometimes miracles do happen," Riley said. The victory was attributed to incumbent Republican David Beasley's indecisiveness on two issues: whether to allow the Confederate flag to fly over the state capitol and whether to eliminate video poker.[8] During the campaign, Donna DeWitt, president of the South Carolina AFL-CIO, had contacted Riley. "She said, 'Hodges is big on education and has a good shot at becoming governor. I would like him to come down and meet you. You can introduce him to the maritime players,'" Riley said. "So he came down and we met. He was a very likable guy; he told me his vision for the state, and we also talked about what was going on with the port authority. I told him that it was a problem for us because all of the members are developers and bankers and other business people who don't know much about the maritime industry. I said that sometimes the port authority doesn't listen to the industry. I said the industry would support him, provided he would pledge to have two seats on the port authority filled by individuals from the port community. We didn't say who at the time."[9]

Kenny Riley and Black Union Labor Power

After winning, Hodges appointed Riley to serve on his transition team, an eye-opener for the black union leader. "We were filling cabinet positions," Riley said. "I hadn't realized that so many jobs had to be filled." When the transition was completed, Riley said the governor asked him, "'Kenny, what can I do for you?' and I said, 'We want those two seats filled,' and he nominated me for one of them. When he did that, the state chamber of commerce went into a frenzy. They felt they could not allow a union guy to sit on a state agency board. So much pressure came down from them, so much blowback, that the governor called me in. He said he could not afford to spend so much political capital on my appointment and he would like me to say that I withdrew my nomination. I told him they can frame it any way they want, but everyone who knows me knows I'm not a quitter."[10]

Following the withdrawal of Riley's nomination, the *Post and Courier* reviewed Hodges's decision making and its impact, concluding that "the governor was attempting to fulfill an election-year promise to waterfront interests—one that blew up in his face." The newspaper reported that

> Hodges has confirmed that last year he told the Maritime Association of the Port of Charleston he would give waterfront interests representation on the nine-member SPA board. Historically, SPA appointees primarily have been lawyers and non-port related business leaders. After the election, maritime association officials sent Hodges two recommendations for the SPA board: harbor pilot Whitemarsh Smith III and Riley.
>
> When controversy erupted over the Riley nomination, Hodges acknowledged in a letter to a state chamber of commerce official that he knew it would be a risky nomination. So before formally nominating Riley, he floated a few trial balloons, including testing the sentiment of local politicians. First, he asked Charleston County's five resident state senators if they would sign a letter endorsing Riley. (The state senate must confirm nominations to the SPA board.) All five, including two Republicans, signed on.
>
> It was after the nomination that negative comments began to flow. The state chamber contended that it would be a bad precedent to have a union man on the SPA in a state that is 98.2 percent union-free. One pro-union vote could damage national and international business recruiting, the chamber warned.... As opposition to Riley's appointment mounted from business leaders, Riley went to Columbia to discuss his confirmation strategy with supportive state senators. Before that meeting, he met with Hodges. The governor has said he told Riley he feared the nomination would fail. The strength of the opposition has become a matter of debate. Some Democrats have said Riley had more than half the Senate in his camp. Democrats hold a 24–22 majority in the Senate, and Riley also had some avowed Republican support. But Hodges said he could foresee the potential for a damaging filibuster. Riley withdrew. Hodges' decision not to fight for Riley drew sharp criticism from within his own party. The Democratic Party chairwoman of

13. A World Beyond Charleston

Orangeburg County, Donna DeWitt, who's also president of the AFL-CIO in South Carolina, resigned her party post.[11]

Riley believed the nomination would have been approved had Hodges gone through with it. Among his backers were state senator Glenn McConnell, a Charleston Republican who was Senate President Pro Tempore and who later became president of the College of Charleston. McConnell came from working-class roots and understood the power of longshoremen at the port.[12] He was a thoughtful leader in the fight to keep the Confederate flag in a prominent place at the state capitol, a man who exemplified the view that one can honor the Confederacy without being racist as a matter of "heritage not hate." It is a position that is widely contested. But Riley accepted it. Of McConnell's support for the flag, Riley said, "He knows what the period represents for us as African Americans, but with him, the issue was truly heritage and not hate. Emotional things like the flag cause people to forget that he is a great friend of the labor movement."

"I know there are many people who say the Confederate flag is a symbol of heritage not hate," Riley said.

> I don't know a lot of those people, but I have spent enough time with Glenn McConnell to know that he means it. I think I have been blessed with discernment enough to know whether someone is being real or modifying their position to appease me, and in my conversations with Glenn—and I spent a lot of time with him—I felt great sincerity.
>
> He is proud of his heritage. There is no denying that members of his family fought and died for the Confederacy. He can't deny that history. He can't denounce his heritage, just as I cannot denounce my forefathers. But he keeps it in perspective. If you still believe in the Confederacy, then it shows up in your treatment towards African Americans, in the bills that you sponsor and support. But you cannot be a friend of the ILA if you are a hater of black people, and Glenn has been a friend of the ILA. I can say this, that when it comes to the state representatives of South Carolina, the only Republican candidate I ever went into my own pocket to write a check for was Glenn McConnell.
>
> He has always been there for us. He once told me that his father had a sheet metal company and was a union employer by choice. [Glenn's father] felt his workers were well prepared due to the union's sheet metal apprentice program. He didn't have to hire people and hope they knew what they were doing. When he hired union labor, he knew what he was getting. So Glenn was a supporter of labor unions.[13]

McConnell had even put Riley on the board of the Save the Hunley Commission, which helped to raise and restore a sunken Confederate submarine. He also backed Riley's appointment to the port authority. "Here is a respected leader in this community, with a positive outlook and a track record of trying to make the port run more efficiently, and he was attacked in an anti-labor campaign by the big business in this state," McConnell told the *Charlotte Observer* in 2000. "I have not the first regret about supporting him."[14] Riley said, "Glenn McConnell and others were fighting for me. Glenn had lined up the votes. Glenn was begging [Hodges] to send the nomination over, but [Hodges] was too spineless to do it."[15]

It was a few years later, in 2004, that Riley became influential in Democratic presidential politics, a result of the move of the South Carolina primary to an earlier date on the party's calendar. The move was partially a result of lobbying within the party by Don Fowler, a Spartanburg native long active in Democratic politics. Fowler headed the South Carolina Democratic Party from 1971 to 1980, oversaw the 1988 Democratic National Convention and then served as chairman of the Democratic National Committee from 1995 to 1997. In 2019, he was busily hosting potential 2020 Democratic presidential nominees at his home. Additionally,

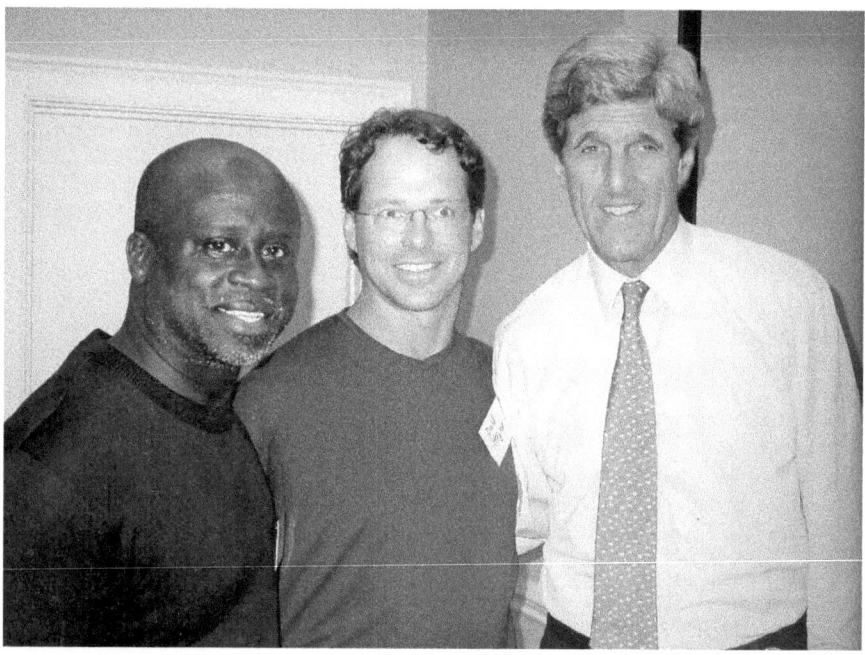

John Kerry (right) visited with Kenny Riley and David Hogan, president of ILA Local 1771, at the union hall. Kerry was campaigning during the 2004 South Carolina presidential primary (ILA Local 1422).

13. A World Beyond Charleston

he was an adjunct professor in the Department of Political Science at the University of South Carolina, where he began teaching in 1964.

Since the 1970s, New Hampshire has held the first presidential primary while Iowa has held the first presidential caucus. The South Carolina primary had long been near the middle of the primary pack when, in 2003, some party leaders thought that perhaps it should move to a more prominent role.

"Iowa and New Hampshire had long held as being the first and second state processes," Fowler said. "They enjoyed a lot of political status, and other states including South Carolina and Alabama and Arizona were jealous. They said, 'Are we going to let [New Hampshire and Iowa] have all the glory?' This came to a head before the 2003 sequence." A series of meetings involved Terry McAuliffe, chairman of the Democratic National Committee, and other Democratic leaders including Fowler, who was on the rules committee. "We were trying to find a formula that would be fairer but nevertheless would be part of a process in which retail candidates, who were not well known, could participate. These are candidates who need smaller population states to pursue their goals."

For its early primaries and caucuses, the Democratic Party wanted not only small-population states where candidates could test their abilities to mix with potential voters, whether or not they had enough money to pay for big market TV advertising, but also diverse racial representation. While Iowa and New Hampshire are largely white states, South Carolina is a state where African American voters account for a large share of Democratic primary voters. "Among states with large African American populations, it was between us and Alabama, and we got selected," Fowler said. Meanwhile, Nevada was chosen to be early in the process because its Hispanic voters account for a large share of primary voters. The proposed changes, developed in a series of eight to ten meetings, gained approval from the rules committee and then from the full Democratic National Committee.

Fowler said various South Carolina African American groups, including Local 1422, have influence in the primary vote. "South Carolina has a lot of local African American leaders, spread throughout the state, a lot of elected officials, mayors and members of city councils, and they all have influence," Fowler said. "A lot more African Americans fill these elective positions than there used to be, and the proliferation of prominent elected officials has diminished the influence of statewide groups."[16] Nevertheless, three groups—the black church, the NAACP and Local 1422 stand out as institutions that can turn out members to vote.

Kenny Riley and Black Union Labor Power

The Charleston union hall had long been a center for Democratic politics in the region. "Since we moved up to third in the primary, nearly every primary Democratic party candidate has visited the union hall," Riley said. "Appearances at the union hall were important because it was clear that to win the South Carolina primary, you had to get the black vote, and to do that you have to go to three places: the black church, the NAACP and the ILA."[17] In 2004, Richard Gephardt and John Kerry visited the union hall: the union endorsed Gephardt, who was perceived as friendlier to labor. Nevertheless, that year North Carolina senator John Edwards won the South Carolina primary and Kerry won the Democratic nomination.

In 2008, the ILA faced a difficult choice because Barack Obama opposed Hillary Clinton, already a friend to the local. "We were in a peculiar situation," Riley said. "I was personally a fan of Hillary Clinton, but we had an opportunity to help elect the first African American president. So I lay quiet; I was conflicted. Then Cory Booker came to see me, and we sat in the board room, and he said, 'Kenny, I'm telling you this guy has a solid chance, we are building a movement and we are going to need an endorsement from you to make this happen.' I said, 'I understand how significant this is, and I knew that if I took this to my membership in an endorsement meeting, they would support an African American candidate, and I would be able to say my members went with Barack Obama.' That was the only time I called an endorsement meeting. It was packed. We told them the situation and they voted overwhelmingly for Obama."

Obama had visited

Hillary Clinton visited Kenny Riley and Local 1422 members at the union hall, while Clinton was campaigning during the 2008 South Carolina presidential primary (ILA Local 1422).

13. A World Beyond Charleston

the union hall early in the campaign, and Riley sought a second visit the night after the endorsement was issued. "A campaign guy promised he would come," Riley said. "But the next morning I got a call from the campaign guy, he said, 'Barack can't make it.' I said okay, but the day after that, I heard that Obama was in a meeting in Charleston with a women's breakfast club. I didn't believe this. I thought, 'You cannot win without the minority vote.' So I called the guy again. I said, 'You better let Barack know. I am very pissed: you come to Charleston and you meet with a women's breakfast club and not with the ILA.' I was in my car, and a minute later my phone rang, and a voice says, 'Barack Obama here. I've got to apologize. I promise I will get by to you guys.' I said, 'Okay, fair enough,' and we hung up. But he never came back. So I am thinking about trying to raise money for the African American Museum and I am hoping he knows that he owes me one, because I plan to remind him of that story."[18]

14

The Charleston Five

Charleston's dockworkers drew the national spotlight in 2000, when their effort to keep non-union workers from working a Danish ship in a union port led to demonstrations, violence, headlines that referred to "riots," arrests, a trial and a slogan—"Free the Charleston Five"—that became known worldwide and that is widely remembered to this day.

The episode on January 19, 2000, provided a pivotal moment in South Carolina labor politics. "Free the Charleston 5" signs became familiar. A protest in Columbia in June 2001 attracted 4,000 people. Some of the state's politicians, especially those from the northwestern part of the state who opposed Charleston's supposed liberal outlook, seized an opportunity to show toughness in the face of a perceived threat from labor and black people. This group was led by South Carolina attorney general Charles Condon, who announced in February 2001 that he was running for governor and who turned the city's misdemeanor cases against the five into state-prosecuted felony cases. In the end, the legal battle fizzled out as the felony charges were reduced to misdemeanor charges with pleas of no contest and small fines.

Unfortunately, the Charleston Five—four blacks and one white—were under house arrest for months as the process played out. During the course of the battle, Local 1422 was strengthened through solidarity and publicity, and Kenny Riley became nationally and internationally recognized.

By 2000, continuing efforts to use non-union labor represented a smoldering problem for Local 1422, just as they did for other longshoremen and other unionized workers in various labor fields throughout the country. At the same time, the Port of Charleston maintained a reputation for rapid growth, high productivity and freedom from labor disputes, thanks largely to Riley. Throughout his career, Riley worked to maintain labor peace, reflecting the need for practicality, the dynamics of Charles-

14. The Charleston Five

ton and his own solution-oriented personality. In fact, it had been three decades since labor battles roiled the port. In 1969, longshoremen had walked off their jobs in a contract dispute with stevedores; in 1971 they did the same during a nationwide strike. But, at least since the end of slavery, no precedent existed for a violent encounter between longshoremen and 600 law enforcement officials.

The Danish shipping line Nordana's effort to work with non-union labor surprised no one. Local 1422 had picketed the company's ships several times during 1999. "Each time, the ship would come in, they would load it and it would sail," Riley said. "My guys were starting to feel that we were having no impact—that what we were doing wasn't working. They said we should forget about the picket line; we should be going in there."[1]

A problem for the January 19 event was that overzealous preparation on the law enforcement side raised the number of police officers and therefore the intensity on both sides. Although some of the lawmen were black, many more were white and rural. They had been bussed into Charleston from surrounding municipalities; some were clothed in riot gear. These circumstances likely served to heighten their concern about lawlessness and their commitment to preventing it. They confronted about 400 union members, most of them black, who were protesting Nordana's effort to load a ship with non-union workers. In its broadest context, the event was one among the myriad of demonstrations, before and since, of the disparity between black protestors and largely white law enforcement entities. However, it cannot be said that all of the demonstrators acted blamelessly.

Eighteen years later, Riley said that beyond the immediate effect of being caught up in a confrontational, widely publicized local news event, the biggest impact of the Charleston Five struggle on him and his members came afterwards, when they were suddenly made aware that their situation could attract international support. Charleston has always been, for its laboring blacks as well as its ruling whites, a sort of cocoon, a city immersed not only

The slogan "Free the Charleston 5" became widely known following the 2000 incident when a ship sought to load in Charleston with non-union labor (Jeff Siner).

131

in its monumental historical role but also in its traditional small-town parochialism. Riley, who had spent most of his life in town and had never left the Eastern United States, was entering his third year as a union president. During the Charleston Five incident, his cause garnered support from pro-labor organizations throughout the world—with a few notable exceptions: support from the International Longshoremen's Association and its affiliates was both delayed and minimal. On the other hand, one of the first phone calls he received after the incident came from the ILWU, the rival union that primarily represented dockworkers on the West Coast.

"Suddenly we had an awakening that there was a whole movement out there, way beyond the ILA," Riley recalled. "It was an awakening for me as well as for my guys. All we'd really known was the ILA and its network. When we got involved with the Charleston Five struggle, we were not in the good graces of the international because of our reform movement. At first, there was no effort on the part of the ILA nor the mainstream labor movement to do anything to help us. When there was news of the incident that first night, the first call we got was from the ILWU office in San Francisco, offering help. Then we heard from dockworkers in Barcelona and Japan. They called because they were in solidarity with the ILWU: They wanted to join in the struggle."[2]

Two days before the Charleston Five event—on January 17, 2000, Martin Luther King, Jr., Day—an estimated 46,000 people rallied in Columbia to protest the flying of the Confederate flag on the state capitol grounds. The Confederate flag has long been controversial, perhaps becoming even more so in the 21st century. In South Carolina, the flag was raised atop the capitol dome in 1961 as a demonstration of hostility to the civil rights movement. In 2000, following the January demonstration, it was relocated to a Confederate war memorial on the statehouse grounds. In 2015, following the mass shooting of nine worshipers at a black church in Charleston, it was removed from the statehouse grounds and moved to a nearby museum.

Riley did not attend the January 17 demonstration, but Local 1422 sent food, as well as people to cook it, in order to feed the demonstrators. The event also required the presence of hundreds of police officers. In fact, the *Skodsborg*, Nordana's ship, was ordered to remain at sea for several days until after the march because "they did not have enough security for both the demonstration in Columbia and the one at the port," Riley said.[3]

On Wednesday, January 19, Riley spent the morning in the port's of-

14. The Charleston Five

fices, negotiating with officials from the port, Nordana and Stevedoring Services of America (SSA), a global logistics company that hires ILA longshoremen. The crux of the problem was that Nordana "was tiny compared to its mega-container ship competitors and was having trouble competing on their scale. To reduce its freight-handling costs, Nordana had dropped SSA and contracted with Winyah Stevedoring Inc., a nonunion stevedoring firm owned by an area businessman [Perry Collins]. That morning, sitting at the port's office negotiating, Nordana officials weren't willing to change their minds and Collins' non-union workers were still unloading the ships for half the wages. The union's three months of picketing and protesting had not altered the company's position. Riley walked out of the fruitless and frustrating talks. As lunchtime approached, [he] ran some errands near his home in West Ashley and headed back across town to the union hall around 3 p.m."[4]

Riley had been forewarned, by a friendly state law enforcement official, that plans had been developed to counter an expected union picket line with a force of 600 police. He recalled his drive to the union hall that Wednesday.

> The ship was scheduled to work that night, and I wanted to be ready for the demonstration As I came off Cosgrove Avenue, getting on to I-26 to head downtown, I saw buses ahead of me going into Charleston. At first, I thought they were tour buses, but when I pulled alongside of them, I saw they were marked "South Carolina Department of Corrections" and thought, "Oh my God, those buses are coming for us." Then when I exited and started getting close to the union hall, I could not believe what I was seeing: police cars from city, county and state and armored cars, completely surrounding the circumference of the terminal. This was very concerning to me. Again I thought, "Oh my God, this is going to be something."
>
> I knew that the Charleston Police Department had been very decent to us. Chief Reuben Greenberg recognized our right to protest and the Charleston police protected us from out-of-town truckers who didn't like unions. We had no quarrel with the Charleston police. But these officers who were coming from small hick towns and everywhere else, they were not familiar with us. That was very concerning to me. When I got back to the hall about 4 p.m. or 5 p.m., we started having discussions. I decided we needed to call a meeting of all our people, so we called them in. About 150 to 200 people came to the meeting. I told them, "You guys see what's going on out there. You see all these police resources: we are making them spend a tremendous amount of money for this. So we are not going to go down there now. Later, when they think we are gone, they will start sending people home to cut expenses. And that is when we will show up." A lot of my guys went home. Some others just hung around. What I didn't realize then was that there were informers inside the hall, repeating whatever we said to law enforcement.[5]

Kenny Riley and Black Union Labor Power

Around 7 p.m., the *Skodsborg*, a 443-foot ship that carried both containers and traditional roll-on, roll-off cargo, docked at Columbus Street Terminal in Charleston. Non-union workers began to unload it. Around 11:30 p.m., many ILA members were returning to the union hall after following Riley's earlier suggestion to go home and return later. By then, Riley said, "The police had the streets blocked. They were hassling folks." At the union's midnight meeting, Riley and the two other local presidents, Johnny Alvanos of the white clerks and checkers local and Ben Parker of the black mechanics local, discussed their members' planned move to the picket line. "Since the police were still out there, I suggested we go back home again and then come back at 3 a.m.," Riley said. "But some guys said we needed to be out there because we had always said we would fight for our jobs. So I said, 'Okay, we did say that, you guys go down on the line, but for god's sake be careful and please don't engage those officers.'"

> So they went back outside, picked up the signs and starting marching and chanting and singing. I went back and sat in my office, with the other two local presidents. We looked at each other and I said, "This is going to be a long night." And as soon as I said that, [Parker's] phone rang, and he said, "Are you kidding me? They are already fighting down there?" As soon as I heard that I ran as fast as I could to the front of the picket line. It was 200 to 300 yards. I never slowed down; I was running on pure adrenaline. When I got there, I saw people with their heads busted open. I saw people rolling on the ground; I was jumping over them. I wanted to get to the front line so I could tell my guys to go back to the hall.
>
> When I looked around, to see if anybody else was in trouble, I turned to my left, and, boom, I got clubbed in the front of the head. My cousin was there, I remember hearing him say, "You didn't have to do that." He was talking to a cop. I didn't fall. I had a cap on. When I lifted that cap, the blood came pouring down. Two guys from the Local took me under their arms and started escorting me out. A female member, Georgette Carr, took a shirt, wrapped it around my head and walked me back to the union hall. Then I walked to my car and drove to the hospital. When I got to the admissions desk, it was a funny sight: there was a cop in front of me, and he was holding the back of his head and I was holding the front of mine. I got a dozen stitches that night.[6]

The incident was termed a "waterfront riot" in the *Post and Courier*'s headline. Riley contests the use of the term "riot," saying police incited disorder at what began as a lawful labor protest. Initially, a few picketers appeared, but in general the atmosphere was calm until around midnight. "At midnight, hundreds of longshoremen returned to the union hall and met for another closed-door meeting," the newspaper reported.

> Moments later, they streamed out the doors and into the parking lot. Many carried signs. Some carried wooden clubs. Others carried beer bottles and appeared to

14. The Charleston Five

be intoxicated, slurring obscenities and accosting reporters. The chant, "ILA, ILA, ILA" could be heard as the crowd marched down the street. "This isn't your fight, get the ... away," one man said, pushing a reporter.

When the mob turned the corner, they were met by the line of police. Standing inches away from the officers, they shouted threats and waved signs. Soon, a hailstorm of rocks, bricks, logs and other debris rained down on the officers who raised their shields to protect themselves. Charleston Police Capt. Thomas Robertson was struck in the back of the head by a railroad tie, officials said. He was taken to the hospital where he received seven stitches. Police did not find the person responsible.

At 12:14 a.m., the crowd knocked over the temporary police light, plunging the scene into darkness. Although the protesters continued to throw debris, police managed to prop up the lights. The situation continued to deteriorate. A freelance cameraman's head and thumb were injured when he was pushed to the ground by workers. Another protester tried to wrestle a camera away from a reporter with The City Paper. At one point, Riley was seen trying to get his men to pull back. He was hit by something and escorted away by three other men.[7]

A cameraman was assaulted. The police chief said Riley was struck by debris thrown by union members, but Riley said, "I got clubbed in the front of the head by a cop." Blood began to pour from his head. At the hospital, Robertson was the cop Riley encountered. "We have to stop meeting like this," Riley said.

"Seeing their president hit, the longshoremen let loose again," said the book *On the Global Waterfront: The Fight to Free the Charleston 5*. "Men who had been lobbing gravel at the light now began to pelt the police. Three men pulled down the temporary light pole while others confronted a cameraman with a local television station and told him to stop shooting.... Demonstrators grabbed the still cameras of the *Post and Courier* photographer who had come too close, but they were secured by the straps around his neck. Police hoisted the photographer behind their line. Far in the back, some longshoremen pushed over a television station van parked along Immigration and it crunched on its side. An occasional shard of rotten railroad tie from the roadbed and a steady stream of airborne gravel flew in the direction of the police. The projectiles bounced harmlessly off their shields."

The actions of some police officers were no less restrained. At one point, after Riley had left for the hospital, "An unmarked state trooper Suburban with lights and a siren followed by an unmarked state trooper Crown Victoria approached the crowd from the rear and forced its way through. When troopers in the Suburban threw a concussion grenade and tear gas canisters out both windows toward the front of the car, it sounded like war had broken out. The crowd cleared, except for one longshoreman who was looking to see what had caused the smoke. The front car slammed into at least one worker, rolling him over the hood where he athletically jumped up and walked over the roof and off the back. Longshoremen surrounded a third car, which quickly shifted into gear and followed the other cars through the crowd."[8]

According to the *Post and Courier*, "Above it all, A police helicopter circled with a spotlight, casting a white glow on the melee. At about 12:45 a.m., police ordered the crowd to disperse, broadcasting over and over on a loudspeaker." Police fired guns containing bean-bag-like projectiles to move the crowd back. At first the men retreated, but a few lingered despite the projectiles, and some overturned a television van. Eventually, using tear gas, police forced the crowd back to the union hall parking lot. "By 1:30 a.m., about 60 or so protesters were still in the parking lot, occasionally shouting at police. Then, as if to punctuate the bizarre turn of events, a rare winter thunderstorm roared through the area at 3 a.m., causing the few remaining protesters to head for their cars. By 7 a.m., the Nordana vessel was loaded and sailing toward its next destination, Baltimore. Police removed barricades on Morrison Drive, and by mid-morning, the terminal had its usual heavy flow of truck traffic."[9]

Riley meanwhile had been treated at the Medical University of South Carolina hospital. "After that, I was lying in a bed in the hospital, and one of my friends was there, and he said, 'Man, Kenny, it got rough out there.' He said, 'After you got hit, guys saw you bleeding and they went ballistic.' He said they called Leonard, my brother, but

A defiant Kenny Riley stands atop railroad tracks that run near the site where the 2000 Charleston Five incident took place (Jeff Siner).

14. The Charleston Five

they couldn't find him. So, of course, I feared the worst and I started to get up. The doctor said, 'What are you doing? You can't go anywhere,' but I said, 'I've got to find my brother' and I headed out the door. That's when my cellphone rang. It was Leonard. He said, 'I am in a police bus; there are 12 of us in here.' I was never so relieved as when I heard that he was in the police bus. I drove back to the hall in the wee hours. It was a cold, rainy night, and the police had the hall surrounded."[10] The next day, Leonard—who had been arrested for trespassing after he found a way onto port property during the protest—and the seven others were released on bail. Eventually, a different set of five workers would head for trial.

In the midst of the anxiety and uneasiness on the morning of the Charleston Five incident, Kenny Riley had one moment of pure exhilaration. It came as he tried to determine how to bail out the eight men who had been jailed. Forbidden to use the union treasury for bail money, he sought an alternative and appealed to Ceasar Wright, the longshoreman who had won a substantial financial settlement in a Supreme Court case. In response to Riley's appeal, "Ceasar Wright came to the union hall with a bank bag full of money, and he said, 'How much do you need?'" Riley recalled. "He was peeling off hundred-dollar bills, and he said, 'Had it not been for Kenny Riley and 1422, I would not have any of this money.'" Riley said Wright posted tens of thousands of dollars in bail for half a dozen people. It is not clear whether Wright was ever repaid. In any case, Wright didn't care, Riley said.[11] Wright died in 2017.

In an interview, *Post and Courier* reporter Tony Bartelme said it was accurate to describe the Charleston Five event as a riot. "People turned over a TV truck and there was tear gas and I watched a guy get run over," he recalled. "I call that a riot." Bartelme said police had decided on "a huge show of force," which initially seemed an overreaction because in the afternoon, "Two guys carrying signs walked out of the union hall, a way to call their bluff," he said. "It was a great moment of non-violence. Then everyone supposedly went home." But over the next several hours, some of the longshoremen who remained at the union hall became unruly. "They were drinking beer and starting to throw bottles," Bartelme said. The full group, which came to number about 400 people, marched towards the police line: eventually, the two sides were face to face. "I went to the side," Bartelme said. "You could see all the energy."

The *Post and Courier* photographer waded into the hostile crowd and was getting pushed around. One of the officers behind the lines suddenly grabbed him and pulled him to safety. "The photographer later said it was as if the hand of God picked him up and moved him behind the police lines," Bartelme said. The scene remained chaotic for several hours. Bartelme, who had an 11:30 p.m. deadline for the next day's paper, called in details for the story while " 'crouching behind a giant piece of concrete' as the police used tear gas." As the standoff dragged on, participants on both sides became exhausted. Then surprisingly, almost miraculously, the rare thunderstorm struck around 3 a.m. "That put out the fire," Bartelme said.[12]

15

Lessons Learned from the Charleston Five

Kenny Riley learned valuable lessons from the Charleston Five incident. One was that a situation involving black dockworkers in a medium-sized southern town could attract international attention. It could, in fact, attract sufficient attention and also indicate that the threat of a global port shutdown loomed if the five workers suffered more than minimal punishment. Riley also learned, to his surprise, that law enforcement surveillance of the Local's activities that day had been extensive. Finally, he realized that the State of South Carolina and the Port of Charleston had little interest in pursuing the case.

On January 20, 2000, the day after the incident at the port, the story was being widely reported in newspapers and on various television stations—local, network and cable—and Riley spent much of the morning taking calls from supporters. Among the early callers were leaders of the ILWU, the West Coast longshoremen's union, which quickly sent $5,000 for legal support, and also the Japanese longshoremen's union leaders, who learned of the event because they had been meeting with ILWU leaders in San Francisco. But nobody from the ILA called.

If the moment when Ceasar Wright walked into the union hall with rolls of cash was exhilarating for Riley, a meeting in an elevator in Savannah the next day was enlightening in providing perspective on the irrationality of the ILA's position.

During the week of the Charleston Five incident, national leaders of the ILA were meeting at the Savannah Marriott to discuss the union's health-care program. Riley, shaken up yet energized by the confrontation on the docks, decided to attend the meeting. "I drove down there in my bloody jacket, with stitches in my head, and I walked into the hotel and checked in," he said. "The [union leaders] were all in the lounge and everybody saw me. As I walked by, all their eyes started turning toward me. But no one got up; no one said anything." Riley went to the elevators and as he stepped into one, he encountered three top executives from the United States Maritime Alliance, which represents East and Gulf Coast longshore industry employers, including ports, container carriers and terminal operators. The alliance negotiates master contracts with the ILA. According to Riley, as the elevator ascended, one of the executives said, "Hi, Kenny—what you did in Charleston was remarkable. We're glad somebody in the ILA has balls, because there are too many of these renegade companies out there and we are sick and tired of the union not taking a stand."[1] The point was that established stevedore and steamship companies found themselves at a cost disadvantage when competitors could hire cheaper, non-union labor. Those companies needed to have national ILA take a stand, as Local 1422 had done in Charleston.

It was particularly odd that the ILA would not insist on a contract with Nordana in Charleston, because the company willingly observed union contracts in Baltimore and Houston. "Nordana didn't seem to have an issue with [union contracts elsewhere], but they made a decision to stop using ILA workers in Charleston and the ILA didn't approve it, but did nothing to stop it," Riley said. "I tried to get [union leaders] to use our leverage, to get with Nordana, to avoid using our members in two ports and not using them in another port. But ILA was not supportive of me fighting for my jurisdiction. They wouldn't do anything and it got to the point where we ended up in that big fight that night. And I realized that it was all about me. I had already started with [the Longshore Workers Coalition]. And now, beyond the shadow of a doubt, they did nothing to stop it because of Kenny Riley."[2]

Just as it was unsupportive in Charleston, the ILA had fallen on the wrong side of the issues roiling European dockworkers. Early support from the Barcelona-based International Dockworkers Council (IDC) drew Riley's attention to the cause of striking Liverpool dockworkers, who, like Local 1422, had seemed unable to garner support from established kingpins of the transport labor movement and who had reacted by joining in the establishment of the dissident IDC. The traditional kingpins, including ILA, were affiliated under the mantle of the London-based International Transport Workers' Federation (ITF).

"The ITF was very bureaucratic," Riley said. "It had a dockworkers division, but the division is one of the smallest in the federation even though ports are very strategic in the global transportation network." Earlier, Riley

15. Lessons Learned from the Charleston Five

thought, the ITF had positioned itself on the wrong side of the Liverpool dockers' strike, one of the most important European labor actions of the time. The strike began in 1995 when Liverpool dockworkers refused to cross a picket line set up by 80 workers who had been fired by a British stevedoring firm. Over the next 13 years, until they agreed to a settlement in 1998, the workers waged an international campaign, gaining support around the world. "The international union did not support that local in Liverpool, and as a result 500 dockworkers lost their jobs," Riley said. "ITF failed them because the British union did not support the strikers and so they lost the whole port."[3]

In the Charleston Five struggle, the Liverpool dockworkers were among the early supporters of Local 1422, which also gained backing from dissident labor groups in Australia, Canada, Spain and Sweden. "We all kept communicating," Riley said. "We felt we could not let what happened in Liverpool happen again. We had to do something different." Backing the Charleston Five became the IDC's first major action. During a 2000 meeting on the island of Tenerife, Spain, Savannah local leader Eddie McBride and Riley became involved with the IDC; Riley eventually became the council's U.S. East Coast representative. "It was not a stretch for me to buy into the philosophy of the IDC," Riley said. "They were saying, 'Never again will we watch dockworkers fall victim to this type of bureaucracy,' and the same thing was about to happen to me."

"We were creating movement within the union," Riley said. "We developed a slogan, 'We will never walk alone again.' They decided that the Charleston Five would be their first test. The IDC and the Longshore Workers Coalition were running a parallel, global reform movement. But no one in the ILA would touch it. They thought the IDC was too disruptive and might even be communist. Later on, the Spanish IDC dockworkers helped us in working out a deal with Nordana. Those Spanish dockworkers went aboard a Nordana vessel, handed the captain a letter and told him that they would not work another Nordana vessel if that vessel had been in Charleston and not worked by the ILA."[4]

In fact, Local 1422 had three legal battles to fight: one against Nordana, one against the non-union stevedore firm it employed in Charleston, and one against South Carolina Attorney General Charles Condon. Condon had filed felony charges against the five dockworkers and was subjecting them to house arrest. Condon's belligerence enabled the slogan "Free the Charleston Five."

Nordana was a small steamship line that historically had operated

Kenny Riley and Black Union Labor Power

Kenny Riley walks through a warehouse that is located beside the site of the Charleston Five incident. The warehouse provides storage for "project cargo," which typically consists of shipments for construction projects (Jeff Siner).

as its larger competitors did, employing stevedore companies that hired unionized dockworkers to load and unload its ships. "But Nordana was tiny compared to its mega-container ship competitors and was having trouble competing on their scale."[5] Seeking to reduce costs, Nordana moved to a non-union stevedore company in Charleston.

From the start, Nordana's owner was not pleased with the furor in Charleston. "Nordana's reputation among its countrymen was at stake; Danes don't take kindly to social injustice and virtually every Danish worker belongs to a union." Claes Rechnitzer, Nordana's executive vice president, had set up the non-union stevedoring arrangement in Charleston. When the unrest in Charleston was reported in a Danish newspaper, "Nordana's owner, a son of the founder and a man twenty years younger than Rechnitzer, stormed into his office and threw the newspaper down on his desk. 'You really put us in a mess here,' he said angrily. 'I cannot accept that we are put on the front page of the papers and customers are getting worried. Do consider the consequences and get us out of this mess.'"[6]

After this conversation, Rechnitzer changed his focus towards finding a solution in Charleston. This endeavor involved complications he had

15. Lessons Learned from the Charleston Five

not foreseen. For instance, he learned that early on Riley had offered to cut Nordana costs under the union contract, but that the SSA, the non-union stevedore, had not passed the offer on to Nordana. Even so, a settlement remained elusive because contractual cost reductions could not be exclusive to one shipper or one stevedore company but rather had to be extended to all those companies that agreed to master contracts. But a possible work-around emerged after a national ILA leader determined that Nordana, operating smaller ships that carried both containers and roll-on, roll-off bulk cargo, fell under contract language that enabled it to hire smaller ILA crews, Erem and Durrenberger wrote.[7]

Meanwhile, pressure on Nordana increased in April 2000 when the *Skodsborg* docked in Barcelona and Spanish dockworkers asked for a word with the captain. The workers said that the ship's cargo had been unsafely lashed down by non-union workers in the United States and that the next time a Nordana ship arrived in the same condition, they would not work it. For Nordana, the message was clear: "The problem was spreading. It was getting out of control. This time they would have to settle."[8] Days later, Rechnitzer agreed that Nordana would operate under an ILA contract and would drop its lawsuit against Local 1422.

The next problem was that WSI (Winyah Stevedoring, Inc.), the non-union stevedore company in Charleston, would not accept the settlement. Rather, it raised the ante in its lawsuit against Local 1422 to $2.5 million, far more than Local 1422 could afford to pay. But in April 2001, Riley and Peter Wilborn—a young Charleston attorney who worked in Derfner's office—flew to Denmark to take Rechnitzer's deposition as they prepared for a trial.

Wilborn presided over two major steps that enabled a favorable resolution of the case. First, he said, "I toiled long nights reading the documents, and I noticed that the contract had a 'liquidated damages provision.'"[9] The provision, which required that if either party breached the contract it had to pay $60,000, vastly reduced the union's potential liability. Among the various attorneys working on the case, Wilborn was the first to realize that the provision could be applied to the Nordana case. "Everyone had seen it, but they hadn't understood that it applied to us," he said. Discerning the provision's relevance was a major achievement for Wilborn, then in his early 30s, working as a junior partner to Derfner, whom he deeply respected. Derfner was "a legal superstar" who had already argued five cases before the Supreme Court. Wilborn said, "I was used to not being a central part of the work."

Kenny Riley and Black Union Labor Power

In Denmark, Wilborn realized just how sensitive the Danes were to the perception that Nordana was trying to break a union in the United States. In taking the deposition, he benefited from his awareness not only that Rechnitzer's "boss was very embarrassed to learn what had happened," but also that Rechnitzer himself "was a lover of African American culture in the South, including blues guitar." Wilborn argued that by harming Local 1422, Nordana would diminish an institution that provided African Americans with an opportunity to achieve comfortable middle-class lives burnished by health care and pension benefits. "The consequences of union busting at the port, starting with break bulk, would have been the beginning of the end of that," he said. "I got him to acknowledge that."[10] Importantly, Wilborn also got Rechnitzer to acknowledge that the union's liability in the event of a breakup was just $60,000.

Unlike the corporate cases, the criminal charges brought by Condon involved a political battle that had to be fought in the court of public opinion. For this, a small South Carolina union local, especially a local that lacked the support of its national union, needed help. Fortunately, help arrived following a May 2000 meeting, in Atlanta, of the Coalition of Black Trade Unionists. There, Riley was introduced to Bill Fletcher, Jr., a longtime labor activist who was an assistant to AFL-CIO president John Sweeney. "Kenny explained to me what the Charleston Five case was, and I was blown away by it," Fletcher said. "I asked what kind of support he was getting, and he responded 'very little.' So I went back to Washington and reported on the case to senior management."[11]

An early challenge to getting the AFL-CIO involved, Fletcher said, was that the organization required a formal invitation from either the ILA or the South Carolina AFL-CIO chapter, and ILA president John Bowers was strongly opposed, but Donna DeWitt, president of the South Carolina AFL-CIO, readily made the request. Soon, Fletcher said, John Sweeney "became very enthusiastic. He decided that this was an important case and that the labor movement needed to mobilize. After that, every time he would see John Bowers, he would ask, 'What's going on with the Charleston Five case?' But Bowers did not appreciate our involvement."

The AFL-CIO set up a national committee nominally headed by Fletcher, but in fact "Kenny Riley was the political leader of the entire project," Fletcher said. "I was the operational leader. I looked at it as I worked for Kenny. We got resources from the AFL-CIO and we reached out to every conceivable ally."[12] The organization worked with media, political allies including Mayor Joe Riley and other Charleston politicians,

15. Lessons Learned from the Charleston Five

and labor groups. A key goal was to lessen support by South Carolina moderates for Condon's aggressive, self-promotional prosecution of the case. A highlight was a demonstration in Columbia on June 9, 2001, which attracted about 4,000 participants. Two months of organizing preceded the event. "The AFL-CIO supplied ten summer interns with room and board for four weeks to help with mailings, visibility, phone calls, and logistics. Staff from the AFL-CIO started writing checks for buses: eight buses from Atlanta, 15 from the rest of Georgia, five from North Carolina and three from South Carolina. All told, the AFL-CIO would spend more than $30,000 on bus transportation for marchers." Meanwhile, "the speakers list would define the rally as a high priority for the AFL-CIO." Besides Kenny Riley, the list included top labor leaders Linda Chavez-Thompson, second in command at AFL-CIO; Cecil Roberts, president of the United Mine Workers; Joseph Lowery, president emeritus of the Southern Christian Leadership Conference; and labor leaders from Sweden and South Korea. The final agenda included more than 20 speakers, "enough to melt even the heartiest rally-goer in the Carolina summer sun."[13]

In fact, Riley's 2001 schedule was crammed with appearances, in the United States and abroad, intended to bolster support for the Charleston Five. One such appearance took place in Boston. It occurred at the behest of a group that included Steve Early, a labor activist and writer, who discussed it in a 2009 book entitled *Embedded with Organized Labor*.

> The sponsoring committee wanted to broaden the turnout beyond the usual suspects on the labor left (us) and the kind of "friends of labor" who would gather in a fashionable Cambridge living room to give generously to any left-initiated "defense fund." So we also contacted the Boston-area affiliate of the International Longshoremen's Association (ILA) to see if they wanted to meet our guest as well. The ILA's local headquarters is in "Southie" the Irish-American neighborhood where public school desegregation and busing was violently contested in the mid–1970s. Both locally and nationally, the scandal-scarred ILA had little past connection to progressive trade unionism. Its rather insular Massachusetts membership was rarely seen on the picket lines of other unions. But when the South Boston ILA official who answered the phone was informed that a union brother named Ken Riley was coming to town, arrangements for a meeting were made quickly. To the surprise of those who attended, the main speaker turned out not to be a fellow son of "the auld sod," but rather a leader from another planet indeed—a black longshoreman from a local union in the Deep South, whose picket-line militancy had triggered a worldwide solidarity campaign.

"The prosecution of the Charleston 5—four blacks and one white accused of rioting—could easily have remained an obscure local problem," Early wrote. Instead, he said, Local 1422 built an international coalition, overcoming barrier after barrier. Early called Riley "the main character in this unusual story" and described him as "a college-educated second-generation longshoreman [who] built a defense campaign with considerable interracial and cross-border appeal. Among those it brought together were labor and civil rights groups in South Carolina (and elsewhere), longshoremen on the East and West Coasts (who belong to two different unions), and dockworkers around the world. Such solidarity does not come naturally. It takes a lot of hard work, organizational arm twisting, and bottoms-up pressure generated by member-to-member networking that often flouted the official protocol of labor bureaucracies, here and abroad."[14]

Among the barriers, Riley's work required convincing blacks in South Carolina that the dockworkers' battle was as much a civil rights struggle as it was a labor struggle. "Although almost entirely African-American, Charleston longshoremen do not fit the usual profile of southern workers under siege," Early wrote. "The latter, more often than not, are low-wage blacks or immigrants picking vegetables, plucking chickens, slaughtering hogs, or tending to farm-raised catfish, under conditions of extreme exploitation. Riley's members who worked full-time earned $1,350 a week."[15]

"For labor, the main lesson of the Charleston 5 campaign is as follows: American unions need all the help they can get from wherever they can get it," Early said. "The example of ILA Local 1422—which gave to and received from the black community, and then made new friends and allies throughout the United States and the world—needs to be widely emulated. In today's increasingly hostile political and economic climate, no union is an island. Any that tries to be one won't survive for long."[16]

Interest in the case was so widespread that even the TV program *60 Minutes* began work on a story that, sadly, never materialized despite months of preparation. The concept had originated when a Harvard classmate of Fletcher's, a woman who worked for the program, called out of the blue to ask whether he knew of any stories that might interest the show. Did he ever! Correspondent Ed Bradley worked on the segment, and producers for the show filmed at the Columbia rally. Kenny Riley recalled that the crew filmed him not only in Columbia but also in Norway and New York. But a roadblock emerged when the producers said they required that one of the Charleston Five defendants appear on the show. Both of the attorneys who represented the defendants said no. "They said their job was to get these guys off; they could not take the risk of having them answer questions," Fletcher said. "It broke my heart."[17]

15. Lessons Learned from the Charleston Five

A year and a half after the Charleston Five event, Riley was gathered in a room with Derfner and other attorneys reviewing surveillance tapes that they had subpoenaed. The review occurred on the morning of September 11, 2001. "We were viewing the tapes, trying to get our defense together, and I saw film of myself running from the union hall to that picket line near the dock," Riley said. "That was the moment I realized they had taped me in video taken from a helicopter. I hadn't even realized there was a light on me, and I wondered how did they know that I would be there, although we also found out later that everything we were planning was being radioed [by informers] to the police. The police knew we were not going out at 7 p.m., that we were going to pretend we were going home and then come back at 11 p.m. I realized something was going on when the guys who started coming back at 11 were being blocked by police officers."[18]

The memory of those sudden realizations in an attorney's office are bound up with Riley's and Derfner's recollections of the events of September 11. Said Derfner, "Several of us were sitting in Andy Savage's law office looking at videos of the night of the Charleston Five event and a secretary came in and said, 'Turn on the TV.' At first, we thought she was talking about the video we were watching. Then we turned that off and what we saw on TV was 9/11. It was eerie."[19]

In fact, watching the surveillance tapes provided a series of revelations for both Riley and Derfner. At one point, they watched film of police preparing for the dockside protest. "Their leaders were trying to pump them up, saying to them, 'There will be a battle tonight,'" Riley said. "There was an equipment room and as they left, they were handed shields and helmets, as if they were heading to the battlefield. I was mesmerized as I watched it: I realized this was what was happening behind the scenes." Riley has consistently disputed the commonly used description of the Charleston Five event as "a riot," noting "there was no riot, there was provocation by police." Among the provocations, he said, was use of the word "nigger" by some police officers: "Some of our guys were told, 'C'mon, nigger, we are going to bust your head tonight,'" he said.[20]

The Charleston Five case ended with a whimper. On November 13, 2001, nearly two years after the incident, three dockworkers pleaded no contest to a misdemeanor charge, "engaging in a riot, rout, or affray when no weapon was actually used and no wound inflicted," several days after the two other dockworkers had entered the same pleas. They paid small fines.

Kenny Riley and Black Union Labor Power

"Tuesday's proceedings could have been more dramatic had prosecutors and defense lawyers failed to make their 11th-hour deal," said the *Post and Courier*. "The five were scheduled to go on trial Tuesday, and union officials from across the world had planned an 'international day of action' to support the dockworkers. The International Longshore and Warehouse Union, which handles cargo on the West Coast, had vowed to walk out in protest, a move that could have temporarily crippled commerce at the nation's busiest ports."[21]

In October, Condon, who increasingly became an obstacle to settlement as the union campaign turned the focus on him, had turned over the case to another attorney, First Circuit Solicitor Walter Bailey of Summerville. Bailey said that "he tried to look at the case as he would any other," the *Post and Courier* reported. "'There was a lot of hype here,' he said. 'I also tried to take into account what the victims wanted. In this case, I felt the victims were the Charleston Police Department and the ports authority, and they both just wanted the case resolved, and this was a way to do it." In the courtroom that morning, three dockworkers—Ricky Simmons, Peter Washington, Jr., and Elijah Ford—were in attendance.

"When their hearing began, Bailey briefly described the clash with police and how previous felony indictments had been tossed out," the newspaper said. "Flanked by [their attorney] Lionel Lofton, and another attorney, Armand Derfner, the three longshoremen answered 'yes' or 'no' to most of Circuit Judge Victor Rawl's questions about the case, but made no statements. Lofton thanked Bailey for his decision to accept a plea in the case. 'This should have been disposed of a year ago,' Lofton told the judge. Rawl then sentenced the dockworkers to 30 days in prison or $309 in fines and court costs. 'Thank you very much for handling it like you have done,' the judge then told Bailey. 'This is over.'"[22] Later, *Post and Courier* reporter Tony Bartelme described the minimal settlement as "What everybody wanted: let's make nice and get along. It's so Charleston."[23]

"We won the case, which was amazing," Fletcher said. "The case imploded for the prosecution. But for me, the saddest part was that the AFL-CIO did not take a victory lap, in part because of 9/11 [two months earlier]. The labor movement needed a victory lap because, with all the layoffs at the time, this was a case we had won. Kenny and others, myself included, wanted a tour around the U.S. to talk about the Charleston Five case, about what we had done and why we won. The AFL-CIO didn't pick up on it and I left the AFL-CIO shortly thereafter."[24]

In a deeper sense, Fletcher said, labor victories often tend to be for-

15. Lessons Learned from the Charleston Five

gotten. The Charleston Five case is remembered in labor circles, he said, but not elsewhere. "I have gone all over the country, in the years since 2001, and I run into people who say I worked on that case," he said. "The people involved have never forgotten. But the officialdom in the labor movement has largely forgotten the Charleston Five case and has underestimated its importance, and that has been very frustrating. The importance was that we organized a national defense campaign, both inside and outside the labor movement, using multiple approaches to put pressure on the government of South Carolina, particularly the attorney general of South Carolina. We succeeded in isolating him. No one wanted to be associated with him."

In Fletcher's view, the stories of all of the key events in South Carolina labor history—the textile strike of 1934, the Charleston hospital workers' strike of 1969, and the Charleston Five events of 2000 and 2001—are either forgotten or misremembered in a way that reflects the lesson of Aesop's fable about the man and the lion. In the fable, a man and a lion encounter one another in the jungle, where they argue about which species is stronger—men or lions. The man argues that mankind had the advantage of greater intelligence. He takes the lion to view a statue of Hercules overcoming a lion. The statue, the man says, proves that men are superior to lions. But the lion responds that the statue proves nothing, because it was built by a man. Had a lion built the statue, the lion said, then the lion would be on top.

Similarly, Fletcher said, it is not working people and labor unions who write history. "History is written by others, who have a bias against the idea of workers and their collective struggles, so historic events like the Charleston Five end up being forgotten," he said. Moreover, he said, such events come to be seen as accidental or random, when in fact they represent labor's consistent ability to achieve success when it mobilizes.[25]

16

A Charleston Guy Finds Allies in New York and San Francisco

Over two decades, from 1997 through 2018, Kenny Riley was elected to the presidency of Local 1422 eight times, defeating his predecessor twice and then notching six consecutive victories over a team of two brothers, one of whom ran four times. Riley's leadership skills, combined with his 60s-inspired passion for change, enabled him to become a prominent Charleston presence for a quarter century. At the same time, he was a defiant advocate for black workers in the International Longshoremen's Association, which, like most of the labor movement, has long been dominated by aging white males.

From the start, Riley very quickly found himself at odds with the union's national leadership. He was South Carolinian, rebellious, young and black, while the New York–based leadership was entrenched, older and white. It did not help that Riley, facing a deteriorating relationship with local presidential predecessor Benjamin Flowers, filed a lawsuit against the union.

The stereotype of a longshoreman has been shaped by Marlon Brando in a 1954 movie, *On the Waterfront,* but the truth is that for decades the majority of U.S. dockworkers have been black. In recent decades, ILA membership has been about 60 percent black. The makeup reflects the predominance of container ports in southern cities led by Charleston, Savannah, New Orleans and Houston, where membership is overwhelmingly black.

John Bowers, a white Irishman who led the union from 1987 to 2007 after serving as executive vice president to Teddy Gleason, became the symbol of entrenched leadership's opposition to Riley and the LWC, the

16. Allies in New York and San Francisco

African American advocacy group Riley and Eddie McBride had organized. "From the time I was elected local president, Bowers and I warred the entire time," Riley said.

National union leaders led by Bowers summoned Riley to a 1999 meeting in New York, where they objected to a letter Riley had written seeking local leaders' support for the LWC. "I got a call from New York one day, Bowers wants you to come to a meeting," Riley said. "I flew up and I ran into Bowers [and a Bowers associate] outside the Downtown Athletic Club, where the meeting was scheduled, and they had the letter and they said, 'Kenny, what is this? We can understand Eddie McBride signing this, but you?' and I said, 'I know my name is on there. I believe in it.' And Bowers lost it. He said, 'You know what, Riley? You are not going to divide my union.' And I said, 'Your union is already divided. I'm just trying to bring it back together.' Bowers then shouted, 'Riley, you are not coming into my meeting.' Then I went back to my hotel and got my stuff and I flew back to Charleston that same night."[1]

Longtime union spokesman Jim McNamara said Bowers and his contemporaries were products of their time, not necessarily anti-black and certainly supportive of Benjamin Flowers. But they were not comfortable with a world where black people were demanding equality and it did not help that one of Kenny Riley's early actions as an emerging leader was to sue the national union. "It was an interesting dynamic," McNamara said. "When Kenny was coming up, the international leadership was elderly and white and very conservative, very traditional, very anti–Communist and very 'pro–American.' They were strong in their beliefs and they believed in protocol. They saw Kenny replacing Ben Flowers, who was an international vice president, very popular and well-liked, part of the leadership with Teddy Gleason and John Bowers, and a great labor leader in his own right. John would have preferred that Ben Flowers remain as president of 1422. So that was hard. Politics in the ILA is like politics anywhere: the enemy of my friend is my enemy. It may have looked as if John was trying to silence Kenny and put him down, but John was just following the traditions and customs of the ILA," McNamara said. "Kenny was a young officer on his way up, and sometimes it's not easy being progressive in a labor union, not easy being the one trying to chip away from the outside. But eventually people open up their eyes to the future." McNamara said the ILA was among the labor unions that supported the civil rights movement, and that in the early 60s, Gleason once pulled a convention meeting out of a Miami hotel because it would not allow blacks to stay there. Nevertheless, he said, "Everybody [here] could have done better. Everybody had their ways. There was definitely a conflict [with Kenny]."[2]

Riley's national profile rose despite, or perhaps because of, the continued conflict with national leadership. In 2004, Riley was elected to be an international vice president, entitling him to become a member of the union's executive council, which has about two dozen members. The election to replace an ailing predecessor was not an easy one; it came in a 12–9 vote by the existing executive committee. At the time, Riley had a pending lawsuit against the ILA. The suit alleged that the union violated its duty of fair representation because some locals, including Houston and New York, had been allowed to negotiate contracts with better pension funding than the national contract that was in place in Charleston and other ports. Riley recalls international leaders led by Bowers "came to me and said, 'Kenny, we will support you, but you cannot be a vice president while suing the union. If you drop the lawsuit, we will make sure you get the pensions improved.' I said OK. The only votes I got were the South Atlantic district and the ones promised to me by Bowers. Nobody in the Great Lakes supported me. But I won and we dismissed the lawsuit and I have been an international vice president ever since."[3] His term extends to 2023.

Peter Wilborn, the longtime attorney for Local 1422, said Riley probably should have become president of the ILA, but that Riley's combination of integrity, commitment and intelligence was never fully valued within the union. "Kenny never played the game," he said. "He was seen as a threat to the power structure." A lesson from the international recognition of the plight of the Charleston Five, he said, was that "the farther Kenny Riley got from home, the more he was appreciated. When he got closer to home, he became a mere mortal."[4]

While Bowers and much of the leadership were Riley opponents, rising union leader Harold Daggett became an important ally. Daggett, a third-generation longshoreman who served in Vietnam while in the Navy, was president of powerful New Jersey Local 1804–1. He added a post, secretary-treasurer of the union's Atlantic Coast Division, in 1991. "I met Kenny Riley when I got involved with the Atlantic Coast district," Daggett said. "When you do four years in the service, you meet a lot of different characters and you get to where you can understand real quickly whether a person is true or just showing off. My first impression of Kenny was that he was very sincere. A lot of people in those days were nervous about him because here you've got an African American, seeing into the

16. Allies in New York and San Francisco

future before a lot of people could see it. But I happened to embrace him. Kenny was head of a coalition that went against Bowers, and behind the scenes, everybody was putting Kenny down," Daggett said. "But I saw a different Kenny, a very intelligent person who came from a family that had strict rules. His dad had made the kids come to Long Island and pick potatoes, made him do a lot of farm work, and made him go to church. Then [his dad] put him through college. When I got to listen to all the things Kenny would say, and I would also listen to the other side, I understood that Kenny and others formed the coalition because they felt they weren't being treated right. They felt they weren't getting representation. I took a back seat and listened to both sides for a long time, and I started to have a relationship with Kenny. Certain people didn't like that, but I said, 'You have to embrace people who are sincere and trying to help.' So Kenny had me in his corner. I was always listening to him, and a lot of the things he was saying were true."[5]

A key difference between Daggett and Bowers was generational. Daggett was a medic in the Vietnam War, where blacks and whites fought side by side. Bowers fought in World War II, where blacks often fought in black regiments. "There was a big difference in the attitudes toward blacks," McNamara said. "Harold always says that all he saw, when he looked at the soldier next to him, was the American flag on his patch. When he became ILA president, there were a lot of open wounds that he was able to repair, to make amends. He was able to eliminate the dissonance and to give people a voice."[6]

Riley's long-standing support was essential to Daggett's quest for union leadership. In the 2007 election for ILA president, "Daggett was ready to challenge the establishment," Riley said. "He didn't like the leadership—it was like a family feud." By that time, affiliates of the Longshore Workers Coalition composed one of the largest voting blocs within the ILA. Daggett had worked his way up through the ranks. "He could match votes with the Bowers people," Riley said. "He had the coalition and he also had a smaller group of guys who ran tugs in the New York harbor."[7] At the 2007 convention in Hollywood, Fla., leadership desperately wanted to avoid a floor fight, so the two sides negotiated a deal to make Baltimore ILA leader Richard Hughes the international president for one term, after which Daggett would succeed him in 2011.

Despite the agreement that Daggett would take over, the 2011 convention—again held in Hollywood—was still contentious. Riley had fought for years for the establishment of a civil rights department within the ILA, while his opponents preferred to establish a civil rights committee. The distinction was meaningful. "You know the saying—if you want to kill something, put it in a committee," Riley said. A committee, he said, would represent an added assignment for existing officers, while a department would be staffed and dedicated to its separate role within the union. "They argued that there was no dedicated funding for a department," Riley said. "I envisioned that, given the strength of the ILA, there would be a department that would be able to get involved in the disparities that still exist in the labor movement and within the union. Our vision was that it would deal with social justice issues both inside the union and outside the union."[8]

Riley cited the United Auto Workers' failed 2017 organizing drive at a Nissan plant in Canton, Miss., as a venue where the ILA might have provided more support to a campaign that targeted a largely African American workforce. The ILA issued a statement supporting the workers, he said, but it could have done more. "Those workers were fighting for a union, and their cars come through our ports. Who is better positioned to help them than the dockworkers?" he said. "But we had only a committee. A real functioning department might have called for a big event to help organize members."

Two of the qualities that characterize Riley were engaged at the convention. On the one hand, he is unyielding regarding his core beliefs, which include opposition to racism. On the other, he is congenial and easily forges relationships: Race is not a factor in his selection of allies. Early in the convention, Riley was a panelist in a discussion of one-man, one-vote union elections. The ILA, like many unions, allocates voting on key issues to local delegates based on the number of local voters they represent. That means that on key issues, voting is by delegate representatives, not by individual members voting in one-man, one-vote representation. For Riley, the arrangement represents a formula for subverting black majorities to a process dominated by whites. This time, he said, "I raised the issue of institutionalized racism in the ILA," Riley said. "I pointed out that there had never been an African American in a top union position of real power, even though the population of the union is around 60 percent African American."

Subsequently, union leaders declared on stage, to the full convention of a few thousand delegates, that they would oppose Riley's bid to remain an international vice president. "I got a tap on my shoulder that they want you on stage," he said. "When I got there, here comes Richard Hughes,

16. Allies in New York and San Francisco

along with all the executive officers, and they said, 'Kenny, we were going to support you for international vice president, but after you talked about racism in the ILA we don't know if we should.' So I responded. I said to Hughes, 'You're mostly white Irish, you are proud white Irishmen, and you have every right to be—Look what you have in this union. But let me say this to you, I am one proud African American and I don't like it when I see what goes on with African Americans in this organization. If you don't want to support me, be my guest. I will go back home and be president of my local.' After that, Hughes said they would support me, even though they thought I had been disrespectful. And then, when the nominations came up, I had a white Irish guy from Canada nominate me, and another Irish guy from Milwaukee who seconded my nomination."

Although Riley was re-elected to be international vice president, he failed in his bid to have the ILA establish a civil rights department. Instead, the union agreed to form a civil rights committee. Then, rather than extend an olive branch, union leadership did not include a single person from the Longshore Worker's Coalition on the committee. "We had drafted resolutions year after year to create a fully funded civil rights department," Riley said. "But when they finally decided to create a committee instead, they appointed ten people, and of the LWC members who fought for it, not a single one was appointed to the committee, not from 2011 until now," Riley said in January 2019.[9]

Still, Daggett's 2011 ascendance to the union presidency represented a vast improvement for Riley and the black longshoremen he represented. Daggett moved quickly to reward those who had backed him. "When I became president of the ILA, I put Kenny on almost every important committee," Daggett said. "I believed in him; he is intelligent and he had helped me in many ways. He had faith in me; I had faith in him." After two decades of negotiating contracts, Riley was well-versed enough that Daggett assigned him key roles in negotiating master contracts in 2013 and 2018. The ILA negotiates contracts with the United States Maritime Alliance, which represents container carriers, direct employers, and port associations serving the East and Gulf Coasts. A previous contract had expired September 30, 2012. The 2013 agreement included wage increases totaling $3 an hour over six years, bringing hourly pay to $35 an hour, as well as restrictions on outsourcing or subcontracting of ILA jobs and job protections for workers displaced due to new technology and automation.

In 2018, when the 2013 contract expired, Daggett and his team, which included Riley, negotiated improvements. "Our union fights automation,"

Daggett said. "On the West Coast and in Europe, automation is killing unions, but we have been able to prevent it. We tell management that if you trust us, we can make between 30 and 35 moves off a ship. [The average in 2018 was about 32.] Fully automated, they can do 20 to 25 an hour, and if you ever get a glitch in the automation, you lose customers. It costs a billion dollars to put in an automated port, and you still have to have the ILA around to help if an automated terminal goes down. So they decided to take a chance on us. They're not putting in any new automation from Maine to Texas."[10] In contrast, ports from Rotterdam and Singapore to Long Beach and Los Angeles are heavily automated.

Early on, Daggett moved to honor Riley's international commitment to the Barcelona-based International Dockworkers Council, which had backed the Charleston Five: In 2018, Daggett called for a boycott of IDC-rival International Transport Workers Federation, which the ILA views as failing to strongly oppose automation. "When Harold got his votes in 2011, he made a promise to me," Riley said. "He said, 'Kenny, you will see a change when I get elected,' and he delivered." As for the ITF, at its international congress in Singapore in October 2018, "they had robots walking around serving hors d'oeuvres," Riley said.[11]

Willie Adams was elected to be the first black president of the International Longshore and Warehouse Union in 2018. The ILWU is the only national union that is based in San Francisco (ILWU photograph).

Besides winning a key friend in New York, Riley also won one in San Francisco, the headquarters of the International Longshore and Warehouse Union, which represents the longshoremen in the West Coast ports. ILA and ILWU have long been opponents with very different histories, particularly racial histories. While the majority-black ILA has always been led by white men, the ILWU, despite being majority white, elected Willie Adams as its first black president in 2018.

In the days when John Bow-

16. Allies in New York and San Francisco

ers was battling Riley and seeking to sidestep involvement in the Charleston Five case, ILWU was among the earliest and strongest supporters of the cause. Early in the campaign, long before the AFL-CIO became involved, Riley visited ILWU headquarters in San Francisco, seeking support and financial backing for the Charleston Five. There, he and Adams became acquainted.

"I felt Kenny was very articulate and very passionate, and he said something very profound that stuck with everybody," Adams recalled. "He said 'I am president of a local and we work on the docks where our ancestors came as slaves.' He was very inspiring to me, coming from the South and leading the struggle in Charleston. I could see he was a visionary, ahead of his time. Then getting to know him, as we became friends, I found him to be very engaging and very politically astute."[12]

Adams, a native of Kansas City, went to Tacoma in 1978 to visit a friend, Leo Randolph, who had been a member of the 1975 U.S. Olympic boxing team. Adams liked Tacoma, went to work as a longshoreman and eventually became active in ILWU Local 23. The Local was predominantly white, but Adams found his way (at first, "It wasn't easy," he said) and was elected to union office in 1998. For several years, while Adams was in Tacoma, Riley visited regularly to participate in Local 23's annual black history program, which Adams called "the best black history program in the country." In 2003, Adams was elected to be the ILWU's international secretary-treasurer, and he moved to San Francisco. He says he is still surprised, when he visits Charleston or Savannah, to see that the ILA locals are so segregated. In the ILWU, he said, "Our locals are mixed. You have people of every race. Our union is the most progressive union in the country."

Adams said that Riley, "coming from the South, probably liked the progressiveness of the ILWU. We're the only international union not based on the East Coast, and we've always been militant and very progressive. We march to the beat of a different drummer." Riley's first visit to the ILWU was specifically to its San Francisco Local 10, which Adams calls "the lightning rod." The local has a long history of battling racism. It boycotted South African cargo, starting in 1962; it displayed early and strong support for Martin Luther King, Jr.; and it led a 2010 shutdown of the port to protest the murder of Oscar Grant, which was portrayed in the movie *Fruitvale Station*.

The commitment reflects the legacy of Harry Bridges who, like the ILA's Teddy Gleason, is remembered as one of the most influential U.S. labor leaders.

Kenny Riley and Black Union Labor Power

Born in Australia, Bridges went to work as a merchant seaman, arrived in the United States in 1920 and became a San Francisco longshoreman in 1922. He joined the ILA and became a leader of its San Francisco local, but in 1937, after a dispute with the union, he led the creation of the ILWU. Before World War II, when Communism had a worldwide appeal as a progressive form of government that sought to enable broad distribution of wealth, Bridges was an avowed Communist. Following World War II, antipathy mounted between the United States on one hand and Russia and China on the other. Nativist Americans seized on the cause of anti–Communism and on the demonization of those, including Bridges, who once backed it.

Besides being a Communist, Bridges showed an early commitment to civil rights. According to Adams, during the 1934 West Coast longshoremen's strike, "The shipping companies were all bringing in blacks from the South to scab, and Harry Bridges went to all the black churches and to the black longshoremen and he told them, 'If you honor our picket line I will integrate this union.' The union was all white at the time, but he said, 'Every time there are two jobs, one will go to a black worker and one will go to a white worker.'" The strike resulted in the unionization of all of the West Coast ports as well as integration of the Locals.

Adams said he has traveled all over the world with Riley, visiting Australia and Europe as well as domestic locations. "Kenny is a global labor leader with a big vision and an understanding of globalization and the need for international solidarity," Adams said. "He can motivate people. What you see in Kenny is the epitome of a true grass-roots working-class labor leader."[13]

17

The Family Politics of Local 1422

Kenny Riley may be a gifted and compelling labor leader who raised the profile of his union, strongly backs civil rights and other social causes, and has consistently improved the lives of his members during two decades as Local 1422 president, but that doesn't mean he has lacked persistent opposition from within the Local.

Strikingly, that opposition is rooted in the families of the two other leading figures in Local 1422's history: founder George Washington German and former 18-year president Benjamin Flowers. In his eight successful elections to the presidency, Riley defeated Benjamin Flowers twice, German's grandson Kenneth Edmondson four times, and German's grandson Richard Edmondson twice. The decades of conflict between the leading families of Local 1422 mirror the narratives of many prominent families throughout history. In 2018, the fulcrum of the conflict at 1422 was the presence of Flowers's daughter Yvette Flowers as the union's financial secretary/treasurer, occupying an office a few doors away from Riley's. A painting of her father is the dominant decoration in the room. She is undoubtedly aware that Riley viewed her father "not as a progressive but as a passivist who had no vision for the future."[1]

In January 2018, Yvette Flowers filed a lawsuit against Local 1422, the ILA pension office and its administrator, and Riley. She alleged that she been deprived of seniority leading to pension benefits because Riley, acting out of ill will towards her father, deprived her of the opportunity to accumulate seniority hours while she worked two union jobs: one as a receptionist and one as a dockworker. As of March 2019, the case was still pending. During a brief interview in November 2018, Yvette Flowers declared that working in close proximity to Riley could be difficult; she subsequently declined a more extensive interview. Benjamin Flowers, Jr., also declined to be interviewed, as did Kenneth Edmondson. It seemed clear that neither family wanted to contribute their words to a book about Riley. Told of his rivals' silence, Riley declared, "I think they are afraid they would be helping me. They don't want to give me any kudos just because someone decided a book ought to be written. A book would tell the story of how things are, with all the political differences—an accurate reporting of reality. Their mindset is, 'I'm not going to help this guy.'"[2]

In April 2009, a *Post and Courier* story described the night when Yvette Flowers was first elected to her post as financial secretary. The headline was "Financial Secretary, Union Have Long History," and the story was filled with discreet references to the conflict between the Flowers family and Riley. It began, "So much history already existed between Yvette Flowers Davenport and Charleston's most powerful maritime union before the night she stood pacing in the back of its community hall 'awaiting election results.'" The story goes on to say that "Davenport, 46, won't say much about the campaign leading to that January night, only that it wasn't always kind, as a woman from the old guard took on an incumbent from the current regime." The story also said, "After the election, Davenport approached union president Ken Riley, the man who ousted her father. She wanted to make peace. 'I have an attitude of service, and Mr. Riley is my president,' she said. 'If one of us fails, all of us fail.'"[3] Riley did not comment for the story. Notably Benjamin Flowers, Jr., ran his sister's campaign. Interviewed for the newspaper story, he said, "Yvette Flowers Davenport is one of the most influential African-American women in Charleston."

Benjamin Flowers, Sr., began working as a longshoreman in 1961 and served as president of Local 1422 from 1980 to 1997. "He missed out on a lot of family things, but he loved ILA," his son told the *Post and Courier*. Five of his six children became ILA members, working on the dock. Yvette Flowers "worked as his secretary but says, diplomatically, she 'left' the job shortly after her father lost a re-election campaign in 1997."[4] After a few years working for a private ocean-transportation company, she returned to the ILA as office administrator and dispatcher for Local 1771, the ILA Charleston chapter that represents about 200 clerks and checkers who direct cargo movements. Unlike Local 1422, Local 1771 consists almost entirely of white men: Flowers became the only black female member. She also went to work on the docks as a part-time casual worker; later, her sister joined her.

Yvette Flowers's lawsuit alleges that Riley and the union sought to prevent her from accumulating seniority hours to which she was enti-

17. The Family Politics of Local 1422

Yvette Flowers works at her desk at the union hall, a photograph of her father, Benjamin Flowers, hanging on the wall beside her (Jeff Siner).

tled. The suit was filed in January 2018 in District Court in Charleston against four defendants: Local 1422, the ILA pension and welfare office, the administrator of the pension and welfare office, and Riley. It lays out Flowers's employment history, noting that between 1989 and 2000, she worked every other weekend as dispatcher/secretary for Local 1422, and that she became vested in the pension plan in 1997. But, the case alleges, once Riley took over as union president in 1997, she "began to experience policies and procedures that were being implemented differently towards her versus when the same policies and procedures were being enforced for other employees of defendant ILA Local 1422." This, the case alleges, was because "the election leading to defendant Riley's election was tumultuous and as a result of defendant Riley's animus toward plaintiff's father, plaintiff became the target of defendant Riley's animus."[5] Then in 2000, Benjamin Flowers, Sr., defeated Riley in an election to be international vice president, and Riley fired Yvette Flowers from her secretarial post "as a means to punish and humiliate" her, the suit argues.

Nevertheless, Yvette Flowers continued to work on the docks for Local 1422, earning a promotion from casual longshoreman to regular longshoreman in 2006. But her election to financial secretary/treasurer in 2009 required her to work Monday through Friday, restricting her ability to accrue hours working on the dock. "This erroneous limitation was implemented, only in regards to her, by defendant Riley (in a) pretextual means to frustrate and limit plaintiff's ability to attain hours," the suit says. Nevertheless, it says, "plaintiff continued to work as defendant ILA Local 1422's financial secretary/treasurer and also worked the docks. Subsequently in 2013, in spite of defendant ILA Local 1422's and defendant Riley's animus towards her, plaintiff was promoted to journeyman." Later in 2013, Flowers tore the rotator cuff in her right shoulder while working. She was initially awarded pro rata pension credit for the 19 months she took off from work to recuperate, but in 2015 the credit was rescinded on the grounds that she was also a union officer. In November 2015 Flowers appealed the decision to the ILA pension fund board—and lost. The lawsuit contended that Local 1422 breached its employment contract with Flowers by "failing to protect plaintiff from the illegal implementation of the seniority classifications, the limitation on the accrual of hours to gain seniority and the outright rebuffing of plaintiff's complaints to Kenneth Riley."[6] The case was dismissed, but then refiled.

Despite the lawsuit and the troubled environment at the local office, Yvette Flowers' relationship with the ILA—at least with the national ILA— remains a positive one. Not only did her employment by two Charleston locals continue, but also in October 2018 she was honored at the ILA's sixth annual Civil, Human and Women's Rights Awards dinner, which took place in Savannah. At the event, ILA president Harold Daggett announced the union's endorsement of Stacey Abrams and Andrew Gillum in the high-profile, racially divisive races for the governorships of Georgia and Florida. "Long before anyone really knew her, Stacey Abrams, the Democratic candidate for Georgia governor, addressed the ILA's Dock and Marine Council meeting," Daggett said. "How great it will be for Georgia to elect an African-American woman as governor."[7] (Both Abrams and Gillum lost to Republican candidates.)

At the dinner, Daggett also honored three regional ILA leaders, including Flowers, declaring in his keynote address that "women in the ILA have become a powerful new voice for all of us to hear. A collective voice that shouts for equal pay, equal opportunity, respect and dignity. Yvette, you have been a labor leader and I think I know where you get your skills and your voice from. As a proud father myself, I am certain Ben Flowers is smiling down from heaven tonight, equally proud of the accomplishments of his daughter. Ben Flowers was my friend and colleague. He was a powerful voice for the ILA in the Port of Charleston and everywhere. Yvette, you honor his memory and speak his voice by your continuing to fight for our ILA members. Thank you for that."[8]

The event was a bit much for Kenny Riley, who sat at one of the two tables Local 1422 had purchased for the event. "Our homegirl was going to be the 2018 recipient and it was appropriate for us to go along with the program," he said. "It would have been small to say 'we aren't going.'"[9] Still, Riley was irritated that the dinner seemed a reaffirmation of the ILA's decision to limit African American enfranchisement by creating a civil rights committee rather than a department, and then to honor those who had not taken a role in civil rights advocacy. Not only were the actual advocates overruled when the committee was created, but also, Riley pointed out, those advocates have never been honored even as the national ILA "has given awards to everybody under the sun, including some who have not shown any real passion for issues of inequality and social justice."

Riley said members of the Flowers and German families have generally not made the connection between holding union office and using those offices to benefit the community, including the civil rights movement. "I would say they were members of the union because they had union cards and got benefits, and they had the sense that my grandfather or father was important to the union, but they did not have the vision to engage in union struggles," Riley said.[10]

Leonard Riley said he and his brother were "better prepared to lead" than the descendants of the union's earlier leaders. The ability to lead, he said, results from three factors: a history of hard work, involvement in the civil rights movement, and higher education. "We had our beginnings as workers," he said. "We worked in the fields locally and then we would go to New York in the summer and work there in the labor camps, and so we valued work and it was natural for us to be advocates for workers." Secondly, he said, both brothers were shaped by the civil rights movement. And third, both had college degrees.

"Formal education helped," Leonard Riley said. "We were able to articulate the difference between what it is now and what it should be. We were looked up to as young, up-and-coming guys. The other union members embraced us as new blood, and we challenged the status quo when we felt it wasn't doing justice to the members. It wasn't so much about our families; it was about having a vision of how the organization could move forward in a productive way."

A college education helped not only in articulating a vision for the union, but also in working on the dock and in contract negotiations. "Rigging the cranes, rigging the wrenches, I understood the science behind it because I took physics," Leonard said. "And when we went into negotiations, we were usually better prepared than our counterparts [whom] we bargained with. We saw that if we didn't rise to the occasion when we saw the industry changing, then we would be taken advantage of in negotiations."[11]

Among the leaders who seek to straddle the divide between Riley and the Flowers family is James Pickney, vice president of Local 1422 since 2012. Pickney, the son of a longshoreman, first worked on the waterfront in July 1984, weeks after graduating from Burke High School. (He was born May 7, 1965.) "I was hanging out with my friends and my dad came around the block and said, 'We have plenty of work—Do you know your social security number?' He took me to the union hall and I got a job as a 'top man,' making sure that top locks are put into the four corners of a container so it can bind to the container stacked above it. The cranes would stack containers, one on top of the other, and you would have to climb up and lock it manually at each of the four corners."[12]

Leonard Riley has been by his brother Kenny's side from their days as children in rural West Ashley to their long stints as leaders of Local 1422 (Ted Reed).

The work provided a summer diversion for several months until Pickney, who had already enlisted, left to join the Air Force. He spent four years on active duty as an administrative specialist, at one point running runway operations at an F-16 fighter base. He was stationed at various sites in Europe, Canada and the United States. Pickney aspired to be a pilot, but he suffered from color-blindness and a lack of depth perception. "I had my life planned out," he said. "I wanted to become a commercial pilot, but it didn't pan out." Instead, he returned home, where his work as a casual longshoreman included loading military cargo for the invasion of Kuwait, in which his Air Force unit participated. Subsequently, he entered

17. The Family Politics of Local 1422

the College of Charleston, graduating in 1999 with a degree in history and a minor in education. He worked as a teacher at a charter school and then ran a masonry business, but the 2008 recession ended the housing boom in Charleston, and Pickney returned to the waterfront full-time. By that time, he had spent a few years regularly attending union meetings, "educating myself about union business." In 2011, he decided to run for the vice presidency. "Normally you would work your way up through the ranks, but I thought having been in the military and served as a trustee at my church and having a lot of experience working with people, I had the necessary leadership skills," he said. He was elected vice president in 2012, then re-elected in 2015 and 2018.

Pickney admires Riley, whom he compares to labor and civil rights icon A. Philip Randolph, but he also speaks favorably of the Flowers and German families. By 2018, Pickney had already said publicly that he hopes to succeed Riley as union president. "Kenny is an extraordinary labor leader; he has a very keen sense of what is right for workers," Pickney said. Pickney recalls an incident that made an impression on him when he and Riley were in a hotel room in Biloxi, Miss. There, Riley pointed out the discrepancy between how hard hotel maids work and how little they get paid, which forces them to rely on tips to make a living. "Kenny has a keen sense," Pickney said. "He picks up on injustice in the world."

A student of labor history, Pickney said Riley's career reflects Randolph's career in that it combines the civil rights struggle and the labor movement. Randolph is revered as an early leader in both; in 1925 he organized the Brotherhood of Sleeping Car Porters, the first predominantly African American national labor union. (Eleven years later, George Washington German presided, as Local 1422 was awarded a charter by the ILA.) Randolph became an influential and enduring voice in Washington; he not only was among the labor leaders who successfully urged President Franklin D. Roosevelt to ban discrimination in defense industries during World War II, but also headed the 1963 March on Washington where Martin Luther King, Jr., delivered his "I Have a Dream" speech. Randolph was an early advocate of nonviolence as a tactic for the civil rights movement.

"The civil rights struggle emanates from the labor struggle," Pickney said. "A. Phillip Randolph piggybacked on what Samuel Gompers did in founding the AFL-CIO; he tapped into that energy with the sleeping call porters. But Randolph also had to fight Jim Crowism. In Kenny's time, there is still institutionalized racism in society, and we still have to struggle for the rights of minorities. From what I can see, Kenny is still focused on the rights of workers. But he has taken this local on a path to global influence, not only in longshore labor but also in the labor struggle overall. This union has a position in the community that is of iconic proportions, which is what motivated me to get into unionism. We are an African American local, brought up from the grass roots by African American men and women."

Riley is not the only one who deserves credit for the local's importance, Pickney said. "The Flowers and Germans have left a great legacy, and the families of the past presidents are still here," he said. He doesn't see generational involvement in the union as unusual. Many organizations have disproportionate representation by certain families, often because descendants follow their parents in selecting careers. "You go to any union, you often see a lot of family members in there," Pickney said. "The ILA is no different. That's because if you see opportunities, you tell your family first. That's not a bad thing. Everybody who comes in here is treated fairly. There may be a lot of familial relationships, but the ILA is governed by its constitution and bylaws."

Asked whether the family loyalties created conflict, Pickney responded, "You call it conflict, but you have to qualify that. There are differ-

James Pickney, Local 1422 vice president, says that Kenny Riley (seated) "picks up on injustice in the world" (Jeff Siner).

17. The Family Politics of Local 1422

ences of opinion and philosophy, but there has never been an organization where everybody in the local agrees with the current leader. I don't agree with every decision that President Riley makes, and I let him know when I respectfully disagree with him." In Pickney's view, the conflicting views of the three families sometimes provide the underpinning for a strong union. "In any organization there are differences of opinions and philosophy," he said. "For me, that's healthy. In every area, differences in philosophy create environments that are healthy for democracy."[13]

18

For Labor, South Carolina Is Tough, but "The Union Is Anomalous"

Among the unique aspects of Kenny Riley's emergence as a national labor leader is that it occurred in South Carolina, one of the least unionized states—and one of the states where the battle over unionization has continued most fervently into the 21st century, even as the battlefield has shifted along with the state's changing economy. "Charleston longshoremen have overcome two of the most seemingly impenetrable obstacles in American politics: Southern hostility to unions and racial prejudice," wrote Eli Poliakoff, in his Harvard thesis on Local 1422. "In arguably the most hostile state in the country for organized labor, [the Local] has commanded respect from local business and civic and political leaders for over 100 years," Poliakoff said.[1]

In South Carolina, "most employers and most politicians are hostile to unions," said Kerry Taylor, associate professor of history at the Citadel. "But in Charleston, the ILA has found this kind of niche. The union is anomalous."

From its earliest days, Local 1422 of the ILA realized that its success was tied to the success of the SCPA, which operates the port of Charleston. The two organizations "have a mutually beneficial relationship," Taylor said. "They share an interest in making sure the port is productive. There is mutual respect and collaboration. The members of 1422 are recognized for their skill and productivity and efficiency: the port authority accepts that. When they bargain, everybody bargains hard, and it can become contentious. But they have a good working relationship. When there are union functions honoring retirees, representatives of the port authority will be there to honor the ILA members."[2]

18. South Carolina Is Tough

Riley has formed positive working relationships with various waterfront leaders, including Barbara Melvin, SCPA chief operating officer, who said Riley "cares a lot about this waterfront. He cares about our reputation for productivity. He advocates for his membership and he has taken the time to teach me about the industry." Melvin went to work for the port in April 1998 as a lobbyist. "When I started, Kenny was one of the first people I got to know," she said. "I didn't have a background in shipping, and he helped me learn about the industry. He is always gracious; he never considered my questions to be dumb questions, and he doesn't hoard information like some people do."[3]

The ILA does not negotiate directly with the port. Rather, it negotiates a master contract with the United States Maritime Alliance, which represents East Coast and Gulf Coast employers, including container carriers, marine terminal operators and port associations including the SCPA. The most recent contract, which covers 14,500 port workers, was signed in 2018 and runs through September 30, 2024.

The port is not a signatory to the master contract, so the relationship between Local 1422 and SCPA is largely an informal one. ILA workers

Barbara Melvin, chief operating officer of the South Carolina Ports Authority, says that Kenny Riley "has taken the time to teach me about the industry" (Jeff Siner).

are hired by the carriers and the stevedores, who work at facilities owned and operated by the port, which—like the ILA—is committed to efficient loading and unloading. "I would highlight the pride in their work product that Kenny and his membership have had for decades on this waterfront," Melvin said.

Despite the positive feelings, Riley and the port face a conflict over Riley's desire to expand the contract to include crane operators and heavy equipment operators at a planned new North Charleston terminal, scheduled to open in 2021. At many East Coast ports, the work is done by ILA members, but at existing terminals in Charleston and Savannah, located in right-to-work states, the work is done by non-union port employees. When the new terminal opens, Melvin said, "The roles will remain the same as they are today. We invested our capital and dollars into constructing that. Kenny and his members will have the same jobs they have in the existing facilities." She added that the port is not a party to the negotiations, which involve the master contract.[4]

Riley sees it differently. The master contract specifies that staffing at any new terminals will be provided by the union, he said, and he is committed to ensuring, as the final piece of his legacy as a local president, that union jurisdiction will extend to the new terminal.

"The port is not the industry," he said. "The industry is the shippers and the truckers and the other businesses and the union. The port is a facilitator of the industry. The port can build whatever terminals it wants, and it can put in the most expensive cranes and infrastructure it wants at any terminal it wants, but if no ships call on that terminal, then it just got a brand-new terminal with nothing there," he said. "All of my contracts are with the steamship lines. The steamship lines recognize the models in place in South Carolina and Georgia and North Carolina. However, if there are any new terminals built, and if they are not in compliance with the contract, the ships will not call on those facilities.

"This issue has been around since before I became a longshoreman," Riley said in March 2019. "Long ago, I saw that, except in Charleston, Savannah and Wilmington, all of those jobs were ILA jobs. I see this as a landmark. I recognize that it will be a challenge. I don't expect the port to roll over; they have to answer to the state legislature in an anti-union state. It will be one of the last fights I ever fight."[5] If he wins, Riley says, Local 1422 could add 400 to 500 Charleston jobs.

"Kenny wants those jobs," said Marty Crosby, a Charleston native who owns a line-handling company that ties up and unties union-manned

18. South Carolina Is Tough

ships that operate in the Port of Charleston. "This is going to be a last hurrah for Kenny before he retires. He wants it to be his legacy."[6]

Crosby's firm has a separate contract with Local 1422, one of a half dozen contracts the local has with local maritime companies. About three quarters of ships in Charleston operate under the master contract. "Kenny is a good labor person," Crosby said. "He looks out for his members and he looks out for the Port of Charleston, which allows the port to be competitive. He's very talented."

If Crosby has a complaint, it's that Riley, particularly in the past few years, seems to have become busier and busier with his other activities, including the trusteeship in Miami, international responsibilities for the union, and his commitment to the orphanage in Liberia. "He is juggling so many things," Crosby said. "He's very talented, but as far as being a Charlestonian like I am, I want his first priority in life to be Charleston. He is doing great things in Africa, but his Charleston boys like us want him to spend more time taking care of the Port of Charleston."

During a meeting (which I attended) at the union hall in November 2018, Crosby and his team of two other executives negotiated with Riley in a friendly manner over a contract that had expired about six weeks earlier. All parties agreed on a key point, that Crosby's crews should be larger in order to tie and untie larger ships. The tone of negotiations was friendly, although the end result was that the two sides would have to keep talking.

"To tie up a ship we have four people; to untie we have two," Crosby said. "But the ships we tie up used to be 700 feet to 900 feet, and now they are 1,000 feet to 1,200 feet. As the ships have gotten bigger, the lines used to tie them up have gotten bigger too. Kenny has been complaining about this for years, and we just kind of put him off. But now it's actually a safety issue for us, and we think it's smart to entertain Kenny's desire for more people."

This is labor negotiations, so Crosby also wants some things, including changes to contract language that calls for restarting a crew assignment every time a ship shifts between berths, even if the new berth is a few hundred feet from the old one. Some longshoremen interpret the contract to mean that every time a ship shifts, Crosby must employ a new gang to work on it. "Some of these longshoremen and checkers, we call them 'waterfront attorneys,' they all have opinions on how our contract should be read," Crosby said. "We want some verbiage to make it clear, because we don't think that it requires a new work order when a ship moves a couple of feet." Sound like a very fine point? "Our contract for line handlers is very simple compared to the stevedore contract," Crosby said.[7]

In any case, Local 1422's relationship with the Port of Charleston and with the various port businesses represents a sharp departure from the tortured history of the labor/management relations in the rest of South Carolina—where the battleground has shifted from the state's textile mills to the Boeing plant in North Charleston, one of only three U.S. sites where large aircraft are manufactured.

South Carolina's anti-union environment and the proximity of Charleston's port and airport were key reasons for Boeing's site selection, and some of the state's political leaders have taken pains to emphatically demonstrate their continued opposition to the labor movement. Most recently, the champion of South Carolina anti-unionism has been Nikki Haley, governor from 2011 to 2017, who has emerged as a national politician. Haley once declared, "I wear heels, and it's not for a fashion statement. It's because we're kicking the unions every day."[8]

Haley's views on labor reflected the views of the majority of her constituents. In 2018, South Carolina was tied with North Carolina for the lowest percentage of workers who were union members—just 2.7 percent, according to the federal Bureau of Labor Statistics. Nationally, 10.5 percent of workers were labor union members in 2018, down from 10.7 percent in 2017 and the lowest percentage of union members since the bureau began tracking the figures in 1983, when union membership totaled about 20 percent. The percentage of U.S. workers belonging to a union peaked in 1954 at about 35 percent, with many employed in manufacturing. Overall U.S. manufacturing employment has declined due to automation and a concerted effort to move workers to areas with lower wages, often foreign countries. Unionized manufacturing has declined even more because jobs have moved not only to foreign countries, but also to the South, which obstructs unions with barriers, including right-to-work laws that enable non-union workers to be covered by union contracts.

As companies flee organized labor, South Carolina has benefited substantially. By 2018 the state was home not only to the Boeing plant but also to the largest BMW plant in the world and five foreign tire makers' operating plants, whose combined capacity was higher than any other state's. Moreover, in 2018 both Mercedes-Benz and Volvo opened manufacturing plants in South Carolina. The move to the South was led by the auto and tire industries, but the establishment of aircraft manufacturing in Charleston by Boeing and in Mobile, Ala., by Airbus vastly expanded

18. South Carolina Is Tough

the scope of non-union manufacturing. Charleston and Mobile now rank with Hamburg, Germany; Seattle; and Toulouse, France as the only sites in the western world where large jet aircraft are assembled. Boeing, which began making planes in the Seattle area in 1916, produced its first 787 wide-body aircraft in Everett, Wash., in 2007. Five years later, it opened a second 787 production plant in North Charleston. "Boeing put a plant in South Carolina in order to break the union," said aerospace analyst Scott Hamilton,[9] publisher of trade journal *Leeham News and Analysis*. At the time, about 35,000 Boeing employees were represented by the International Association of Machinists (IAM).

In 2007, the IAM won a narrow and unanticipated election victory at the North Charleston facility of Boeing contractor Vought, gaining the right to organize about 120 workers. But labor law enables decertification if a company doesn't sign a contract within a year. Vought stalled, the union signed a less-than-optimal contract, and in 2009 workers voted 199–68 to decertify. They seemed to be motivated largely by fears that Boeing might not expand in Charleston if the union stayed in place. In October 2009, shortly after the decertification, Boeing selected the North Charleston site for its 787 final assembly and delivery line. The first aircraft was completed in 2012.

The IAM tried again to organize the Boeing plant but suspended the effort in April 2015, citing threats and a dangerous environment for organizing. By 2017, the plant had about 3,000 workers, and the IAM tried again to unionize. It failed badly, winning only about 26 percent of the vote. Haley's opposition was considered a factor in the one-sided outcome. "Boeing's Best Union Buster Is South Carolina's Governor Nikki Haley"[10] was the headline of a 2015 *Bloomberg Business Week* story that detailed Haley's use of Facebook and Twitter to attack the IAM. Haley also appeared in a pro–Boeing radio ad and voiced support for anti-union voters in her State of the State address. In January 2017, Haley resigned as governor. She subsequently served two years as U.S. Ambassador to the United Nations. Soon after she resigned from that post, Boeing announced that she had been nominated for a seat on its board of directors.

During the IAM's efforts to organize Boeing workers, "Haley was the most powerful person in the state, with her salary paid by taxpayers, and she used her position to fight organized labor," said Bill Wise, an IAM general chairman who was active in several Charleston organizing efforts. "That flies in the face of your right to organize. South Carolina is a right-to-work state, but the law protects your right to organize."[11] Wise is among the Carolinas' foremost labor leaders, a South Carolina resident and aircraft mechanic who spent a dozen years as president of IAM Local 1725, which represents American Airlines workers in Charlotte. In 2012, Wise became general chair for the union's District Lodge 142, overseeing and enforcing union contracts at various companies in the Northeast and Southeast.

Organizing in the South is difficult. "I went down to Charleston several times when they needed people to door knock, to go door-to-door and talk with people," Wise said. "It's grueling. In the South, people just don't have a knowledge of what labor unions do. It's a night and day difference. In Philadelphia, places like that, unions are an accepted way of life. Even in West Virginia, where I spend a lot of time, you see signs in the front yards that say 'proud union member.' You just don't see that in the South. In fact, sometimes people who don't know me ask me, 'What do you do?' and when I say, 'I'm a union rep,' they start walking away. They move to another area of the room." Most southern politicians have a similar view. "In the North, some congressmen and senators are labor friendly, but in South Carolina you don't have that," Wise said. "It's beyond me how people down here think."

Wise became acquainted with Riley in the early 2000s when both men were members of the South Carolina AFL-CIO executive board. Although the U.S. Airways maintenance base was in Charlotte, several hundred of the airline's mechanics and related workers lived in South Carolina, so Wise advocated for membership on the state board. "There were 300 or 400 mechanics and [workers in related fields] who lived in South Carolina, and also retirees who had moved to Myrtle Beach, so we worked on dual affiliation with North Carolina and South Carolina for Local 1725," Wise said. The North Carolina AFL-CIO opposed the move because several thousand dollars in annual dues money would be redirected to the South Carolina chapter, but Wise felt South Carolina workers should be represented in South Carolina.

"What first impressed me about Kenny Riley was that he commands respect; he can get everybody in the rowboat rowing in the same direction," Wise said. "In the Charleston Five incident, he was able to go on TV and say that the day this comes to trial is the day that all commerce stops all over the world. He could say that because he took months to fly all over the world to get it set up. That's true power there. He is at the head of the local chapter of the ILA, which is one of the strongest unions I know of.

18. South Carolina Is Tough

When I go into Charleston, everybody there knows Kenny Riley. Everybody knows about the longshoremen. That's accepted down there."

Wise, who lives in a rural area in South Carolina, recalled that the first time he visited the ILA hall in Charleston in the late 1990s was also one of the first times his young daughters were exposed to black people. "Kenny had said anytime I was in Charleston I should drop in, so we did," he said. "I remember we were the only white people on the whole block, and they had a waiting room with a machine that made popcorn, and one of the longshoremen took the kids to that machine and helped them get popcorn. At first my girls were intimidated, but they were treated like princesses in that union hall. I don't like dwelling on whether someone is black or white, but that made a big impression on me." Wise also recalled that during the U.S. Airways bankruptcy in 2005, he feared that the airline might never emerge, and Riley sought to ease his fears. "Kenny said, 'Don't worry about it. You're a mechanic. If you need a job come and see me.' In my mind, I got prepared to pull my camper down to Charleston and go to work there."[12]

Riley praised Wise and the IAM for keeping up the fight at Boeing, but he also fears that the labor movement as a whole was not sufficiently involved. "I don't think the labor movement has focused on Boeing like it should have, like the IAM has, to help ensure a successful campaign there," he said. "When it comes to Boeing, all of labor should have been in." Riley said labor leaders tend to get deeply involved in determining which political candidates to back, and then back those candidates with money and manpower, but they have not devoted the same level of energy to organizing Boeing in South Carolina.

"I don't care what labor union convention you go to, at every single one of them everyone talks about how important the South is," he said. "But those at the helm don't put together a coordinated effort. The other side is always out there. No matter who runs a campaign in the South, the manufacturers, the chambers of commerce, and the politicians will all be out there united against labor, all saying that unionizing is bad for the business environment. But we in labor don't pool our efforts in the same way. When it comes to Boeing, Nissan, Volkswagen and now Volvo, I barely hear a peep from labor beyond the union that is organizing there. Yet when the [2020] political season heats up, when we get beyond the primaries you will see hundreds of millions pumped into the campaign."[13]

Eli Poliakoff wrote that "South Carolina's majority anti-union sentiment is tied to the failure of class-based politics in the state," enabled by

Pitchfork Ben Tillman, who ran for governor in 1890 as a populist challenger to the business establishment. Once elected, the anti-elite populist sentiment was subsumed under Tillman's segregationist platform and "efforts at a bi-racial, class-based, political movement in South Carolina were thwarted." Poliakoff also notes the irony that, "later, Tillman indirectly aided the development of unionized Charleston longshoremen" by backing the development of the Charleston Navy Yard. "This federal spending aided the entire port's growth, which in turn generated work for members of the fledgling dockworkers organization."[14]

Another obstacle to organized labor in South Carolina has been the structure of state government. "Until the mid–1970s the state senate was apportioned one seat per county, giving rural, thinly populated districts disproportionate representation relative to urban, industrialized counties," Poliakoff wrote. "Representation was even more unbalanced considering that African Americans, who comprised over 60% of several Lowcountry counties, were generally excluded from the political process before the 1960s."

Poliakoff emphasizes that Charleston Local 1422 is in a unique position. "Since 1869 organized Charleston longshoremen have overcome South Carolina's racial dynamic and anti-union sentiment to maintain economic, political and social influence unsurpassed in the state's labor community," he wrote. "From its earliest days, this predominantly African-American union has enjoyed significant links with local political and business elites, many of whom looked upon the union favorably. Through Reconstruction, Jim Crow and after, Charleston longshoremen used solidarity forged by racial prejudice to disarm anti-union pressures. Their successful interaction with a Southern mix of race, class, politics and anti-union sentiment has produced a unique South Carolina institution noted for its longevity and influence."[15]

Riley's approach and influence were evident in a 2004 incident where he briefly shut down a port terminal because a port policeman behaved improperly towards a union member. In June 2004, Riley was temporarily working on the docks. It was a time when the union treasury was depleted, so five union officials went back to work, enabling their salaries and benefits to be paid by employers rather than by the union. One Saturday evening, Riley went to work at the North Charleston terminal and found a parking spot beside the truck of a union foreman, who had gone onto a ship to get his crew set up. The foreman, Richard Brown, had neglected to post his parking decal in his window. Just after Riley parked, a white Port

18. South Carolina Is Tough

Kenny Riley with Joe Biden. Biden visited Local 1422's union hall in August 2019 (courtesy Kenny Riley).

of Charleston policeman pulled up and began writing tickets for every vehicle that lacked the proper parking decal.

Riley called Brown on his cellphone. Then he told the policeman that Brown would return shortly to present his decal, which was on the car seat. The policeman seemed hostile. "He said, 'You need to keep your mouth shut,'" Riley recalled. "I called Richard and said, 'You need to get down here, he is writing a ticket.' When Richard came, he showed the cop the decal. But then the cop asked to see a driver's license and Richard refused and started back to the dock." The situation escalated. When Riley told Brown to show his license, "the cop said to me, 'I told you to shut up,' starting screaming at me, and called for backup to escort me off the property. Then he went after Richard. When I walked over there, I saw that he had Richard's face down on the ground, with blood coming from [Richard's] head. Folks were saying to him, 'You didn't have to do that.' By then he was spraying his mace and he had his gun out and I could hear police sirens. I pointed my finger at the cop and I said, 'You are finished.' And I said to my guys, 'Shut everything down—every ship. Shut them down.' I said, 'Nothing [at this terminal] is moving until this is resolved.' When all the sergeants and the people above him came, I said the same thing."[16]

Later, the *Post and Courier* reported that the policeman "jammed his gun into Brown's neck and slammed the burly longshoreman to the ground, witnesses said. Brown lay flat on his stomach, struggling to see, his eyes burning from a close-range blast of the officer's pepper spray."[17]

An ambulance arrived. Medics began to treat Brown, then put him in the ambulance for a trip to the hospital. Then the policeman got in a police cruiser, which followed behind the ambulance. When Riley asked why, the sergeant in charge said Brown would have to go to jail after being treated. Riley responded, "If that guy goes to jail, nothing is moving in this entire port." Various officials from the port and the police force urged Riley to relent, but he declined. Rather, he called the union's vice president, Robert Ford, who was working at the Mount Pleasant terminal, closer to the hospital. He asked Ford to go to the hospital and stay until Brown was released. "I said, 'If he comes out in handcuffs, let me know, and the entire Port of Charleston, not just North Charleston, will be shut down.'"[18]

The outcome was that the North Charleston terminal was shut down for two hours, the amount of time it took for Brown to be released. Nine months later, the *Post and Courier* ran a story entitled "Problem Cops: A Systematic Failure," in a series called "Tarnished Badges." The Port of Charleston police officer who accosted Brown and Riley was named. It turned out he had a history of improper conduct, which had not been known to the port police force.

He later left the port. Riley agreed not to press charges in return for an assurance that he would never again carry a gun or a badge in South Carolina.

19

Riley Looks to Retirement

Like it or not, Kenny Riley understands that time is creeping up on him.

Riley realized by 2019 that as much as he was shaped by what he learned and did as a young man in the 1960s, he was no longer young. He became eligible at 66 for full Social Security, his four children were growing up, and his first wife had died. He also had a few aches and pains from working on the docks for nearly five decades. Once the young controversial radical of the ILA, he had become an elder statesman. Looking to the future, he wanted to remain involved in the union, but also to pursue other interests, including more time with his children, a favorite charity in Africa, and classic cars. He must decide whether to retire as president of Local 1422 when his term ends in February 2020. His current term as an international vice president ends in 2023.

Riley is the father of three girls and a boy. They are close, he said, even though they all have different mothers. Riley's first child, daughter Maya Michelle Holingshed, was born in 1979, soon after Riley graduated from College of Charleston. Her mother was still a student. Holingshed graduated from the University of South Carolina with a degree in journalism, but after working briefly for a newspaper, she returned to Charleston and worked for a year as a clerk for ILA Local 1771. Then she earned a master's degree and began work as a librarian at the Medical University of South Carolina.

In 1981, Riley married his first wife, Maxine Laverne Frazier, who was working in the library at the Grice Marine Laboratory at the College of Charleston. The couple had a daughter, Marnique, who graduated from Tennessee State University and works as an occupational therapist in Nashville. The marriage lasted four years, ending in divorce. "It was my fault," Riley said. "I don't think I was ready for marriage. Both Leonard and I lived at home until we were 28 years old—we had three longshoremen living in the same house, which meant a lot of income for one house, and we had some good times—but Leonard decided to get married that April. So I was left in the room by myself, and I was thinking, 'What are you and Maxine waiting on?' And we got married in December."[1]

Riley and Maxine remained close until she died January 1, 2019, of lung cancer. She had not smoked since college.

Riley's son, Kenneth Riley II, was born in 1992. His dad and his mother, Rosalind, met at College of Charleston, split up, and got back together in 1989. Their marriage, Kenny Riley's second, lasted until 1994. After graduating from high school, Kenny, Jr., attended Atlanta Art Institute and majored in sound engineering. He continues to pursue his passion for music design. He went to work with the ILA in 2013.

After the divorce, Riley and his girlfriend, Harriett Doctor, had a daughter. Born in 1996, Alice Sheree Riley graduated from Coastal Carolina University in 2018 and went to work as an area manager for Amazon in Charlotte.

Riley concedes he has not been successful at marriage. "My mom

Corine and Kenny Riley look over photographs at Corine's home (Jeff Siner).

19. Riley Looks to Retirement

said to someone after my second divorce that she thought that, of all her kids, 'one would not get married, and that was Kenneth.'" Asked if that was because he valued his time alone so highly, Riley responded, "I'm not anti-social, but I do love my space. I love my quiet time." Those times are sometimes spent with his cars: he has four, including a 1969 Impala station wagon and a 1970 Chevrolet Chevelle convertible. In the past, he has had three Corvettes. Now, he envisions adding a high-horsepower muscle car. "I love speed," he said. "My dream is I will go to the dealership once more and buy a super car." After retirement from the local, he said, he will go to car shows. "I would relax more, certainly, and in between trips to Liberia and working on assignments for the ILA, I would be free to drive my cars and go to car shows and swap meets and see classic cars, and maybe to bring a few of them back and drive them."

Despite the logistical challenges posed by each of his children having a different mother and his frequent travel, Riley believes he has been a good dad. "I was at every event I could attend," he said. "I always wanted to be there and for them to know how much I love them and care for them. At Christmas or Valentine's Day, when they wanted to buy gifts for their mom, I would take them all shopping one at a time. Now they are older. I love them, they love me, and they respect what I have done."[2]

An important affirmation came on Christmas Eve 2018 when daughter Marnique Riley Strickland organized a dinner for her father and his four children. (Her husband also attended: At the time she was Riley's only married child.) Because "my dad loves burgers," Strickland selected Rutledge Cab Company, a popular Charleston restaurant that serves American food. "We've been trying to get everyone together for a long time," Strickland said. "This was the first time in years we could get all the siblings lined up in one place. It was very important that everybody made it. Dad was pretty excited; he smiled the whole time. He took a video of all of us, sitting and laughing. We all have a similar, very contagious sense of humor, so that if you say something and you think it's funny, then one laugh turns to another and it builds all around you. It was a great day."[3]

Riley was clearly pleased. "Getting together like that, that was the reward for me," he said. The dinner, he said, demonstrated that "in spite of not being in a traditional home setting, we are going to be okay."[4]

Strickland said the family structure worked partially because "all the moms got along; they would all do things to make sure everybody was OK; they worked together to help each other work out." For example, the mothers would babysit for one another's children. Strickland also recalls times she spent with her father. One favorite activity was attending car shows. "He had a very nice, navy blue truck, and we'd ride to Charlotte and go to the car show. When Kenny [her brother] got old enough, he would be in the back seat." Her father regularly drove her in the 1970 Chevelle convertible to Baskin Robbins to get ice cream. Sometimes he would sing the 1973 song "Drift Away," by Dobie Gray.

Other memories are connected with social justice. Strickland recalls that her mother would drive her to ILA picket lines protesting the use of non-union workers to load ships with poultry for NOCS Group, a New Orleans–based cargo management company, most likely in 1997 when Strickland was 12. "My mom would drop me off, stay there for a little while, and then go home, but I wanted to stay," she recalled. "It was on East Bay Street, all those guys would line the street with signs, and they would chant 'Cold turkey, cold heart, NOCS must depart.' We would stand there; people would drive by and blow their horns."

Later, Strickland participated in Charleston Five demonstrations. She remembers the night that her father was hit in the face and her uncle was arrested. The atmosphere at the NOCS picket line "was kind of friendly, but with the Charleston Five it was different," she said. "It was more inflamed. It had more law enforcement, more agitation." At school, she was noticed. "There were not many Rileys in Charleston," she said. "Just Joe the mayor and Kenny Riley, the longshoreman. Two doors down from me, there was another kid, whose dad was also a longshoreman. We would talk and try to figure things out. We were not really sure what it meant. We just knew that for some reason our dads were doing something different; they were fighting for something. The other kids would say, 'Hey, man, your dad is cool.'"

Today, in her work as an occupational therapist, Strickland is sometimes confronted with instances where a slight alteration in the way she files insurance claims could make a difference regarding how much someone is paid. She thinks of her father then, how he would always tell her, "Do what's right. Don't sell your soul. Keep it honest so that you will be able to live with yourself."[5]

Another of Kenny Riley's abiding passions is his work with Christ Children's Home, an orphanage in Gbarnga, Liberia, that came to his attention when leaders of the orphanage visited Charleston in December 2014 during a fundraising effort in the United States. The orphanage is operated by the family of a woman named Neyor Karmue. In the 1990s, Karmue, accompanied by her five children, was fleeing war on foot when

19. Riley Looks to Retirement

child soldiers accosted them. She prayed as a female soldier was about to execute her. When her five-year-old daughter ran to her, the soldier relented, rather than kill a mother in front of her child. Years later, Karmue was reunited with her husband in the United States. In 2003, more than a decade after the civil war in Liberia ended, the couple returned to Liberia and opened the orphanage, fulfilling Karmue's promise to God.

At the time of the 2014 visit, Liberia faced a new threat: Ebola. Karmue's son "was canvassing in the United States, trying to get rice and medicine and supplies at a time when Ebola was making everything harder, more orphans were showing up because their parents were dying of Ebola, and aid groups were pulling out of the country," Riley said. "They needed money to purchase a used container to ship goods to Africa." Charleston mayor Joe Riley and other Charleston leaders, including Kenny Riley, were moved by the story. Karmue, as she faced death, "had prayed that if God would save her life, she would come back to Liberia and adopt as many of these children as she can, to save them from brutality," Kenny Riley said. "When we heard her story, there wasn't a dry eye in the room. I was so moved. I said, 'Take the money you raised for the container, use it to buy food and medicine, and I will get you four or five containers. I will get them donated.' I worked with truckers and freight forwarders and a steamship line, Mediterranean Shipping Co., and we got that done."[6]

In 2015, as the ship carrying the containers was about to sail, Karmue's son invited Riley to visit, saying that various people associated with the orphanage, including village elders, wanted to thank him. Riley agreed to make the trip, joined by Mark Bass, the longtime president of ILA Local 1410 in Mobile, Ala. The visit required nearly a dozen immunization shots, Riley said. "We got them all. We arrived there late at night, and a welcoming group from central Liberia came to Monrovia to meet us. A guy says, 'Where's Mr. Riley?' They were looking for a tall white Irishman, and they got a short, dark-skinned guy. They were not accustomed to this level of aid being headed by a black." As they watched the goods being distributed in various villages, Riley and Bass witnessed large celebrations that included dancing and expressions of thanks. "It was very festive, very alive," Riley said. "They gave Mark and me dashikis and head gear and names in Kpelle," a local language.

The orphanage has become an important component of Riley's life. Starting in 2015, he and Bass have visited it two to four times annually, including a pre–Christmas trip. Each time, they carry thousands of dollars of their own money, which they give away. Riley said he spent his entire

2018 bonus, about $20,000, on supplies and contributions for Liberian orphans as well as for orphanage staff. "We look at the staff, the cooks, people who are doing menial jobs and never seem to be much appreciated," he said. "People come and look at the kids, and that's fine, but these people are working night and day, taking care of the kids, and we try to make them feel that they are loved also. They don't get paid regularly. When you put a $50 bill in their hands, that is more than they get paid in a month."

"We have a close bond with a lot of these children," Riley said. "A lot of time, I see myself in them, the way I was as a young boy, with some of the same conditions. Many times, the children will pull us aside and say other people have come through here; they have said they will come back, and you never see them again. But you and uncle Mark are different, you always come back. Each time, I promise them that this will not be the last time for me."

Riley expects the ILA to continue to support his efforts even after he retires from the local. He noted that the union raised about $60,000 for the orphanage in 2018 and that union president Harold Daggett "has been very generous in sponsoring the trips—he has done that for two years." Riley fully realizes that his ability to help Liberian orphans has been enabled by the union and by contacts he has made as a result of his position in the union, but he also likes to think the work can continue. "This is all because of the platform I've been given within the ILA, and I want to be able to do more of this kind of thing, hopefully with the support of the ILA and under ILA auspices."[7]

Still, retirement won't be all children and charity, and it won't last forever.

On April 23, 2019, Riley spoke at the funeral of Anthony Lovejoy Shuler, Jr., known as "TJ," his longtime secretary's son, who died at 35, following a two-hour workout, of an apparent heart attack. The memorial service took place at the union hall. Shuler worked at the Department of Transportation in Washington, D.C.; on the day of the memorial service, he had been poised to start a new job at the Office of Congressional Affairs. "I am told that TJ had already spruced up his wardrobe and had even bought some new shoes," Riley said.

Riley's talk combined sorrow, humor and faith, born of his deep Christianity. He began by saying, "I want to give honor to our risen Lord and Savior Jesus Christ, whose resurrection we just celebrated two days ago on Easter Sunday." He thanked guests who had come from Washington, both for "demonstrating your love for TJ by traveling this far distance to be here

19. Riley Looks to Retirement

Kenny Riley surveys the Port of Charleston Wando Terminal from his 2014 Chevrolet Impala. Riley has spent nearly 50 years working on the port (Jeff Siner).

with us today," and "for having names I can pronounce." He spoke of his long relationship with Fran Shuler, who had worked in an adjacent office for 22 years: "It is only natural that we would share accounts of what was going on in the lives of our children," he said. "I knew when TJ placed first, second or third at a track meet." The essence of the talk was Riley's effort to reconcile TJ's early death and promising future. "Last Monday while TJ was preparing his physical body for the challenges of this life, working out, keeping his body fit and strong, God was preparing for him another body, a body not susceptible to pain, sickness, and diseases, but God was preparing him a glorified body."

"The new position that TJ would have received yesterday would have been great and well deserved, no doubt about it," Riley said. "But it does not even compare, and it pales in comparison with, the reward that TJ received on last Monday." Riley then quoted a Bible verse he knew by heart. "I imagine TJ heard the words recorded in Matthew 25:21: Well done TJ, thou good and faithful servant: you have been faithful over a few things, now I will make you ruler over many, enter into the joy of the Lord."

"Like TJ, we weren't called to save the world, but like him, we were called to make a difference in this world," he said. Riley believes he himself has also made a difference, but he does not believe he has done all he might have. He still believes that the ILA will be fully able to empower its African American members only when it shifts to a one-man, one-vote model for union offices. As it is, members elect delegates, typically local officers, who vote for national officers. Changing the procedure "is a struggle that has to take place. If there was awareness that this is the fair and right thing to do, there could be a vote to change the constitution, and by the next convention one man, one vote would be the process. But no one in the higher echelons has embraced it; it has always been shot down." Riley does not blame Daggett for the resistance to change; "He is the most progressive president I have dealt with, but I use the analogy, when these big ships are in the channel and it is time to turn them around and get them out of here, the small tugs get beside that ship and start pushing. For a while it doesn't look like they are doing any good, but slowly that ship begins to turn in the right direction."

"We have been effective in changing a lot of things," Riley said. "But some issues are difficult. And now Eddie McBride has retired, and Leonard and I are getting to the end of our careers. God knows we made a difference, but it is up to the next generation now. Hopefully they will create some type of pressure going forward, because no one gives up power willingly. People give up money, but no one gives up power."[8]

ILWU president Willie Adams says that while Riley may give up the presidency of his local, "I don't think that Kenny will ever actually retire. I hear him say all the time that he will retire. He tries to tell himself that. But Kenny knows he has too much work to do. He doesn't do it for the money. This work is part of his life, just like an actor has to act and a musician has to perform. Kenny has never gone and looked for a struggle," Adams said. "But struggles look for Kenny."[9]

Chapter Notes

Introduction

1. Leonard Riley interview, March 5, 2019, Charleston, S.C.
2. Bill Wise interview, Jan. 9, 2019.
3. Harold Daggett interview, Nov. 22, 2018.
4. Leonard Riley interview, March 5, 2019.
5. Joe Riley interview, Nov. 26, 2018.
6. Marnique Riley Strickland interview, Jan. 26, 2019.

Chapter 1

1. Kenny Riley interview, Nov. 19, 2018, Charleston, S.C.
2. Marnique Riley Strickland interview, Jan. 26, 2019.
3. Kenny Riley interview, May 29, 2018.
4. Leonard Riley interview, Jan. 29, 2019.
5. Kenny Riley interview, May 29, 2018.
6. Corine Riley interview, Nov. 19, 2018, Charleston, S.C.
7. Kenny Riley interview, May 29, 2018.
8. Kenny Riley interview May 29, 2018.
9. Kenny Riley interview, May 29, 2018.
10. Marnique Riley Strickland interview, Jan. 26, 2019.
11. Leonard Riley interview, Jan. 29, 2019.
12. Corine Riley interview, Nov. 19, 2018, Charleston, S.C.
13. Corine Riley interview, Nov. 19, 2018, Charleston, S.C.
14. Marnique Riley Strickland interview, Jan. 26, 2019.
15. Kenny Riley interview, May 29, 2018.
16. Kenny Riley interview, May 29, 2018.
17. Leonard Riley interview, Jan. 29, 2019.
18. Leonard Riley interview, Jan. 29, 2019.
19. Leonard Riley interview, Jan. 29, 2019.
20. Kenny Riley interview, May 29, 2018.
21. Kenny Riley interview, June 20, 2018.
22. Kenny Riley interview, June 20, 2018.
23. Kenny Riley interview, April 8, 2019.
24. Corine Riley interview, Nov. 19, 2018, Charleston, S.C.
25. Kenny Riley interview, June 20, 2018.

Chapter 2

1. Kenny Riley interview, June 11, 2018.
2. Leonard Riley interview, Jan. 28, 2019.
3. Kenny Riley interview, June 11, 2018.
4. Leonard Riley interview, Jan. 28, 2019.
5. Kenny Riley interview, June 20, 2018.
6. Kenny Riley interview, June 20, 2018.
7. Kenny Riley interview, June 26, 2018.
8. Kenny Riley interview, June 26, 2018.
9. Leonard Riley interview, Jan. 28, 2019.
10. Leonard Riley interview, Jan. 28, 2019.
11. Kenny Riley interview, June 26, 2018.
12. Susan Hill Smith, "Kenneth Riley: ILA President Dedicated to Keeping Union Progressive," *Post and Courier*, Dec. 19, 1998.

Chapter Notes—3 and 4

Chapter 3

1. The town of Sullivan's Island hosts its own web site at http://www.sullivansisland-sc.com/. Various online commercial real estate rental web sites provide extensive listings for Sullivan's Island residencies with costs.
2. Encyclopedia Britannica, "Middle Passage Slave Trade," https://www.britannica.com/topic/Middle-Passage-slave-trade.
3. Robert N. Rosen, *A Short History of Charleston* (Columbia: University of South Carolina Press, , 1982), pp. 36–37, hereafter cited as "Rosen."
4. Rosen, pp. 65–70.
5. Walter J. Fraser, *Charleston! Charleston! A History of a Southern City* (Columbia: University of South Carolina Press, 1989), p. 49, hereafter cited as "Fraser."
6. Fraser, p. 110.
7. Fraser, p. 110.
8. Peter H. Wood, *Black Majority: Negroes in Colonial South Carolina from 1670 Through the Stono Rebellion* (New York: W. W. Norton, 1974), Appendix C, pp. 333–341, hereafter cited as "Wood."
9. Wood, Appendix C, pp. 333–341.
10. The history of Gadsden's Wharf is detailed on three web sites: http://charlestonjusticejourney.org/locations/gadsdens-wharf/, https://greenbookofsc.com/locations/gadsdens-wharf/, and https://www.ccpl.org/charleston-time-machine/story-gadsdens-wharf.
11. Rosen, p. 67.
12. Fraser, pp. 187–188.
13. Adam Parker, "A Brief History of Gadsden's Wharf," *Post and Courier*, Oct. 22, 2017.
14. Encyclopedia Virginia, "Transatlantic Slave Trade," https://www.encyclopediavirginia.org/Transatlantic_Slave_Trade_The.
15. National Archives at Atlanta, "Slave Manifests for Charleston," https://www.archives.gov/atlanta/finding-aids/slave-manifests/charleston.
16. GenDisasters.com, "Charleston, SC Gadsden Wharf Fire, Jul 1875," http://gendisasters.com/south-carolina/2824/charleston%2C-sc-gadsden-wharf-fire%-2C-jul-1875; CAD Details, "Gadsdenboro Park, Charleston, S.C. U.S.A.," https://www.caddetails.com/Project/miracle-recreation-equipment-company-inc/94/gadsdenboro-park/1165.
17. Joe Riley interview, Nov. 26, 2018.
18. IAA Museum, "Accolades," https://iaamuseum.org/wp-content/uploads/2018/02/Digital-Booklet-3-17.pdf.
19. Melissa Gomez, "Charleston Apologizes for City's Role in Slave Trade," *New York Times*, June 19, 2018.
20. Kenny Riley interview, March 5, 2019, Charleston, S.C.

Chapter 4

1. Fraser, p. 3; Skip Johnson, *Charleston: The Brief History of a Remarkable City* (Charleston, S.C.: Meeting Street Press, 2016), pp. 1–2, hereafter cited as "Johnson"; Rosen, pp. 9–12; Rodney and Loretta Carlisle, *Charleston in History: A Guide to More Than 100 Sites in Historical Context* (Sarasota, Fla.: Pineapple Press, 2016), pp. 7–10, hereafter cited as "Carlisle"; Everything2, "Charleston, South Carolina," https://everything2.com/title/Charleston%252C+South+Carolina; Wikipedia, "Charleston, South Carolina," https://en.wikipedia.org/wiki/Charleston,_South_Carolina.
2. Fraser, p. 3; Johnson, pp. 1–2; Rosen, pp. 9–12; Carlisle, pp. 7–10; Wikipedia, "Charleston, South Carolina."
3. Wikipedia, "Charleston, South Carolina"; Carlisle, p. 13.
4. Fraser, p. 3; Johnson, pp. 1–2; Rosen, pp. 9–12; Carlisle, pp. 7–10; Wikipedia, "Charleston, South Carolina."
5. Wood, p. 198.
6. Wood, p. 203.
7. Wood, p. 203.
8. Wood, p. 4.
9. Fraser, p. 28.
10. Fraser, p. 3; Johnson, pp. 1–2; Rosen, pp. 9–12; Carlisle pp. 7–10; Wikipedia, "Charleston, South Carolina."
11. Fraser, p. 23.
12. Wood, p. 127; Fraser, pp. 32–37.
13. Wood, pp. 127–130; Rosen, pp. 36–37; Fraser, p. 54.
14. Fraser, p. 42.
15. Wood, p. 146.
16. Fraser, p. 42.

17. Rosen, p. 22.
18. Fraser, p. 51.
19. The 20 percent estimate comes from Shelia Hempton Watson, *Images of America: South Carolina Ports, Charleston, Georgetown, and Port Royal* (Charleston, S.C.: Arcadia Publishing, 2004), p. 23. The 40 percent estimate comes from Wikipedia, "Charleston, South Carolina."
20. Fraser, p. 42.
21. Fraser, p. 67.
22. https://www.britannica.com/event/King-Georges-War.
23. Walter R. Borneman, *The French and Indian War: Deciding the Fate of North America* (New York: Harper Perennial, 2006), pp. xxiv, 1–7, 19–22; William M. Fowler, Jr., *Empires at War: The French and Indian War and the Struggle for North America, 1754–1763* (New York: Walker & Company, 2005), pp. 27–48.
24. Fred Anderson, *Crucible of War: The Seven Years' War and the Fate of Empire in British North America, 1754–1766* (New York: Alfred A, Knopf, 2000), hereafter cited as "Anderson."
25. Tom Pocock, *Battle for Empire: The Very First World War 1756–63* (London: Michael O'Mara Books Limited, 1998), p. 194.
26. Rosen, p. 44.
27. Fraser, pp. 86–88.
28. Fraser, p. 89.
29. Fraser, p. 93.
30. Anderson, p. 461.
31. Carlisle, p. 12.
32. Carlisle, p. 12.
33. Fraser, p. 105.
34. Fraser, pp. 105–106.
35. Fraser, p. 106.
36. Rosen, pp. 48–50.
37. Wikipedia, "Christopher Gadsden," https://en.wikipedia.org/wiki/Christopher_Gadsden.

Chapter 5

1. Wood, p. 152, "Table IV Population Trends in Colonial South Carolina."
2. Mark Jones Books, "Today in Charleston History, Dec. 3, 1737," https://markjonesbooks.com/2014/12/03/today-in-charleston-history-december-3/.
3. Wikipedia, "Henry Laurens," https://en.wikipedia.org/wiki/Henry_Laurens; South Carolina Encyclopedia, "Henry Laurens," http://www.scencyclopedia.org/sce/entries/laurens-henry/; Biographical Director of the United States Congress, "Henry Laurens," http://bioguide.congress.gov/scripts/biodisplay.pl?index=L000121.
4. Fraser, p. 127.
5. Fraser, p. 110.
6. Fraser, pp. 115–117.
7. Rosen, p. 69.
8. Dan L. Morrill, *Southern Campaigns of the American Revolution* (Baltimore, Md.: Nautical & Aviation Publishing Company of America), p. 31, hereafter cited as "Morrill."
9. Rosen, p. 77; William R. Ryan, *The World of Thomas Jeremiah: Charlestown on the Eve of the American Revolution* (New York: Oxford University Press, 2010).
10. Rosen, p. 70; Alphonso Brown, *A Gullah Guide to Charleston: Walking Through Black History* (Charleston, S.C.: History Press, 2008), Kindle edition, chapter titled "Gullah History."
11. Thomas B. Allen, *Tories: Fighting for the King in America's First Civil War* (New York: HarperCollins, 2010), p. 151, hereafter cited as "Allen."
12. Rosen, p. 53.
13. Estimates vary. See Morrill, p. 15.
14. Fraser, p. 148.
15. Mark M. Boatner III, *Encyclopedia of the American Revolution* (Mechanicsburg, Pa.: Stackpole, 1994), pp. 199–200.
16. Fraser, p. 143.
17. Fraser, pp. 144–145; J. William Harris, *The Hanging of Thomas Jeremiah: A Free Black Man's Encounter with Liberty* (New Haven, Conn.: Yale University Press, 2009).
18. Encyclopedia Virginia, "Lord Dunmore's Proclamation," https://www.encyclopediavirginia.org/Lord_Dunmore_s_Proclamation_1775.
19. Morrill, p. 33.
20. Joseph Plumb Martin, *A Narrative of a Revolutionary Soldier: The Memoir Previously Published as Private Yankee Doodle* (New York: Signet Classics, 2010), pp. 49–50, hereafter cited as "Martin."
21. Fraser, pp. 154–158; Rosen, p. 54.
22. David K. Wilson, *The Southern Strategy: Britain's Conquest of South Carolina and Georgia, 1775–1780* (Columbia:

University of South Carolina Press, 2005), p. 54, hereafter cited as "Wilson"; Morrill, pp. 20–25.
  23. Frazier, pp. 161–162.
  24. Morrill, p. 76.
  25. Fraser, p. 164.
  26. Allen, p. 324.
  27. Martin, p. 207.
  28. Henry Lee (Light Horse Harry Lee), *The American Revolution in the South*, edited, with a biography of the author, by his son, Robert E. Lee (New York: Arno Press, a *New York Times* Company, 1969), p. 566, hereafter cited as "Lee."
  29. Allen, p. 326.
  30. Lee, p. 567.

Chapter 6

  1. Rosen, p. 59.
  2. John Holton Fant, ed., *The Travelers' Charleston: Accounts of Charleston and Lowcountry, South Carolina, 1666–1861* (Columbia: University of South Carolina Press, 2016), p. 107, hereafter cited as "Fant."
  3. Fant, p. 114.
  4. Carlisle, p. 29.
  5. Fant, p. 184.
  6. Philip S. Foner and Ronald L. Lewis, eds., *The Black Worker to 1869 (The Black Worker: A Documentary History from Colonial Times to the Present)* (Philadelphia: Temple University Press, 1978).
  7. Wikipedia, "Charles Cotesworth Pinckney," https://en.wikipedia.org/wiki/Charles_Cotesworth_Pinckney.
  8. Ralph Ketcham, ed., *The Anti-Federalist Papers and the Constitutional Convention Debates* (New York: Penguin, 1986), p. 163, hereafter cited as "Ketcham."
  9. Ketcham, p. 163.
  10. Ketcham, p. 375.
  11. Rosen, p. 84.
  12. Carlisle, p. 29.
  13. Fraser, pp. 181–190.
  14. Wikipedia, "Act Prohibiting Importation of Slaves," https://en.wikipedia.org/wiki/Act_Prohibiting_Importation_of_Slaves.
  15. Donald R. Hickey, *The War of 1812: A Forgotten Conflict* (Urbana: University of Illinois Press, 1989), pp. 154, 204.
  16. Rosen, p. 76.
  17. Rosen, p. 77.
  18. Rosen, p. 79.
  19. Robert N. Rosen, *Confederate Charleston: An Illustrated History of the City and the People During the Civil War* (Columbia: University of South Carolina Press, Columbia, 1994), p. 16. To avoid confusion between this book and Rosen's other volume used in this work, *Confederate Charleston* is cited hereafter as "Rosen/2."
  20. Rosen, pp. 75–76.
  21. National Park Service, *Fort Sumter, Anvil of War* (Washington, D.C.: Division of Publications, U.S. Department of Interior, 1984), pp. 13–14, hereafter cited as "NPS"; M. Patrick Hendrix, *A History of Fort Sumter: Building a Civil War Landmark* (Charleston, S.C.: History Press, 2014); Derek Smith, *Sumter After the First Shots: The Untold Story of America's Most Famous Fort Until the End of the Civil War* (Mechanicsburg, Pa.: Stackpole, 2015), pp. 2–3, hereafter cited as "Smith"; Civil War Talk, "Fort Sumter—Construction and Ownership," https://civilwartalk.com/threads/fort-sumter-construction-and-ownership.7395/.
  22. Johnson, p. 17.
  23. Johnson, p. 18.
  24. Rosen/2, pp. 46, 94, 121.
  25. Rosen/2, pp. 46, 94, 121.
  26. Fraser, p. 260.
  27. Robert Hendrickson, *Sumter: The First Day of the Civil War* (Chelsea, Mich.: Scarborough House, 1990), p. 202.
  28. Smith, pp. 19–24, 101–102; Fraser, p. 260; E. Milby Burton, *The Siege of Charleston 1861–1865* (Columbia: University of South Carolina Press, 1970), p. 84, hereafter cited as "Burton"; Stephen R. Wise, *Gate of Hell: Campaign for Charleston Harbor, 1863* (Columbia: University of South Carolina Press, 1994), pp. 129–131, hereafter cited as "Wise."
  29. Wise, pp. 44–52; William H. Roberts, *Now for the Contest: Coastal & Oceanic Naval Operations in the Civil War* (Lincoln: University of Nebraska Press, 2004), p. 121; Ivan Musicant, *Divided Waters: The Naval History of the Civil War* (New York: HarperCollins, 1995), p. 57, hereafter cited as "Musicant"; Spencer C. Tucker, *Blue & Gray Navies: The Civil War Afloat* (Annapolis, Md.: Naval Institute Press, 2006), pp.

7–8, hereafter cited as "Tucker"; Wise, pp. 44–52.
30. Fraser, p. 259; Wise, p. 131; Tony Gibbons, *Warships and Naval Battles of the U.S. Civil War* (Surrey, Great Britain: Dragon's World, Ltd., 1989), p. 53; Tucker, p. 15; Musicant, pp. 74, 131–132. One free black crew of coal heavers gained some notoriety by foiling the attempt of a Confederate skipper who was trying to sink his ship, the *Ellis*, to prevent capture. They stopped the demolition charge and then defected to the Union Navy.
31. Rosen/2, p. 121; Burton, p. 252.
32. House Divided Project, "Emancipation Among Black Troops in South Carolina," http://housedivided.dickinson.edu/sites/emancipation/2012/11/06/emancipation-among-black-troops-in-south-carolina/.
33. Rosen, p. 118.
34. Fraser, p. 213.
35. Smith, p. 307.
36. Fraser, pp. 269–272; Rosen/2, p. 150.
37. Rosen/2, pp. 139–153; NPS, pp. 102–105.

Chapter 7

1. John F. Hassell III, *Imagine What Tomorrow Holds* (Charleston, S.C.: Evening Post Books, 2017), p. 23, hereafter cited as "Hassell."
2. Fraser, pp. 274–275.
3. Fraser, pp. 273–279.
4. Fraser, pp. 275–279.
5. Walter Edgar, *South Carolina: A History* (Columbia: University of South Carolina Press, 1988), pp. 387–389, hereafter cited as "Edgar."
6. Fraser, pp. 275–276.
7. Fraser, p. 285.
8. Lester Rubin, William S. Swift and Herbert R. Northrup, eds., *Negro Employment in the Maritime Industries* (Wharton School, University of Pennsylvania, 1974), p. 33, hereafter cited as "Rubin."
9. Rubin, p. 95; Rosen, p. 138; George Brown Tindall, *South Carolina Negroes 1877–1902* (Baton Rouge: Louisiana State University Press, 1966), p. 138.
10. Eli Poliakoff, "Against the Grain in the Palmetto State: The Improbable Political Influence of Organized Labor in Charleston County, South Carolina," B.A. thesis, Harvard College, 2000, pp. 44–46, hereafter cited as "Poliakoff thesis."
11. Poliakoff thesis, p. 45.
12. Bernard E. Powers, Jr., *Black Charlestonians: A Social History 1822–1885* (Fayetteville: University of Arkansas Press, 1944), pp. 131–132, hereafter cited as "Powers."
13. Powers, p. 132.
14. Donald Nieman, ed., *African Americans and Non-agricultural Labor in the South 1865–1900* (New York: Garland, 1944), pp. 145–146, 151.
15. Charleston Currents, "Ever Wonder Why It's Called Ashley Phosphate Road," June 15, 2015, https://charlestoncurrents.com/2015/06/history-ever-wonder-why-its-called-ashley-phosphate-road/.
16. Poliakoff thesis, p. 48.
17. Poliakoff thesis, p. 49.
18. Fraser, p. 296.
19. Fraser, p. 299.
20. Poliakoff thesis, p. 49.
21. Poliakoff thesis, p. 49.

Chapter 8

1. Hassell, p. 25.
2. Hassell, p. 25.
3. Hassell, p. 26.
4. Fraser, p. 327.
5. Charleston Chamber of Commerce, *The Advantages of the City of Charleston as a Port of Import and Export for the Trade and Commerce of the Ports of the Northwestern States of the United States and of Central and South America, The West Indies and Europe* (Charleston, S.C.: News and Courier Book Presses, March 29, 1880), hereafter cited as "Chamber."
6. Chamber, p. 14.
7. Fraser, pp. 308–309.
8. Fraser, pp. 307–308.
9. Fraser, pp. 314–315.
10. Edgar, p. 426.
11. Robert P. Stockton, *The Great Shock: The Effects of the 1886 Earthquake on the Built Environment of Charleston, South Carolina* (Easley, S.C.: Southern Historical Press, 1986), hereafter cited as "Stockton."
12. Fraser, p. 318.

Chapter Notes—9 and 10

13. Rosen, pp. 135–137.
14. Fraser, p. 327.
15. Fraser, p. 320.
16. Rosen, p. 138.
17. Carlisle, pp. 74–75.
18. Wikipedia, "Charleston Naval Shipyard," https://en.wikipedia.org/wiki/Charleston_Naval_Shipyard.
19. Rosen, p. 139.
20. Wikipedia, "NAACP," https://en.wikipedia.org/wiki/NAACP#Formation.
21. Carlisle, p. 75.
22. Kieran W. Taylor, *Charleston and the Great Depression: A Documentary History, 1929–1941* (Columbia: University of South Carolina Press, 2018), p. 51, hereafter cited as "Taylor."
23. Taylor, pp. 89–92.
24. Wikipedia, "Porgy and Bess," https://en.wikipedia.org/wiki/Porgy_and_Bess. Another touching example is the 1938 painting by Charleston artist Norma Mazo. It movingly reflects the dire nature of the time. It portrays a group of black longshoremen waiting for their pay in front of the offices of the United Fruit Docks, surrounded by the dilapidated remnants of the dock area, recently devastated by a tornado. It is reproduced in color on the cover of Taylor's book and again on p. 48 of Taylor.
25. Charleston Naval Shipyard, http://www.charlestonnavalshipyard.com/1.html.
26. Charleston Naval Shipyard, http://www.charlestonnavalshipyard.com/1.html.
27. Charleston Naval Shipyard, "Charleston Naval Shipyard," www.Charlestonavalshipyard.com.
28. Frazier, p. 380.
29. Charleston Naval Shipyard, www.Charlestonnavalyard.com.
30. Charleston Naval Shipyard, www.Charlestonnavalyard.com.
31. Robert Behre, "After 25 Years Charleston's Shuttered Navy Base Still Has "a Long Way to Go," *Post and Courier*, Feb. 10, 2019.
32. Hassell, p. 26.
33. Hassell, p. 26.
34. Rosen, pp. 140–141; Wikipedia, "Port of Charleston," https://en.wikipedia.org/wiki/Charleston_Naval_Shipyard.
35. Hassell, p. 27.
36. Hassell, p. 29.

Chapter 9

1. Wikipedia, "Textile Workers Strike (1934)," https://en.wikipedia.org/wiki/Textile_workers_strike_(1934).
2. Eli Poliakoff interview, March 4, 2019.
3. Wikipedia, "Honea Path, South Carolina," https://en.wikipedia.org/wiki/Honea_Path,_South_Carolina.
4. Eli Poliakoff interview, March 4, 2019.
5. Eli Poliakoff, "Charleston's Longshoremen: Organized Labor in the Anti-Union Palmetto State," *South Carolina Historical Magazine*, July 2002, p. 250, hereafter cited as "Poliakoff article."
6. Poliakoff article, p. 250.
7. Taylor, p. xxvi.
8. Poliakoff article, p. 251.
9. Fraser, p. 394.
10. Fraser, p. 394.
11. Isabel Liggins, interview by Eli Poliakoff, Jan. 2, 2000, Charleston, S.C.
12. Marion Turner, interview by Eli Poliakoff, Dec. 2001, Charleston, S.C.
13. Poliakoff article, p. 251.
14. Poliakoff thesis, p. 54.
15. Poliakoff article, p. 253.
16. Poliakoff article, pp. 253–254.
17. Poliakoff article, pp. 251–252.
18. Poliakoff article, p. 252.
19. "George German; Undisputed Boss," *News and Courier*, Jan. 18, 1965, quoted by Eli Poliakoff.
20. Poliakoff thesis, p. 59.
21. Jack Bass interview, March 8, 2019.
22. Arthur Ravenal interview by Eli Poliakoff, Jan. 3, 2000, Charleston, S.C.
23. Wikipedia, "Voting Rights Act of 1965," https://en.wikipedia.org/wiki/Voting_Rights_Act_of_1965.
24. Isabel Liggins interview by Eli Poliakoff, Jan. 2, 2000, Charleston, S.C.
25. Joe Riley interview, Nov. 26, 2018.
26. Leonard Riley interview, Jan. 28, 2019.
27. Kenny Riley interview, Jan. 5, 2019.
28. Poliakoff thesis, p. 63.

Chapter 10

1. Kenny Riley interview, July 23, 2018.
2. Kenny Riley interview, July 23, 2018.
3. Kenny Riley interview, July 28, 2018.
4. Kenny Riley interview, July 28, 2018.

5. Kenny Riley interview, July 28, 2018.
6. Tony Bartelme, "A New Leader Found on the Waterfront," *Post and Courier*, Feb. 8, 1997.
7. Kenny Riley interview, July 28, 2018.
8. Kenny Riley interview, July 28, 2018.
9. Kenny Riley interview, Sept. 13, 2018.
10. Armand Derfner interview, Nov. 9, 2018.
11. Armand Derfner interview, Nov. 9, 2018.

Chapter 11

1. Kenny Riley interview, July 28, 2018.
2. Richard Pearson, "Malcolm McLean Dies," *Washington Post*, May 27, 2001.
3. Ken Younger, quoted by Ted Reed in "How Charleston Port's Rise Began in 1960s: Response to Sea-Land Put It on Track to Growth," *Charlotte Observer*, April 30, 2000.
4. Malcolm McLean, quoted by Ted Reed in "How Charleston Port's Rise Began in 1960s: Response to Sea-Land Put It on Track to Growth," *Charlotte Observer*, April 30, 2000.
5. History of the Port of Charleston, quoted by Ted Reed in "How Charleston Port's Rise Began in 1960s: Response to Sea-land Put It on Track to Growth," *Charlotte Observer*, April 30, 2000.
6. Ken Younger, quoted by Ted Reed in "How Charleston Port's Rise Began in 1960s: Response to Sea-Land Put It on Track to Growth," *Charlotte Observer*, April 30, 2000.
7. Hassell, p. 37.
8. Alan Abrams, "Gone But Not Forgotten," *Joc.com*, Jan. 10, 1993.
9. Harold Daggett interview, Nov. 8, 2018.
10. Jim McNamara interview, Nov. 15, 2018.
11. Kenny Riley interview, July 28, 2018.
12. Kenny Riley interview, July 23, 2018.
13. Tony Bartelme, "Behind Battle Lines: ILA vs. Non-union Labor," *Post and Courier*, Jan. 10, 2000.

Chapter 12

1. Tony Bartelme, "A New Leader Found on the Waterfront," *Post and Courier*, Feb. 8, 1997.
2. Kenny Riley interview, Sept. 13, 2018.
3. Kenny Riley interview, Sept. 13, 2018.
4. Kenny Riley interview, Sept. 13, 2018.
5. Suzan Erem and E. Paul Durrenberger, *On the Global Waterfront: The Fight to Free the Charleston 5* (New York: Monthly Review Press, 2008), p. 21, hereafter cited as "Erem and Durrenberger."
6. Eddie McBride interview, May 5, 2019.
7. Kenny Riley interview, Oct. 27, 2018.
8. Tony Bartelme, "Dockworkers to Demonstrate—Muddy Waters: The Use of Non-union Labor to Load a Chicken Ship Here Has Sparked the Wrath of ILA Local 1422," *Post and Courier*, June 17, 1997.
9. Tony Bartelme and Herb Frazier, "Dockworkers Protest Ship Unloaded by Non-union Members at SPA," *Post and Courier*, Dec. 2, 1999.

Chapter 13

1. Kenny Riley interview, March 30, 2019.
2. Kenny Riley interview, March 30, 2019.
3. *Wright vs. Universal Maritime Service Corp.*, U.S. Supreme Court ruling, Nov. 16, 1998.
4. "Dockworker Wins in Supreme Court Discrimination Actions," *Post and Courier*, Nov. 17, 1998.
5. Kenny Riley interview, March 30, 2019.
6. Kenny Riley interview, March 30, 2019.
7. Kenny Riley interview, Oct. 27, 2018.
8. Wikipedia, "Jim Hodges," https://en.wikipedia.org/wiki/Jim_Hodges.
9. Kenny Riley interview, Oct. 27, 2018.
10. Kenny Riley interview, Oct. 27, 2018.
11. Schuyler Kropf, "Trial Balloons Failed to Warn Hodges," *Post and Courier*, April 26, 1999.
12. Erem and Durrenberger, p. 64.
13. Kenny Riley interview, March 30, 2019.
14. Glenn McConnell, quoted by Ted Reed in "Union Leader Balances Camps, Friends Say," *Charlotte Observer* story republished in *The State*, Columbia, S.C., Sept. 4, 2000.
15. Kenny Riley interview, March 30, 2018.

16. Don Fowler interview, March 22, 2019.
17. Kenny Riley interview, Oct. 27, 2018.
18. Kenny Riley interview, Oct. 27, 2018.

Chapter 14

1. Kenny Riley interview, Sept. 8, 2018.
2. Kenny Riley interview, Sept. 8, 2018.
3. Kenny Riley interview, Sept. 8, 2018.
4. Erem and Durrenberger, p. 16.
5. Kenny Riley interview, Sept. 5, 2018.
6. Kenny Riley interview, Sept. 5, 2018.
7. Tony Bartelme and Glenn Smith, "Riot's Aftermath: Assessing the Long Term Fallout of the Waterfront Riot," *Post and Courier*, Jan. 21, 2000.
8. Erem and Durrenberger, pp. 28–29.
9. Tony Bartelme and Glenn Smith, "Riot's Aftermath: Assessing the Long Term Fallout of the Waterfront Riot," *Post and Courier*, Jan. 21, 2000.
10. Kenny Riley interview, Sept. 5, 2018.
11. Kenny Riley interview, March 30, 2019.
12. Tony Bartelme interview, March 26, 2019.

Chapter 15

1. Kenny Riley interview, Sept. 8, 2018.
2. Kenny Riley interview, Oct. 27, 2018.
3. Kenny Riley interview, Oct. 27, 2018.
4. Kenny Riley interview, Oct. 27, 2018.
5. Erem and Durrenberger, p. 16.
6. Erem and Durrenberger, p. 65.
7. Erem and Durrenberger, p. 80.
8. Erem and Durrenberger, p. 86.
9. Peter Wilborn interview, April 30, 2019.
10. Peter Wilborn interview, April 30, 2019.
11. Bill Fletcher interview, March 11, 2019.
12. Bill Fletcher interview, March 11, 2019.
13. Erem and Durrenberger, p. 126.
14. Steve Early, *Embedded with Organized Labor* (New York: Monthly Review Press, 2009), pp. 92–93, hereafter cited as "Early."
15. Early, p. 94.
16. Early, p. 96.

17. Bill Fletcher interview, March 11, 2019.
18. Kenny Riley interview, Oct. 27, 2018.
19. Armand Derfner interview, Nov. 9, 2018.
20. Kenny Riley interview, Oct. 27, 2018.
21. Tony Bartelme, "Charleston 5 Case Ends with No-Contest Pleas," *Post and Courier*, Nov. 14, 2001.
22. Tony Bartelme, "Charleston 5 Case Ends with No-Contest Pleas," *Post and Courier*, Nov. 14, 2001.
23. Tony Bartelme interview, March 4, 2019.
24. Bill Fletcher interview, March 11, 2019.
25. Bill Fletcher interview, March 11, 2019.

Chapter 16

1. Kenny Riley interview, Oct. 27, 2018.
2. Jim McNamara interview, Nov. 15, 2018.
3. Kenny Riley interview, Jan. 11, 2019.
4. Peter Wilborn interview, April 30, 2019.
5. Harold Daggett interview, Nov. 22, 2018.
6. Jim McNamara interview, Nov. 15, 2018.
7. Kenny Riley interview, Jan. 11, 2019.
8. Kenny Riley interview, Jan. 5, 2019.
9. Kenny Riley interview, Jan. 5, 2019.
10. Harold Daggett interview, Nov. 22, 2018.
11. Kenny Riley interview, Jan. 11, 2019.
12. Willie Adams interview, March 19, 2019.
13. Willie Adams interview, March 19, 2019.

Chapter 17

1. Kenny Riley interview, July 28, 2018.
2. Kenny Riley interview, Jan. 3, 2019.
3. Allyson Bird, "Financial Secretary, Union Have Long History," *Post and Courier*, April 13, 2009.
4. Allyson Bird, "Financial Secretary, Union Have Long History," *Post and Courier*, April 13, 2009.

Chapter Notes—18 and 19

5. *Yvette Flowers vs. International Longshoremen's Association Local 1422 et al*, Court of Common Pleas, Charleston County, S.C., filed Jan. 24, 2018.
6. *Yvette Flowers vs. ILA Local 1422 et al*.
7. Harold Daggett, speech to ILA Civil, Human and Women's Rights Awards dinner, Oct. 27, 2018.
8. Harold Daggett, speech to ILA Civil, Human and Women's Rights Awards dinner, Oct. 27, 2018.
9. Kenny Riley interview, Jan. 5, 2019.
10. Kenny Riley interview, Jan. 5, 2019.
11. Leonard Riley interview, Jan. 28, 2019.
12. James Pickney interview, Nov. 19, 2018, Charleston, S.C.
13. James Pickney interview, Nov. 19, 2018, Charleston, S.C.

Chapter 18

1. Poliakoff thesis, p. 1.
2. Kerry Taylor interview, Feb. 22, 2019.
3. Barbara Melvin interview, March 28, 2019.
4. Barbara Melvin interview, March 28, 2019.
5. Kenny Riley interview, April 5, 2019.
6. Marty Crosby interview, March 27, 2019.
7. Marty Crosby interview, March 27, 2019.
8. Nikki Haley, quoted by Ted Reed in "Audacious Union Eyes Southern Sites of Boeing, Delta and Airbus," *The Street*, March 19, 2015.
9. Scott Hamilton interview, Jan. 14, 2019.
10. "Boeing's Best Union Buster Is South Carolina's Governor Nikki Haley," *Bloomberg Business Week*, April 17, 2015.
11. Bill Wise interview, Jan. 9, 2019.
12. Bill Wise interview, Jan. 9, 2019.
13. Kenny Riley interview, Jan. 31, 2017.
14. Poliakoff article, p. 256.
15. Poliakoff article, p. 247.
16. Kenny Riley interview, April 24, 2019.
17. Ron Menchaca and Glenn Smith, "Problem Cops; a Systematic Failure," *Post and Courier*, March 5, 2005.
18. Kenny Riley interview, April 24, 2019.

Chapter 19

1. Kenny Riley interview, Jan. 23, 2019.
2. Kenny Riley interview, Jan. 23, 2019.
3. Marnique Riley Strickland interview, Jan. 26, 2019.
4. Kenny Riley interview, Jan. 23, 2019.
5. Marnique Riley Strickland interview, Jan. 26, 2019.
6. Kenny Riley interview, Jan. 5, 2019.
7. Kenny Riley interview, Jan. 5, 2019.
8. Kenny Riley interview, Jan. 5, 2019.
9. Willie Adams interview, March 19, 2019.

Bibliography

Books

Allen, Thomas B. *Tories: Fighting for the King in America's First Civil War.* New York: HarperCollins, 2010.
Anderson, Fred. *Crucible of War: The Seven Years' War and the Fate of Empire in British North America, 1754–1766.* New York: Alfred A. Knopf, 2000.
Boatner, Mark M., III. *Encyclopedia of the American Revolution.* Mechanicsburg, Pa.: Stackpole, 1994.
Borneman, Walter R. *The French and Indian War: Deciding the Fate of North America.* New York: Harper Perennial, 2006.
Brown, Alphonso. *A Gullah Guide to Charleston: Walking Through Black History.* Charleston, S.C.: History Press, 2008.
Burton, E. Milby. *The Siege of Charleston 1861–1865.* Columbia: University of South Carolina Press, 1970.
Carlisle, Rodney, and Loretta Carlisle. *Charleston in History: A Guide to More Than 100 Sites in Historical Context.* Sarasota, Fla.: Pineapple Press, 2016.
Cecelski, David S. *Waterman's Song, Slavery & Freedom in Maritime North Carolina.* Chapel Hill: University of North Carolina Press, 2001.
Charleston Chamber of Commerce. *The Advantages of the City of Charleston as a Port of Import and Export for the Trade and Commerce of the Northwestern States of the United States and of Central and South America, the West Indies, and Europe.* Charleston, S.C.: News and Courier Book Presses, March 29, 1880.
Detzer, David. *Allegiance, Fort Sumter, Charleston, and the Beginning of the Civil War.* New York: Harcourt, 2001.
Early, Steve. *Embedded with Organized Labor.* New York: Monthly Review Press, 2009.
Edgar, Walter. *South Carolina: A History.* Columbia: University of South Carolina Press, 1998.
Erem, Suzan, and E. Paul Durrenberger. *On the Global Waterfront: The Fight to Free the Charleston 5.* New York: Monthly Review Press, 2008.
Fant, John Holton, ed. *The Travelers' Charleston: Accounts of Charleston and Lowcountry, South Carolina, 1666–1861.* Columbia: University of South Carolina Press, 2016.
Foner, Philip S., and Ronald L. Lewis, eds. *The Black Worker to 1869 (The Black Worker: A Documentary History from Colonial Times to the Present).* Philadelphia: Temple University Press, 1978.
Fowler, William M., Jr. *Empires at War: The French and Indian War and the Struggle for North America, 1754–1763.* New York: Walker & Company, 2005.
Fraser, Walter J., Jr. *Charleston! Charleston! The History of a Southern City.* Columbia: University of South Carolina Press, 1989.

Bibliography

Gibbons, Tony. *Warships and Naval Battles of the U.S. Civil War.* Surrey, Great Britain: Dragon's World, Ltd., 1989.

Harris, J. William. *The Hanging of Thomas Jeremiah: A Free Black Man's Encounter with Liberty.* New Haven, Conn.: Yale University Press, 2009.

Hassell, John F., III. *Imagine What Tomorrow Holds.* Charleston, S.C.: Evening Post Books, 2017.

Hendrickson, Robert. *Sumter: The First Day of the Civil War.* Chelsea, Mich.: Scarborough House, 1990.

Hendrix, M. Patrick. *A History of Fort Sumter: Building a Civil War Landmark.* Charleston, S.C.: History Press, 2014.

Hickey, Donald R. *The War of 1812: A Forgotten Conflict.* Urbana: University of Illinois Press, 1989.

Johnson, Skip. *Charleston: The Brief History of a Remarkable City.* Charleston, S.C.: Meeting Street Press, 2016.

Ketcham, Ralph, ed. *The Anti-Federalist Papers and the Constitutional Convention Debates.* New York: Penguin, 1986.

Klein, Maury. *Days of Defiance, Sumter, Secession, and the Coming of the Civil War.* New York: Vintage Books, 1999.

Lee, Henry (Light Horse Harry Lee). *The American Revolution in the South.* Edited, with a biography of the author, by his son, Robert E. Lee. New York: Arno Press, a *New York Times* Company, 1969.

Martin, Joseph Plumb. *A Narrative of a Revolutionary Soldier: The Memoir Previously Published as Private Yankee Doodle.* New York: Signet Classics, 2010.

Morrill, Dan L. *Southern Campaigns of the American Revolution.* Baltimore, Md.: Nautical & Aviation Publishing Company of America.

Musicant, Ivan. *Divided Waters: The Naval History of the Civil War.* New York: HarperCollins, 1995.

National Park Service. *Fort Sumter, Anvil of War.* Washington, D.C.: Division of Publications, U.S. Department of Interior, 1984.

Nieman, Donald, ed. *African Americans and Non-agricultural Labor in the South 1865–1900.* New York: Garland, 1944.

Pocock, Tom. *Battle for Empire: The Very First World War 1756–63.* London: Michael O'Mara Books Limited, 1998.

Powers, Bernard E., Jr. *Black Charlestonians: A Social History 1822–1885.* Fayetteville: University of Arkansas Press, 1994.

Roberts, William H. *Now for the Contest: Coastal & Oceanic Naval Operations in the Civil War.* Lincoln: University of Nebraska Press, 2004.

Rosen, Robert N. *A Short History of Charleston.* Columbia: University of South Carolina Press, 1982.

Rosen, Robert N. *Confederate Charleston: An Illustrated History of the City and the People During the Civil War.* Columbia: University of South Carolina Press, 1994.

Rubin, Lester, William S. Swift, and Herbert R. Northup, eds. *Negro Employment in the Maritime Industries.* Wharton School, University of Pennsylvania, 1974.

Ryan, William R. *The World of Thomas Jeremiah: Charlestown on the Eve of the American Revolution.* New York: Oxford University Press, 2010.

Smith, Derek. *Sumter After the First Shots: The Untold Story of America's Most Famous Fort Until the End of the Civil War.* Mechanicsburg, Pa.: Stackpole, 2015.

Stockton, Robert P. *The Great Shock: The Effects of the 1886 Earthquake on the Built Environment of Charleston, South Carolina.* Easley, S.C.: Southern Historical Press, 1986.

Taylor, Kieran W. *Charleston and the Great Depression: A Documentary History, 1929–1941.* Columbia: University of South Carolina Press, 2018.

Tindall, George Brown. *South Carolina Negroes 1877–1902.* Baton Rouge: Louisiana State University Press, 1966.

Bibliography

Tucker, Spencer C. *Blue & Gray Navies: The Civil War Afloat*. Annapolis, Md.: Naval Institute Press, 2006.
Watson, Shelia Hempton. *Images of America: South Carolina Ports, Charleston, Georgetown, and Port Royal*. Charleston, S.C.: Arcadia Publishing, 2004.
Wilson, David K. *The Southern Strategy: Britain's Conquest of South Carolina and Georgia, 1775–1780*. Columbia: University of South Carolina Press, 2005.
Wise, Stephen R. *Gate of Hell: Campaign for Charleston Harbor, 1863*. Charleston, S.C.: University of South Carolina Press, 1994.
Wood, Peter W. *Black Majority: Negroes in Colonial South Carolina from 1670 Through the Stono Rebellion*. New York: W. W. Norton, 1974.

Interviews

Ted conducted a series of about two dozen interviews on the telephone with Kenny Riley, beginning on June 20, 2018, and also met with him in Charlotte in September 2018 and in Charleston in November 2018 and March 2019. They exchanged a few hundred e-mails and text messages.
Willie Adams, with Ted Reed, by telephone, March 19, 2019.
Tony Bartelme, with Ted Reed, Charleston, S.C., March 4, 2019.
Jack Bass, with Ted Reed, by telephone, March 8, 2019.
Marty Crosby, with Ted Reed, Charleston, S.C., March 5, 2019; by telephone, March 27, 2019, and subsequent.
Harold Daggett, with Ted Reed, by telephone, Nov. 8, 2018.
Armand Derfner, with Ted Reed, by telephone, Nov. 9, 2018, and subsequent.
Bill Fletcher, with Ted Reed, by telephone, March 11, 2019.
Yvette Flowers, with Ted Reed, Charleston, S.C., Nov. 19, 2018.
Donald Fowler, with Ted Reed, by telephone, March 22, 2019.
Scott Hamilton, with Ted Reed, Montreal, Jan. 14, 2019.
Isabel Liggins, with Eli Poliakoff, Charleston, S.C., March 3, 2000.
Eddi McBride, with Ted Reed, by telephone, May 5, 2019.
Jim McNamara, with Ted Reed, by telephone, Nov. 15, 2018.
Barbara Melvin, with Ted Reed, Charleston, S.C., Nov. 19, 2018; by telephone, March 28, 2019.
Eli Poliakoff, with Ted Reed, Charleston, S.C., March 4, 2019.
Corine Riley, with Ted Reed, Charleston, S.C., Nov. 19, 2018.
Joe Riley, with Ted Reed, by telephone, Nov. 26, 2018.
Leonard Riley, with Ted Reed, by telephone, Jan. 28–29, 2019; Charleston, S.C., March 5, 2019.
Marnique Riley Strickland, with Ted Reed, by telephone, Jan. 26, 2019.
Kerry Taylor, with Ted Reed, by telephone, Feb. 21, 2019.
Marion Turner interview by Eli Poliakoff, Dec. 12, 2001, Charleston, S.C.
Peter Wilborn, with Ted Reed, by telephone, April 30, 2019, and subsequent.
Bill Wise, with Ted Reed, Charleston, S.C., by telephone, Jan. 9, 2019.
David Wren, with Ted Reed, Charleston, S.C., March 4, 2019.

Newspapers and Magazines

The authors relied heavily on reporting by the *Post and Courier* and also referred to an article by Eli Poliakoff in the *South Carolina Historical Magazine*.
We also referred to articles in the *Charlotte Observer*, the *Journal of Commerce*, the *New York Times*, and the *Washington Post*.

Bibliography

Other Source Materials

The authors referred to online encyclopedias, including EncyclopediaBritannica.com, EncyclopediaVirginia.org, Wikipedia, and Everything 2.com and to the website Charlestonnavalshipyard.com.

Two university theses were of value: John D. Duncan, "Servitude and Slavery in Colonial South Carolina, 1670–1766," 2 vols., Ph.D. dissertation, Emory University, 1972; and Eli Poliakoff, "Against the Grain in the Palmetto State: The Improbable Political Influence of Organized Labor in Charleston County, South Carolina," B.A. thesis, Harvard College, 2000.

Index

A. Phillip Randolph Institute 120
Abernathy, Ralph 89
Abrams, Stacey 162
Act Prohibiting Importation of Slaves (1807) 56
Adams, Willie 156-158, 186
A.E. Holleman Stevedoring Company 84
AFL-CIO 91, 106, 122, 145, 148, 157, 165; North Carolina 174; South Carolina 123, 125, 144, 174
Airbus 172
Alvanos, Johnny 134
American Revolutionary War 6, 35, 48-53, 54
Anderson, Robert 64
Angola 33, 34, 38, 50
Armstrong, Louis 26
Ashley River Creative Arts Elementary School 15
Ashley Street (Jacksonville, Fla.) 26
Atlanta, Ga. 10, 63

Bailey, Walter 148
Bankhead, Walter 96, 97, 99, 100
Barr, Capers 104-106
Bartelme, Tony 110-112, 137, 138, 148
Bass, Jack 89, 91
Bass, Mark 183, 184
Beasley, David 123
Beauregard, P.T. 59
Bible Way Baptist Church 19
Black Majority, Negroes in Colonial South Carolina from 1670 Through the Stono Rebellion 33, 40
Blease, Coleman 77
The Blinding of Sgt. Isaac Woodard and the Awakening of President Harry S. Truman and Judge J. Waties Waring 85
BMW 172
Boeing 172, 173, 175

Booker, Cory: visits Charleston 128
Bowers, John 144, 150-153, 156
Bradley, Ed 146
Bradley, William 88
Brando, Marlon 150
Bridges, Harry 157, 158
Brotherhood of Sleeping Car Porters 165
Brown, Richard 176-178
Brown v. Board of Education of Topeka 21, 85
Bull, William, Jr. 45
Burke High School 15, 164

Calhoun, John C. 58
Calvary Episcopal Church 18, 19
Campbell, William 50
Carolina Marine Handling 117
Carr, Georgette 134
Chamberlain, Daniel 71, 72
Charleston City Council 37, 50, 67
Charleston City Railway Corporation 69
Charleston Five 4, 110, 115, 120, 130-149, 152, 156, 157, 174, 182
Charleston hospital strike 82, 89, 149
Charleston Navy Yard 62, 74, 77-80, 176
Charleston police 69, 73, 78, 84, 86, 90, 118, 133-137, 147, 148
Charleston Southern University 28
Charleston Terminal Company 81
Charleston Vigilance Association 59
Charlotte, N.C. 10, 174, 180, 182
Charlotte Observer 89, 105, 126
Chavez-Thompson, Linda (visits Columbia) 145
Cherokee 44, 45
Christ Children's Home 182
Citadel 69, 168
Civil War 4, 6, 36, 47, 54, 59-65, 69, 80, 110
Clinton, Hillary: visits Charleston 128
Coalition of Black Trades Unionists (CBTU) 91, 92, 120, 144

201

Index

College of Charleston 4, 24, 27-30, 125, 165, 179, 180
Collins, Perry 133
Colored People's Convention of South Carolina 69
Columbia, S.C. 59, 124, 130, 132, 145
Columbus Street Terminal 134
Condon, Charles 130, 141, 144, 145, 148
Confederate flag 7, 123, 125, 132
Confederate States of America 60, 125
Conroy, John 90
Cooper River 35, 36, 41, 75, 80
Cornwallis, Lord Charles 52, 53
Crosby, Marty 170-172

Daggett, Harold 5, 106, 107, 152, 153, 155, 156, 162, 184, 186
Delaney, Martin 69
DeLarge, Robert C. 69
Derfner, Armand 101, 102, 122, 143, 147, 148
DeWitt, Donna 123, 125, 144
Doctor, Harriet 180
Dyssli, Samuel 48

Edisto Island 13, 15
Edmondson, Kenneth 159, 160
Edwards, John 128
Ellington, Duke 26
Emancipation Proclamation 62, 67
Emanuel African Methodist Episcopal Church 7, 132
Embedded with Organized Labor 145

Fifteenth Amendment 68, 90
Fletcher, Bill, Jr. 144, 146, 148, 149
Flowers, Benjamin 97-100, 102, 112, 113, 115, 150, 151, 159-166
Flowers, Benjamin, Jr. 159, 160
Flowers Davenport, Yvette 159-163
Ford, Elijah 148
Ford, Robert 178
Fort Sullivan 52
Fort Sumter 6, 54, 58-60, 63, 64
Fourteenth Amendment 68, 90
Fowler, Don 126, 127
Frazier, Maxine Laverne 179, 180
Freedmen's Bureau 65, 66
French and Indian War 44, 45, 47
Fruitvale Station, 157
Fugitive Slave Act 56

Gadsden, Christopher 34, 35, 47
Gadsden's Wharf 34, 35, 36, 47, 56; Kenny Riley visits 37

Gambia 18, 33, 48
Gates, Henry Louis, Jr. 37
Georgetown, S.C. 33, 38, 103
Georgia Ports Authority 105
Gephardt, Richard: visits Charleston 128
German, George Washington 82-89, 91, 159, 162, 165, 166
Gethers, Celia 11, 14, 15, 17
Gillum, Andrew 162
Gleason, Teddy 5, 106-108, 114, 150, 151, 157
Glen, James 44
Gompers, Samuel 165
Gone with the Wind 10
Grace, John 81
Graham, the Rev. Price 19
Grant, Earl 22
Grant, Ulysses S.: visits Charleston 67
Great Earthquake of 1886 36, 74-76
Green, Mary 24
Greenberg, Reuben 119, 133
Gregory, Dick: visits Charleston 113
Guar Gum 95
Guinea-Bissau 3
Gullah 50

Haley, Nikki 7, 172, 173
Hall, Margaret Hunter 55
Hamilton, Scott 173
Hampton, Wade 71, 72
Heyward, Elizabeth 25
Hodges, Jim 123-126
Holingshed, Maya Michelle 179
Hollywood, Fla. 153
Honea Path, S.C. 83
Hughes, Richard 153-155
Hurricane Hugo 36

IAM Local 1725 174
ILA Local 1410 183
ILA Local 1414 116
ILA Local 1422 3-5, 11, 29, 84, 86-88, 90, 91, 96, 97, 99, 103, 108-115, 117-121, 127-134, 137, 140, 141, 143, 144, 150-152, 155; family politics 159-167; in state politics 167-178, 182
ILA Local 1422A 110
ILA Local 1771 110, 111, 160, 179
ILA Local 1804-1 152
ILWU Local 10 157
ILWU Local 23 157
Indians 39, 41, 44, 45, 51
International African American Museum 36, 129

202

Index

International Association of Machinists (IAM) 4, 173-175
International Dockworkers Council (IDC) 40, 141, 156
International Longshore and Warehouse Union (ILWU) 83, 87, 108, 132, 139, 148, 156-158
International Longshoremen's Association (ILA) 3-5, 7, 10, 83, 84, 87, 88, 91, 97, 100, 102, 103, 106-108, 114, 116, 120, 125, 132, 139, 140, 143, 145, 150-156, 158-163, 166, 169, 170, 179, 181, 184, 185
International Transport Workers Federation (ITF) 140, 141, 156
Irish Echo 108

Jacksonville, Fla. 25-27, 83, 97
Jefferson Street projects (Jacksonville) 25-27
Jenkins Woods 11
Jeremiah, Thomas 51
Jim Crow racist laws 20, 22, 37, 68, 87, 165, 176
Johnson, Andrew 67
Johnson, Olin 83
Jones, Phoebe 14, 15

Kappa Alpha Psi 29
Karmue, Neyor 182, 183
Kerry, John (visits Charleston) 128
King, Coretta Scott: visits Charleston 89
King, Martin Luther, Jr. 89, 157, 165
Kirkland, Lane 108
Ku Klux Klan 68, 71, 89

Lambert, John 54, 55
Laurens, Henry 33, 48, 49, 51
Lee, Light Horse Harry 53
Lee, Robert E. 53
Liberia 3, 171, 181; Gbarnga 182, 183, 184
Liggins, Isabel 86, 87, 90
Little Carpenter (Cherokee chief) 45
Liverpool dockers strike 140, 141
Lofton, Lionel 148
Longshore Workers Coalition (LWC) 117, 140, 141, 150, 151, 153, 155
Longshoremen's Protective Union Association (LPUA) 65, 68, 70, 71, 73, 83
Lowery, Joseph: visits Columbia 145

Mackey, the Rev. Stephen 18, 19
Madison, James 56
Magwood, Amos 14
Martin, Joseph Plumb 51, 52

Massey Business College 25-27
Mathew 25:21 185
McAuliffe, Terry 127
McBride, Eddie 116, 117, 141, 151, 186
McConnell, Glenn 125, 126
McLean, Malcolm 5, 103-105
McNamara, Jim 108, 151, 153
Medical University of South Carolina 28, 89, 136, 179
Melvin, Barbara 169, 170
Mercedes-Benz 172
Middle Passage 31
Middleton High School 8, 21, 24, 25, 27
Mobile, Ala. 172, 173
Montgomery bus boycott 20
Morris Island 59, 60
Morrison, William 87
Mount Pleasant Terminal 178

NAACP 77, 122, 127, 128
Nashville, Tenn. 10
Negro Seaman's Act (1822) 58
New Negro Act (law) 43, 46
News and Courier 71, 88, 89
NOCS Group 117, 118, 182
Nordana 118, 119, 131-133, 136, 140-144
North Charleston terminal 170, 176-178

Obama, Barack 128; visits Charleston 129
Obama, Michelle 36
On the Global Waterfront: The Fight to Free the Charleston 5 115, 133, 135, 136
On the Waterfront 150
Orleans Road 12

Parker, Allen 22
Parker, Ben 134
Pawleys Island 19
Pickney, James 164-167
Pinckney, Charles 56
Pinckney, Charles Cotesworth 55, 56
Poliakoff, Eli 70, 83, 87, 168, 175, 176
Porgy and Bess 78-79
Port of Charleston 4, 5, 32, 33, 73, 74, 83, 85, 87, 91, 103-106, 109, 111, 130, 139, 170-172, 178
Port of New York 100, 107, 111
Port of Wilmington, N.C. 104-106
Port Royal 33, 38
Post and Courier 30, 80, 99, 110, 113, 117, 118, 122, 124, 134-137, 148, 160, 178
Prentiss, A.D. 78

Quill, Mike 106

203

Index

Raleigh-Durham, N.C. 10, 67, 104
Randolph, A. Phillip 165
Ravenal, Arthur 90, 100
Rawls, Victor 148
Rechnitzer, Claes 142-144
Reconstruction 15, 65, 67-71, 84, 90, 91, 176
Riley, Alice Sheree 190
Riley, Corine (Gethers) 8, 12, 14-17, 19, 20, 180
Riley, Dick 97
Riley, Joe 7, 36, 85, 90, 97, 144, 182, 183
Riley, Kenny, Jr. 13, 180, 182
Riley, Laurie 16
Riley, Leonard, Jr. 3–9, 12, 13, 15, 16, 19, 20, 22-24, 27-29, 90, 91, 97, 115, 136, 137, 163, 164, 180, 186
Riley, Leonard, Sr. 8, 12, 13, 15, 16, 19, 94, 96, 98, 99, 102, 110, 114
Riley, Michael 16
Riley, Rosalind 180
Riley, Sonya 16
Rivers, Benjamin 78
Roberts, Cecil: visits Columbia 145
Robertson, Thomas 135
Roosevelt, Franklin D. 78, 83, 165; visits Charleston 79

St. Andrew's Episcopal Mission 18, 19
St. Andrew's High School 21-25, 27
St. Andrew's Parish 9, 11, 15, 21, 42
St. Andrew's Parish Church 18
St. Andrew's School (black grade school) 15
Sam Rittenberg Boulevard 9, 10
San Francisco, Ca. 156-158
Saunders, Bill 90
Savage Road 11, 12, 14, 17, 25
Savannah, Ga. 52, 53, 63, 68, 74, 77, 80, 83, 100, 105, 111, 116, 117, 139, 141, 150, 157, 162, 170
Save the Hunley Commission 125
Scalia, Antonin 122
Schackenborg (ship) 118
Sea-Land 104, 105, 107, 111
September 11th 147, 148
Service Employees International Union (SEIU) 106
Sherman, William 63; visits Charleston 69
A Short History of Charleston 43
Shuler, Anthony Lovejoy, Jr., "TJ" 184, 185
Shuler, Fran 185
Sickles, Edgar 67, 68
Sierra Leone 50
Simmons, Ricky 148

Simonton, C.H. 71
60 Minutes 146
Skodsborg (ship) 132, 134, 143
Smalls, Robert 60
Smith, Whitemarsh III 124
Smith v. Allwright (1944) 85
South Carolina Chamber of Commerce 123, 124
South Carolina Department of Corrections 133
South Carolina Electric and Gas busses 20
South Carolina Primary Election 126-128
South Carolina State Ports Authority 82, 89, 104, 111, 112, 124, 125, 133, 148, 168, 169
South Carolina State Ports Authority Board of Directors (commission) 120, 123, 124
Southeastern (stevedoring) 96
Stephen, Adam 44
stevedores 55, 69, 70, 78, 89, 96, 98, 111, 131, 133, 140, 142, 143, 170, 172; Ceasar Wright case 121-123
Stevedoring Services of America 133, 143
Stono Rebellion 43
stow factor 96
Strickland, Marnique Riley 8, 10, 13, 15, 179, 181, 182
Sullivan's Island 31, 32, 35, 36, 40, 43, 50, 56, 59
Sweeny, John 106, 144

Tacoma, Wash. 157
Taylor, Kerry 168
textile workers strike (1934) 82, 83, 149
Thirteenth Amendment 56
Tillman, Ben 77, 176
Transport Workers Union 106
Truman, Harry S. 85
Turner, Marlon 86

United Auto Workers 154
US Airways 174, 175
United States Maritime Alliance 140, 155, 169
United States Supreme Court 101, 120-123, 143
University of South Carolina 127, 179

Vesey, Denmark 58
Vietnam War 27
Volvo 172, 175
Voting Rights Act of 1965 90, 101
Vought 173

Index

Wallace School (black grade school) 15, 20-22, 24
War of 1812 57, 58
Waring, J. Waties 6, 7, 84-86
Washington, George 44
Washington, Peter, Jr. 148
Washington Post 104
West Africa 37, 39, 42
West Ashley 9, 133
West Coast longshoremen's strike (1934) 158
Wilborn, Peter 143, 144, 152

Winyah Stevedoring Inc. (WSI) 133, 143
Wise, Bill 4, 173, 174, 175
Woodard, Issac 85
Wright, Ceasar 121-123, 137, 139
Wright vs.Universal Maritime Service 122

Yamasees 41
Young, Andrew: visits Charleston 89
Younger, Ken 104, 105, 106

Zion Presbyterian Church 69